Manual of Revivals Practical Hints and Suggestions From Histories of Revivals and Biographies

G. W. Hervey, Funk and Wagnalls

BIBLIOLIFE

MANUAL OF REVIVALS.

PRACTICAL HINTS AND SUGGESTIONS

FROM

HISTORIES OF REVIVALS AND BIOGRAPHIES OF REVIVALISTS,

WITH

*THEMES FOR THE USE OF PASTORS AND MISSION-
ARIES BEFORE, DURING, AND AFTER
SPECIAL SERVICES,*

INCLUDING THE TEXTS, SUBJECTS, AND OUTLINES OF THE
SERMONS OF MANY DISTINGUISHED EVANGELISTS,

BY

REV. G. W. HERVEY, M.A.,
AUTHOR OF "A SYSTEM OF CHRISTIAN RHETORIC," ETC.

NEW YORK:
FUNK & WAGNALLS, PUBLISHERS,
10 AND 12 DEY STREET.

PREFACE.

In this volume the writer has attempted to accomplish two new and important objects. One is to embody the many practical suggestions which have occurred to him in the study of the literature of revivals. The other object is to give the reader an extensive variety of revival themes, outlines, and texts, and so to illustrate, by the example of the most successful evangelists, the peculiar excellences of the best revival sermons.

In the first part the writer has tried to avoid prejudice and onesidedness. Instructive as the life of one man may be, yet the blended light of many men's observation and experience is the clearest and safest, the most far-shining, and the fullest of warmth and inspiration.

The more strictly homiletical part is also intended to fill a vacancy. We possess many books of texts, themes, and sketches, some of which are so large as to be called cyclopædias. These may be of more or less service by way of suggestion and reminder to such pastors as think for themselves; but not one of these collections was made with special reference to the exigencies of pastors and evangelists in times of revival. It is for the purpose of meeting these demands (often as unexpected as they are exacting) that these examples have been prepared for the press. The chief object of the writer is to suggest proper texts and themes. Among them will be found the texts of Wesley, Whitefield, Edwards, Griffin, Knapp, Spurgeon, Moody, and many other revivalists of eminence and great success. These texts have been gathered not only from published sermons, but, in some cases, from volumes of letters and journals. In this way, and now for the first time, have been made out tolerably complete lists of the revival texts of Wesley, Whitefield, and Brainerd. Having for many years been an enthusiastic student of all sorts of homiletical literature, the writer has been able to draw many of his materials from sources various and curious, as well as remote and obscure. In order to make the circle of subjects more nearly complete, he has, now and then, consulted his commonplace-book of texts and subjects—a book enriched by the fruit of many years of study. Only as a last resort has he presumed to add texts, themes, and sketches from his own store of revival sermons.

Our field of view, it will be observed, is not confined to revivals in progress. The writer has included such texts and subjects as may serve to prepare the way for, and profitably follow, seasons of special service. The brilliance of noonday wisdom should not be allowed to blind us to the value of morning and evening wisdom.

G. W. H.

CONTENTS.

PART I.

SUGGESTIONS FROM THE RECORDS OF REVIVALISM.

CHAPTER I.

WORKING AND WAITING FOR A REVIVAL.

CHAPTER II.

PRAYER IN ITS RELATION TO AWAKENINGS.

CHAPTER III.

CHAPTER IV.

CHAPTER V.

CHAPTER VI.

CHAPTER VII.

CHAPTER XIII.

INQUIRY MEETINGS CONSIDERED.

CHAPTER XIV.

THE AGENCY OF TRACTS AND LETTERS IN REVIVALS.

CHAPTER XV.

THE MANAGEMENT OF DISTURBERS AND RIOTERS.

CHAPTER XVI.

THE INTRUSIONS OF THE FEEBLE-MINDED AND THE INSANE.

CHAPTER XVII.

SOME OF THE EVILS INCIDENT TO TRUE REVIVALS.

CHAPTER XVIII.

FEEDING THE LAMBS OF THE FLOCK.

CHAPTER XIX.

SHALL WE JOIN THE REAPERS OR NOT?

CHAPTER XX.

WAITING FOR POWER FROM ON HIGH.

CHAPTER XXI.

THE TEMPTATIONS TO WHICH EVANGELISTS ARE EXPOSED.

CHAPTER XXII.

THE RELATIONS OF THE PASTOR AND THE EVANGELIST.

PART II.

OUTLINES, THEMES, AND TEXTS USED BY EVANGELISTS OF NOTE.

INTRODUCTION

It is too late in the day to apologize for revivals or to attempt to establish their importance. We are indeed well aware that there is a certain class of pastors who take but a languid interest in this subject. They consider that their call is not to say to men, " Be ye reconciled to God," but rather to say to the sacred Scriptures, " Be ye reconciled to science, to reason, to intuition, to consciousness." If in their dreams they should have a vision of a valley full of bones, such as Ezekiel saw, they probably would not concern themselves with the question, " Can these bones live?" but with the question, " Where among all these fossils is the skeleton which forms the missing link between man and the baboon?" The more reasonable theory is not that of modern evolution, but the old rabbinical one of degeneracy. For it really appears as if some of us were going forth, like Nebuchadnezzar, to browse with cattle. Such men do not know what a revival means, and were one to commence among their people they would, like the apes in the Oriental fable, sit shivering round an expiring fire, which they know not how to feed with wood ; or, like the baboons in the old Sanscrit fable, that in a cold, stormy night mistook a glow-worm for a spark of fire, and threw dry sticks upon the poor, flameless creature. It is every way true that the angel who has power over fire comes out from the altar.

Other pastors hold revivals in real regard, but keep the serious examination of the subject in abeyance. Jointly and equally with the people of their charge, they pray for the conversion of souls, while exhortations and invitations to sinners run as golden threads through the tissue of many of their sermons ; but still they consider themselves called to feed the sheep rather than the lambs. They are continually occupied with discourses which seem to be demanded to meet the present necessities of the brotherhood. So that, in their judgment, they could not commence a course of revival sermons without the painful conviction that many hungry members of their flock would suffer and justly complain. Some of these and other pastors have come to regard a revival as a kind of Christian saturnalia, during which order and propriety are set aside for the purpose of reaping all the advantages which liberty and familiarity can bestow. They know how distressing it is for persons of good taste to adjust themselves to the irregularities which too often attend such seasons, and how much more distressing to readjust themselves to the manners of a revolutionized church. One of the standing questions for debate in a famous theological seminary is : " How are we to treat the disinclination of refined culture to sympathetic awakenings ?" *

One difficulty to be overcome arises from a growing tendency to elaborate fixity in the order of worship, and to expect uniformity in the length, if not the quality, of sermons. " There is," says the Rev. Calvin

* " Theory of Preaching," by Rev. Dr. A. Phelps, p. 597.

Colton,* "a pulpit vice (and the pulpit has its vices) which is unfriendly to revival preaching and a great obstacle to its success. It owes its origin to the popular demand that every religious service should have a certain kind of completeness." This is one of the things which prevent the preacher from saying what he thinks best, or from saying it in the most effective manner, and from stopping the moment the best impression is made.

But in churches not a few, the highest and steepest difficulty is of a social kind. Their meetings are largely arranged with a view to attract young people and to maintain social amusements. Reunions, festivals, fairs, sociables, and all that, succeed each other so rapidly, and with such momentum, that church life vies with the world of fashion in keeping out of the mind all thought about our Christian duties and interests. A revival crossing the track of such a train of festivities would be as unwelcome as a fire that is devouring a railroad bridge.

Foremost among those whose theories deserve early consideration, are pastors who labor for continual ingatherings from month to month, or every year, without high excitement or subsequent reaction, and the dangers of lethargy. They hold, with an eminent professor in one of our theological seminaries, that "to a people trained under instructive and discriminating preaching, revivals of religion may come and go as the most natural process of religious experience, creating no morbid excitement, and leaving behind them no perils to be feared and no evils to be corrected. They may be as natural as the tides—themselves a

* "American Revivals," p. 272 (London : 1832).

purifying agency, instead of needing, as actual revivals often do, to be themselves purified." They give examples of pastors and churches that have enjoyed a long succession of ingatherings without the aid of evangelists. Their study and aim are so to educate a church that it may have a harvest of souls every year. To this end they search out and train Christian workers among themselves, and organize daily meetings for the winning of souls. These meetings are separate but permanent services, and young converts find in them a sphere for efficient evangelistic work.

It is but fair to add that some of these friends of pastoral evangelism favor professional revivalists, and would not hesitate, upon an emergency, to invite their co-operation. Having the charge of churches which have been taught and trained in revival labors, they consider that they have nothing to fear from the occasional visits of evangelists who, so far as they are concerned, come and go as auxiliaries and not as revolutionists. Among these pastors the Rev. Dr. William W. Newell, of New York City, may be classed as an honorable representative. Converted under the ministry of Rev. Dr. Lyman Beecher, in Boston, he has been the successful pastor of several churches, in which he has established what he styles evangelistic meetings. While pastor of the Allen Street Presbyterian Church, N. Y., these services were held every evening for three or four months every year. In their chief features they resembled the Fulton Street Prayer-Meeting. They were held for one hour; the prayers, exhortations, and hymns were very brief; variety was studied, and liberty was given to each one to take an active part in the service. The pastor led these meetings, and on Monday evenings gave a discourse, which was intended to be attractive to outsiders, and to follow up the impressions of Sunday. Any one was free to ask the prayers of the faithful. The chorister, or some one familiar with a large number of appropriate hymns and tunes, struck a tune and verse suitable for the end of every prayer, Scripture reading, or address. The leader sometimes announced that speeches and long prayers were out of place. Whenever, amid so much freedom, there was a marked disregard of decorum, brevity, or appropriateness, the transgressor was privately and kindly spoken to. Everything was short ; men dropped the usual beginnings and endings of prayer, and simply asked for what they most wanted. Sometimes the leader would say, '' Now, Christians, tell us how you came to Christ. What led you to decision ? Can you commend Him to these friends ?'' Then men of all ages would take part, and each would give a word of testimony.

In answer to the question, How are converted men led to take part in the meetings ? Rev. Dr. Newell says : '' The duty is at once urged upon them privately. During the meeting the leader may say to the men, ' Have you recently received anything from God for which you would praise Him ?' or, ' What has the Saviour done for you ?' or, ' How did you find Him precious ?' If these methods fail, a person may sometimes be called by name. . . . The easiest and best time for a man to speak in a prayer-meeting is when he commences his Christian life. Let churches never forget that this is the golden time ; and with multitudes it is now or never.''

But some one asks, Why not be content with one good week night meeting ? Rev. Dr. Newell answers, Because each of the continuous meetings brings together twice the number that one evening service would. These constant meetings draw; they are very attractive; there is something doing; it is a daily business of absorbing interest and enjoyment. Again, amusements and unnecessary affairs are surrendered. It is not the meeting one night, and the theatre or the Masonic lodge the next. The mind is held steadily to solemn truth until the soul is saved. These young men feel that it is *their business* to bring their companions to these services, and to labor for their salvation.*

An annual harvest was reaped by this kind of work in the Allen Street Church. One year, two hundred and twenty persons expressed a hope in Christ. During seven other years there was annually an average of eighty-five hopeful conversions. This revival continued for twelve years. Rev. C. H. Spurgeon, with the help of Christian agencies differently organized, has for the last thirty years had large annual ingatherings. That original and earnest pastor, Ludwig Harms, of Hermannsburg, near Hanover, Germany, had large accessions annually for seventeen years. Meetings for prayer or inquiry were held every evening. Many other examples from every evangelical denomination might be cited.

But desirable as such a state of continual growth in numbers is, and laudable as is the aim to lead forward a church to this state, to many pastors the privilege is never given to realize this beautiful ideal; and some who do realize it for several years are at length compelled to adopt evangelistic measures and instruments

* "Revivals: How and When?" by Rev. William W. Newell, D.D., pp. 133-149. This author is an earnest advocate of continual revivals, and yet his attractive volume is marked by candor, good sense, and a judicious largeness of views.

for the conversion of people whom they have failed to reach by ordinary means and agencies. This is not the place to ask the reader to stop and gaze fixedly at this important problem ; but the writer must venture, in passing along, to make one remark which, he has reason to fear, will, in some quarters, meet with a cold if not a freezing reception. Young pastors would, in the judgment of the writer, make their sermons more conducive to the ideal in question, if they would study to apply their themes with love, skill, and thoroughness. One has only to look into recent volumes of sermons and works on homiletics to convince himself that the homiletical study of applications is much neglected. This remark is intended for pastors who are, as they think, reduced to the necessity of depending on stated Sunday services for gradual and continual ingatherings from the world.

But to return and take another glance at the practice of such churches as aim to hold evangelistic services every year. Let not our statements be so understood as to mislead any one in any direction. We are not to suppose that these revival services were held every week throughout each year. During one or two months of the summer most city parishes are scattered. The mass of churchgoers are out of town, and of those who remain not a few are exhausted by the heat or prostrated by disease. In most sections of the country at this season, men, women, and children are overworked gathering in the harvests. A zealous evangelist of our acquaintance has always contended that we are everywhere to seek and expect a revival in the time of summer, and it is not to be denied that he has been blessed with several great awakenings during the hot season. But we have observed that the

meetings were held in villages and cities along the
New England coast, to which multitudes had fled
from the killing heat of the West and South. We do
not intend to maintain that there have been no revivals in very warm weather or in places oppressed with
tropical heat. Generally, however, the case stands
otherwise.* The preacher gives not the Gospel invitation, unless the people assemble to hear it ; but those
who cannot be easily attracted to places of worship in
the most pleasant weather, cannot usually be expected
to go to church daily at a time when many of the most
earnest communicants are fleeing from discomfort and
disease to the mountains or the ocean. And yet,
every Christian laborer may privately do much evangelistic work during the summer, and were this the place
for it, we might point to examples of those who, by
their prayers and serious talks, have turned to righteousness many whom they providentially met on the
lake, or the river, or the ocean, or the mountain, or
in the wilderness. We therefore concur with Rev.
Dr. Newell, while he is answering the question, Why
not gather a harvest of souls at all seasons of the year ?
"On this subject," says he, "there is some senseless
talk. . . . The late fall and winter come ; the evenings are long ; the air is bracing ; business is slack ;
the city is filled with attractive amusements, and

* The same remark applies to Scotland. The great awakenings
that have occurred there in summer have either been near the coast
or among the mountains, while the exceptional cases have, for the
most part, been the revivals at the great communion meetings held in
the open air, which so nearly resemble the American "camp-meet-
ings." These last are, it is true, held in the summer, but very seldom
in the warmest part of it, and when they are so held the airy situation of the spot, together with the shadows of tents and groves, defend
the people from the heat of noonday.

Christians find that God in His sovereignty has made this season of the year most favorable to evangelistic meetings. And while we are planning, praying, and preparing for that time, we feel that God is always blessing us, and that we are striving to be as wise as the children of light ought to be." In New York City, for example, those churches which hold continuous revival services usually commence the first or second week in January, and close before the first of July. In one or two of these churches, at least, we are glad to know, the evenings of late spring and early summer are largely occupied in addresses and talks designed for the growth of young disciples in Christian wisdom and knowledge.

And this suggests another caution : the success of continual revival services is dependent in part on the places where they are held. After a pretty careful review of experiments of this kind, we reach the conclusion that they are very suitable for large and growing cities and villages, or in such sections of old and declining towns as, from any cause, are filled with young people. In many a large city the population rolls in and out and round about so rapidly that the stationary evangelist may reap as rich an annual harvest as he would were he to visit many settled communities ; in the former case his audiences come to him ; in the latter he journeys in quest of his audiences.

Just here arises the question whether churches thus situated and so deeming themselves called to devote themselves to the conversion of the multitudes that are drifting around and past them, are not in danger of taking one-sided views of the mission of a church and its ministry? In answer to this question we must confess that many facts do point toward this danger. It is a mistake to suppose that the promotion of revivals, and consequently of the conversion of souls, is the supreme business of the Gospel ministry. It is only a part of their supreme business ; and every definition of the ends of Christian preaching is defective which does not state in substance that they are to glorify God by the conversion of souls and the edification of the church. The neglect of either of these views or objects is very liable to be visited by its regular penalty. In what way or how soon the penalty will descend is often determined by the government of the church. For example, we have known churches, whose polity was congregational or independent, to give themselves almost exclusively to revival meetings from year to year. What followed? These churches grew indeed in numbers, but, alas ! also in a proselyting spirit and in an emotional and sympathetic habit of mind unenlightened by Scripture knowledge and unfortified by true patience and meekness. Consequently they became so enfeebled by the accession of such a membership, that when important church business was to be discussed fierce disputes and incurable divisions arose ; disintegration followed, and Bishop Berkeley's theory of the infinite divisibility of matter was very nearly realized. We are not here, be it observed, writing in disparagement of these particular forms of church government. Under other kinds of ecclesiastical polity the evils now under consideration might possibly have made their first appearance in the home, in society, or in the place of business.

As a guard against these effects of religious dissipation, seasons of devotional retirement are of no secondary importance, more particularly in large cities. Our blessed Lord's own example and His precepts on this subject (among which is that concerning *secret* prayer, to which is joined the promise of *open* rewards) should teach us the necessity and advantage of stated times of secret communion with God. Nor can we find, in the force of circumstances or the special calls of any ripe spiritual harvest-field, any substitute for this duty and privilege. Hear Cecil : " I am fully persuaded that most religious tradesmen are defective in this duty, those especially in this great city (London). I tell every one of them so with whom I am intimately acquainted."* Hear Tholuck, writing in a quiet university town in Germany : " Men now live in the fleeting present, and have no longer time to think either of the past or of the future. The consequence is that even in the present they do not live as they ought." We are well aware that it would be very objectionable to advise certain classes of young converts to pass more time in their secret chambers. Doubts about doctrines are often removed by a prompt discharge of duties ; fledglings learn their own buoyancy and the various assistance they can receive from the atmosphere only by stretching their wings and sailing away from their nest. But still when the neophyte has such doubts on important doctrines as evidently proceed from a defective Scripture knowledge concerning these doctrines, the wisest course is to encourage him in a more thorough and prayerful investigation of the subject ; otherwise the interruption of his inquiries, by a resort to good-doing or evange-

---

* " Remains of Rev. Richard Cecil." See his remarks " On Religious Retirement" and " On a Spiritual Mind."

listic services, may fail to remove preplexities for good and all. The clouds may return so long as the intellect shall remain logically unsettled. This appears to have been the case of Dr. Arnold, of Rugby. While he was a Fellow at Oxford, he had distressing doubts on certain points in the Thirty-nine Articles. As a remedy for these difficulties he was advised to pause in his inquiries and turn himself more strongly than ever to practical duties. This counsel has generally been thought to have been very wise ; the more so because it was temporarily successful. We say temporarily, for after repeated readings of his life and correspondence, we are convinced that it would have been more expedient to have allowed Arnold to go on battling with his scepticism until he had vanquished it, once for all. This would have increased his knowledge of theology, with which, as it was, he never gained a tolerable acquaintance. It was by his subsequent preaching that he was kept in the habit of studying the Scriptures, and so, as we think, saved himself from that extreme rationalism into which, had he followed a vocation totally secular, he would probably have drifted ; although he would not, perhaps, have wandered into that mire (the Slough of Despond was nothing to this) through which his eldest son Matthew is wading—a mire which seems to be a compound of ignorance, prejudice, misbelief, and miserable fudge. From the known reputation of Mr. Matthew Arnold as a poet, a classical scholar, and an educator, one would have expected something far less chaotic, wretched, and dismal than his religious writings so often reveal. A general acceptance of his dogmas would be to toll a moral curfew—to sound a signal to extinguish all revealed lights, to cover up the last embers of Christian zeal, and to bid all consciences go to sleep in the prospect of a threatening hereafter.

There is another class of converts, real or supposed, who should not be encouraged to put themselves forward in frequent and public meetings. They are of the character commonly advertised as " the greatest sinner in the city," " the blackest infidel in the city," and others of the same genus. All Protestants and many Catholics would, no doubt, concur in the opinion of Carlyle that Loyola ought to have followed his supposed conversion by a life of modest seclusion—" to cower, silent and ashamed, into some dim corner, and to resolve henceforth to make as little noise as possible. That would have been modest, salutary ; that might have led to many other virtues and gradually to all." Which is more damaged, the good cause or the men themselves, by their forwardness, it were hard to determine.

But still there are some to whom practice is the best proof. Among these are such as are full of doubts and fears about their conversion, and such as are naturally very timid and cautious, or those who pass for " old hopers." Richard Baxter, Henry Venn,* and Andrew Fuller agree in their testimony in behalf of the efficacy of Christian work as an antidote for despondency and chronic sadness.

As for the question of the admissible use of the outlines and sketches in the second part of our volume, we do not presume to speak in any preceptorial tone. Writers on scientific subjects have always adopted, without acknowledgment, what they consider the best

---

*" Life of Rev. Henry Venn." See his paper on " Mistakes," etc., last paragraph.

methods of those who went before them in the same walks of knowledge ; and they have eschewed above all things the adoption of methods which sound criticism would regard as second-best. In like manner, students of theology are, for the most part, permitted to borrow such rhetorical partitions or chief-heads as they find most suitable for their object. Thus the young evangelist Burns,* educated at Aberdeen and Glasgow universities, and a vigorous and independent thinker though he was, did not hesitate to put on record the fact that in preaching on Deut. 32 : 35, he once on a memorable occasion availed himself of many hints in Jonathan Edwards's great sermon on the same text. A spring-tide of grace attended its delivery at Perth : "an extraordinary measure of the Holy Ghost ; and the feeling of the hearers became so intense that when one man in the gallery exclaimed, ' Lord Jesus, come and save me ! ' the great mass of the congregation gave expression to their emotion in a universal wailing." The student will find these outlines and sketches profitable exercises in methodology ; and if he shall learn, not slavishly to copy, but freely to imitate them, he may hope that they will serve to discipline him in original thinking and furnish fuel for an earnest ministration of the Word.

We have been guided, as far as possible, by the light of the past. The men of our day, particularly the most ardent men of the period, give no heed to the lessons of the past. They set no value on any experience except their own, not considering that this will be of less service to them than that of others. "Human experience," as Coleridge regretfully says,

---

* "Memoir," by Rev. Dr. Islay Burns, pp. 150, 151.

"like the stern-lights of a ship at sea, illumines only the path which we have passed over." But, he might have added, such lights are of manifold use to the inward man, while they serve to direct and cheer those who follow in our wake.

There is one objection which, to one who merely glances at this volume here and there, may be judged to be well taken. It is this : you appear to satisfy yourself with partial inductions ; not unfrequently you lay down a rule which you support with only one historical or biographical fact. You seem to forget that " one swallow does not make spring." But the reader may be assured that the facts here given are almost all of them representatives of large classes. But it would have been a heavy tax upon the patience of the reader to have paraded across these pages all the facts known to him, which go to support the many suggestions he has made. It has been our purpose to handle the subjects in such a way that when we cite testimony any veteran evangelist who may read it would be able to say : " This agrees with my own experience and observation."

We have set the highest estimate on such recorded facts as either convey or impress the lessons of wisdom. And yet the writer has not been deaf to the voice of the passing hour ; he has hearkened diligently to the counsels of several evangelists now living. He has not always been able to make references to books, because some of the facts and hints here recorded for the first time are of the nature of oral traditions. Occasionally, no doubt, the reader will say, " Oh, I knew that very well before you told me ;" but, after all, the very things we all know so well are apt to lie forgotten just when we most need their assistance. Thus, more than once, have we met with incidents like the following : " In my early ministry an elder of a country church came to me and said, ' Our pastor and church are very desirous you should come out and labor with them.' ' What is the condition of the church?' ' They are thoroughly prepared to work for a revival.' I trusted his word, left my own parish, and went out and preached every evening for two weeks. The community was aroused ; the sanctuary and inquiry room were filled ; but there was scarcely a single conversion ; the church were simply interested *spectators*. This was the last time I ever labored for a revival among the unconverted until my own heart and some members of the church were prepared for the effort." He knew better, but did not remember.

There is, let me add, another and not less advantageous use to be made of revival narratives, which requires that the pastor or evangelist read them for himself—I mean the selection and employment of them for matter of explanation, proof, and persuasion. No fact is better established than that the rehearsal of the incidents of other revivals has been of great service in many a work of grace. Let a single example stand forward in behalf of many. It was while the young Scottish evangelist, William C. Burns, was calling to mind the great achievements of the Spirit at the Kirk of Shotts, in 1630, under the preaching of the celebrated John Livingstone, that his congregation at Kilsyth was overwhelmed with a flood of commingled sorrow and joy. " The power of the Lord's Spirit became so mighty upon their souls as to carry all before it, like the rushing mighty wind of Pentecost." And in the revival meetings he afterward so successfully conducted in Dundee, he read as a part of the exercises Robe's narrative* of former revivals in the same part of Scotland. To reproduce a great number of the most affecting incidents in the history of revivals does not fall within the scope of the present work ; but we have given a long list of the most valuable narratives and biographies in evangelistic literature. Many of them are of great interest and profit ; some of them read much as if they were continuations of the Acts of the Apostles.

In the mean time, new chapters in the history of revivals are in the course of composition. Evangelists who have won abundant success in Christian lands are going beyond the borders and invading heathendom. In his évangelistic zeal Varley has visited Australia, and Taylor is heard of now in India and now in South America. Burns, after laboring with the richest results in Scotland and in Canada, carried the message of salvation to China, saw an awakening at Pechuia, which reminded him of a similar one at Kilsyth, and laid down his bones at last in Manchuria, an obscure but vast kingdom beyond the northern limits of China. Regular missionaries in their tours among heathens are adopting, more and more, the theories and practices of home evangelists. The day is not distant, we hope, when thousands of evangelists will visit the remotest shores, repeating to weary and restless multitudes our Lord's compassionate and universal invitation : '' Come unto me all ye that labor and are heavy

---

* '' Memoir of Rev. William C. Burns, M.A.,'' by Rev. Dr. Islay Burns, pp. 95, 113 ; also '' Evangelists in the Church,'' by Rev. P. C. Headley, p. 325, and Rev. James Robe's '' Narrative of the Work of the Spirit at Cambuslang, Kilsyth, etc., in 1742.''

laden, and I will give you rest. Take my yoke upon you, and learn of me : for I am meek and lowly in heart ; and ye shall find rest unto your souls For my yoke is easy and my burden is light.''

PART I.

PRACTICAL
HINTS CONCERNING REVIVALS.

CHAPTER I.

WORKING AND WAITING FOR A REVIVAL.

Preparation by prayer and beneficence—Relation of missions to revivals—Our Sunday-schools need reconstruction—Unanimity not to be expected at the outset—The ideal Pentecost—Dr. Duff's hint—The time to wait—The call of Providence—The alternations of judgment and mercy.

MANY there are who imagine that a revival is not to be deliberately sought and worked for, but that it is to be waited for, as it must come as the season of spring or a shower of summer comes, without man's bidding, and in spite of his opposition. Nor is it to be doubted that not a few revivals have thus commenced. The churches and communities which they blessed abundantly had made no preparation for them, were not expecting them ; they could only confess that they were in desperate need of them, while they were totally unworthy to receive anything from the Lord, except His judgments. But the blessed Redeemer comes to His people at different seasons, from opposite quarters, and while they are looking for Him, as well as while they are asleep, or awake only to the service of the world or Satan. Fully persuaded, therefore, that very many revivals have been preceded by fitting preparation, we think it prudent to examine its kinds and degrees.

The foremost means of getting ready for a general awakening is prayer. This means is so important that we make it the subject of an entire chapter. Next follows giving for benevolent objects, especially for the

conversion of the heathen. We say of the heathen, because the reports which come to us in response to dona-
tions have a direct tendency to revive a practical interest in the work of conversion, and to lead sinners
among us to contrast their own unregenerated state
with the regenerated state of many who never enjoyed
their privileges and opportunities. Besides, this kind
of beneficence is likely to be the most unselfish. If we
work, pray, and give for our own family, congregation,
or country, we may do this from motives that are
largely selfish ; whereas, if we are beneficent toward
the distant heathen, we rise superior to and fly far beyond ourselves. Witness the experiment in the Mount
Holyoke Seminary and in the Baptist Church at Ket-
tering. Read the observations of President Edwards,*
and look at the decay of those churches which do little
or nothing for preaching the Gospel among idolaters.

It is now in order to suggest the reform of many of
our prayer-meetings. Our space forbids the mere
mention of the abuses to be corrected and the improve-
ments to be introduced in too many of the stated meetings for prayer and exhortation.†

Of scarcely less importance is the entire revolution
of very many of our Sunday-schools. Whatever industry, talent, and wealth can do to make them attractive
has in many schools been done, and yet, alas ! in
Scripture knowledge there is very slow growth, and in
the Redeemer's inward kingdom no growth at all.
But the revolution demanded should begin with the

* " Recollections of Mary Lyon," by Fidelia Fisk ; " The Memoirs
of Andrew Fuller ;" the works of President Edwards, " Thoughts on
the Revival of Religion," Part V.

† Fail not to read " The Prayer-Meeting," by the Rev. L. O.
Thompson.

superintendents and teachers. It may be of little advantage to displace them. It is better, if the church can afford it, to have none but hired superintendents, of approved piety and intelligence, with a sense of obligation and of strict accountability both to Christ and the Church. At any rate, there should be a two-fold aim : to cultivate the conscience and to lead to the Saviour. The study of the Old Testament will promote the former ; of the New Testament, the latter. With all its faults, it must still be said that the Sunday-school of to-day is the Church of the future. At teachers' prayer-meetings the leader may request the mention of the names of any whom the teachers desire to carry to the Throne of Grace. They may be divided into classes, as the insensible, the convicted, those with whom the Holy Spirit appears striving, such as seem to be hardening under affliction, etc.

Here we subjoin the preparation of the Church in the matter of confessing faults, composing differences, " breaking up the fallow ground," taking out of the way stones and stumbling-blocks, endeavoring after a positive no less than a negative goodness, and the fostering of forbearance and compassion toward such fellow-disciples as we cannot regard with complacency.

In almost every church there are found, at times, some who have, for no sufficient reason, abandoned the habit of going to church. If the pastor has any reason to suspect that they have come to dislike him or his preaching, he can, nevertheless, while visiting his flock, urge them to come to the prayer-meetings, more especially if the church has tried to make them more attractive, instructive, and cheering.

Rare indeed are the churches that at the beginning of a work of grace unanimously give their voices in favor of it. The young pastor who means to win souls will do well to commence with securing the co-operation of a few prudent and trustworthy helpers. And if the principal burdens of the work fall to their share, from first to last, let him not wonder. Let him remember how the army of Gideon was purposely reduced to a small company, and what a decisive and glorious victory was won over Sisera, for all the tribes of Israel, by the two tribes Zebulun and Naphtali. Consider, too, how excellent men may be misled by the delusion that all revivals of God's work are just alike, and are prejudiced by the memory of some great awakening that came, all of a sudden, upon a whole nation. We have somewhere read of a Scottish minister who was always praying for a true revival, while he found fault with the recent American, Irish, and Scottish revivals. Such men forget that there was but one day of Pentecost, and that the apostles did not refuse to go forward because they could not have a second.

In addition to week-day meetings for prayer, praise, and exhortation, there should be on Sunday new preaching services, and if possible, in new places. The course recommended by the late eloquent and renowned missionary, the Rev. Dr. Alexander Duff,* is intended for cities, but is even more practicable in village and country churches. It is this : The pastor is to say to his people, " We must cease to be selfish ; and therefore in the afternoon I will get another person to take my place in the pulpit. He will give you wholesome truth on which to feed. While he is addressing you, I will be down yonder,

* " Life," by Dr. George Smith, vol. ii. p. 304.

speaking to poor souls who have never had any of the bread that came down from heaven ; and therefore in your prayers remember them and me."

In the ordinary affairs of life, the time to wait is after we have done all we can by word and deed to accomplish our object. But as in the kingdom of Christ we cannot work to any good purpose without His gracious assistance, our best exertions, at times, partake of the nature of waiting. In seasons of weariness and discouragements, this is the principal duty that remains for us to do. Then we must "rest in the Lord, and wait patiently for Him." * According to the Hebrew idiom, we are to "be silent to the Lord"—that is, if we rightly understand the meaning, we are to desist from our importunities, and occupy ourselves in thanks and praise. We are to cease attempting to serve him by a troubled and murmuring excitement, but rather make melody in our hearts unto the Lord. It is while engaged in this part of worship that the long-expected blessing sometimes comes.†

And this accounts for the fact that in some instances, when the prayer-meeting has been changed into a praise-meeting, there has been heard "a sound of abundance of rain."

This brings us to the place where we can glance at the relations of revivals to the severe and gracious providences of God. As the vicissitudes of day and night are friendly to the material world, so the prosperous and adverse events of providence are beneficial to the moral world. But the co-operation of providence and grace suggests many problems that are too

* Comp. Ps. 65 : 1 ; 62 : 1-5 ; 37 : 7.
† 2 Chron. 5 : 13, 14 ; 2 Kings 3 : 15.

mysterious for us to solve. The subject is sublimely and profoundly illustrated in the first chapter of Ezekiel, where Jehovah is represented as riding in His chariot ; while on the human and practical side it is illustrated by the 107th Psalm. This psalm teaches many things, but reiterates the lesson that hearty praise is better than the petitions which are pressed out of our troubled hearts by the heavy hand of adversity ; and in the closing lines we are taught that afflictions are dictated by the loving-kindness of the Lord. The history of revivals proves that great works of grace have gone before and followed great national calamities, and this has been the case of lesser awakenings in churches and small communities. Very instructive are those successive visions of the Apocalypse, 14 : 14–20, in which we behold the Lord Jesus crowned with gold, as King of the harvest, sitting on a white cloud—the emblem of holiness and peace— holding in his hand the sharp sickle of the effectual Gospel. He reaps the ripened wheat of the land—in other words, converts part of the passing generation. Then follows the angel of justice with a sharp sickle, and goes into the vineyard and cuts off the clusters of grapes, and casts them unto the wine-press of the wrath of God. Now, as always, mercy goes before judgment ; while prayer, whether it be the deep-voiced intercession for pardon or the bitter cry for avengement, marks and calls out the harvest hour for both. Some of the following chapters are discussions of the same subject, although with more unity and detail ; while many of the preparatory texts and subjects are classified in the indexes.

CHAPTER II.

PRAYER is the right arm of evangelism. Very many are the instances of revivalists who in emergencies, and especially when the work of God in a community seemed to pause, or after long and apparently unavailing labor have passed whole nights and days in secret prayer. Indeed, such cases are not uncommon. There will be times when the providence of the Spirit says to the evangelist, Cease for a while to deal with the people on behalf of God, and give thyself tonight or to-day to dealing with God in behalf of the people and thyself. We do not say that such prayers will always prevail for the objects urged. Sometimes the answer has been : Pray no longer for a continuance of the work of reviving grace in this place. But in most cases such importunities and pleadings have been answered soon, and with fresh manifestations of saving power.

Much is it to be desired that numbers agree to meet and pray for the blessing of the Spirit upon the coming revival and the expected meetings. The Divine favor has almost always approved such assemblages. One example is as familiar as it is impressive. It is that of the young John Livingstone, whose sermon on Monday, the 1st of June, at the Kirk of Shotts, when nearly five hundred were converted, was preceded by a prayer-meeting, which continued through the Sunday night preceding. And when Whitefield was travelling through Scotland in 1771, "the Lord countenanced him in a very convincing manner, particularly at a place called Lundie, five miles north of Dundee. Scarcely had he begun when the presence of Divine power was very discernible." "Never," adds his fellow-traveller, "did I see such weeping in any congregation."

Whence, according to human judgment, came the beginnings of his success in Lundie? From a meeting of a considerable number of serious Christians, who, hearing that he was to come that way, spent most part of the preceding night in prayer. Well known are the immediate and lasting effects of the sermon entitled, "Sinners in the Hands of an Angry God," which President Edwards preached at the time of the "Great Awakening." It was believed that the sermon owed much of its success to the earnest petitions of a few believing persons who spent the whole of the previous night in a prayer-meeting in the vicinity (Enfield). These prayers were made the more earnest by the fear that God, who was blessing other places, would in just indignation pass them by. A short time before the great revival that took place at East Hampton, Long Island, in the summer of 1764, some of the good people became wrestling Jacobs in their determination to receive the blessings of salvation.* Similarly was prayer instrumental in the Scottish revival at

* The Rev. Dr. Samuel Buell's "Narrative," p. 28.

Moulin in 1800, at Arran in 1813, at Skye in 1814, at Lewes in 1834, and at Kelsyth during the early stages of the Spirit's majestic doings in that town.* We would not, of course, be understood as saying that every instance of the Lord's gracious returns to His people is totally dependent on known importunities. The real human sources of many revivals are more secret and remote. They have often been traced to some poor sick disciple, praying at home for years, or to a little band of believers meeting according to mutual pledges, and at times and places unknown or unconsidered by the mass of formal professors. The great harvesting of souls which in 1859 began in Ireland and advanced thence to Scotland and England, had its obscure source in a meeting of four young men for prayer in an old country school-house.†

When, therefore, a pastor or evangelist is about to commence special meetings, he will do well to inquire whether any are or have been secretly or quietly praying for a gracious visitation of the Lord. If he shall be so happy as to find out such hidden ones, it would not always be wise to proclaim his discovery. It will suffice if it move him to obtain from others the promise that they will secretly and, if possible, unitedly remember the anticipated services at the throne of grace. Nor should he be satisfied with cold and formal requests and responses. He should urge the importance and necessity of such intercession and importunity from the Scriptures of truth and the history of revivals.

Ordinarily it is not prudent to seek at the outset of

---

* " Lectures on Revivals by Ministers of Scotland," p. 335.
† " The Year of Grace," by Professor Gibson, p. 41.

special services a general discussion of the expediency of the undertaking, and then call for a vote on the question. So far from this, it is very seldom wise to talk much about a revival, even while one is in progress. Rather should we unite all our forces to pray that the Lord may continue and extend His own saving work, and to co-operate with Him in the use of all the means of grace.

There may be a great deal of cant and formality in preparing for special services. Revival hymns are, perhaps, learned and repeated in an unfeeling and unseasonable manner. Such as have assisted in former revivals take every opportunity to talk about, rather than to pray and work for the Lord's gracious visitation ; while overvaluing their own narrow individual observation and experience, they are very positive that if certain means and measures are adopted, many sinners will be brought to repentance, and the Church be elevated to a Pentecostal power and joy. But let us hearken to the voice of a venerable pioneer of thirty-five years' experience,[*] and all the more attentively because it is in accord with the voices of many other revivalists : '' Sometimes a church will send for an evangelist, in order that they may have what they call a good time. They will pray, sing, and talk with a great deal of emphasis, but they do not possess that peculiar state of mind which prepares them to be workers with God. It is often necessary, in the first place, to take away from the church all human dependence, just as much as it is to endeavor to take away the sinner's dependence, or that in which he trusts. This I have never known to fail, that when-

---

[*] '' Life and Times of the Rev. Thomas S. Sheardown,'' p. 198.

ever a church, under the proclamation of God's truth, was led to cry out as Rachel did, 'Give me children or I die,' sinners have been converted to God, and Zion has been increased by an addition of living members."

While, therefore, cant is to be carefully avoided, it is very promotive of a revival to obtain and communicate facts concerning special works of grace in other places. Plain and unexaggerated statements of this kind have many a time caused "great searchings of heart," driven a church to renewed prayer, and kindled a flame of zeal in hundreds of hearts and homes. The news of the revival of 1858 in the United States, wafted across the Atlantic in every steamer, was plainly instrumental in enlisting the hearts of thousands in a similar work in Ireland, Scotland, and England. In a single and incomplete narrative of this awakening in Great Britain,* there are a dozen passages which serve to fix a proper value on this means of advancing the work. Among these influences were the reports which good men, fresh from the work of winning souls in other places, made to communities that were praying for a gracious visitation of the Spirit. Two things greatly add to the effect of this means : the newness of the intelligence, and the readiness of the people to receive it. Accounts of awakenings in former times given to a formal or dead-alive people will, perhaps, do more harm than good. The spread of a fire depends much on the nature and condition of the fuel.

* "Authentic Records of Revival," edited by the Rev. William Reid, with an introduction by the Rev. Dr. Horatius Bonar (Nesbet, Lond., 1860).

The preparations of Divine Providence are often still more remote. Events apparently the most adverse are ultimately found to have been the mysterious beginnings of a state of great spiritual prosperity. At times there seems to be a conflict between the course of Providence and the ways of the Divine Spirit. In such seasons of perplexity, let us ever pray that all clouds may be driven from our sky, so that, with Ezekiel, we may see the wheels and the spirits moving in close connection and in one direction. While the Rev. Dr. Daniel Baker was travelling in Virginia, his horse stumbled, and in falling broke a shaft of his gig. Detained at Charlotte Court House until the injury was repaired, he was invited to preach in the place. He consented to do so, and this led him to hold an unbroken series of meetings in Virginia, which continued a whole year, and resulted, it was thought, in the conversion of about a thousand persons. It was only a slight illness that detained Charles Simeon for a summer's day at Dunkeld, in Scotland. But this led to another more vexatious delay ; for it brought him to Pitlochrie to be detained for another day, on account of what was to him an unexpected fast in the little parish of Moulin. And yet both these delays were parts of the Lord's gracious design in making Mr. Simeon the instrument of converting the parish minister, and in preparing the way for a revival in Moulin and other parts of the Highlands—a revival that eventuated in the conversion of Alexander Duff, who afterward became the eloquent and renowned missionary to India. Once Whitefield had made every preparation to embark for America. He had preached a farewell sermon to his friends in London, and had set out for the sea-coast, where he was to begin his voyage, but an unlooked-for embargo disconcerted his plans, and compelled him, for a time, to resume his labors in England. Such, however, was the success of his preaching in several cities, while the ship was shut up in port, that he was ultimately moved to thank God for the embargo.* It was an accident that led to the great revival in 1630, at Shotts, in a sequestered corner of Scotland. Some ladies of rank were one day passing the manse, when their carriage broke down. The minister, Mr. Hance, invited them to remain in his house until it could be repaired. During their stay in the manse they noticed that it was small and dilapidated. In gratitude for the minister's kind attentions to them, they built a new house and on a better situation. Whereupon Mr. Hance thanked the ladies, and asked them how he could worthily testify his gratitude. They desired him to invite some ministers of their acquaintance to assist him at the next communion. Accordingly a large number of people from all parts of the country assembled. On the following Monday, June 21st, John Livingstone preached that sermon which made him and the obscure little place among the most famous in the history of revivals. These special providences of the Holy Spirit in reference to revivals are worthy of careful observation and grateful acknowledgment. These are shown in the accidents of life not only, but in our relations to parents, teachers, and pastors as well. Books read, strangers talked with, loss of wealth or employment, disappointments, loss of children or others very dear to us, severe sickness, or threatened death, may be so ordered by the Spirit

---

* "Life," by Dr. George Smith, vol. ii., p. 327 See Whitefield's "Journals," No. V., p. 7.

as to disengage the mind from this world, and draw attention to the next.   They may be the pre-arranged means of removing obstacles in our way to the hearing of the Gospel, and thus serve as a negative preparation for the work of regeneration.   They may go far to shape the terrene form of the new man, so that it may receive the divine breath of a new life.*   Two happy deaths heralded one great revival.†   But to return and make an end.   Intercession for particular persons has often been observed as a sign of the near presence of the mighty Saviour.   Large and comprehensive petitions do not offer so hopeful an omen.   When we pray for the speedy conversion of a whole city or nation we can hardly ask in faith, nothing doubting.   Few such prayers were ever answered, and for one very good reason : such vast results are almost always reached gradually, through a long course of time.   If we are deeply moved by the Spirit of all grace, our prayers become personal and individual.   We single out friends and relatives as the subjects of intercession and unceasing importunity.   " Why do you expect a revival ? ' rejoined a pastor to a wise and zealous member of his flock.   " Because," was the reply, " I have learned this evening that three members of our church are praying for the same individuals.   Each is ignorant of the strong desires of the others.   It is the Spirit of God alone that can thus operate simultaneously on these minds."   This tendency to individualize becomes habitual with some winners of souls ; so much so, at times,

---

* The Rev. Dr. William Anderson, in his treatise on " Regeneration," distinguishes between the providence of the Spirit and inspiration in this gracious change.   His discussion of the subject is original and instructive, pp. 133-137.

† The Rev. Dr. S. Buell's Narrative, p. 136.

that they indulge in public and shocking personalities.

We will only add, that whenever the pastor contemplates special services he will best prepare the way for these, not by trying to enlarge his Sunday congregations, but his week-day prayer-meetings. In his pastoral visits he may meet with many neglecters of the Sunday services, who will perhaps be able to make very fair excuses for neglecting these services, and some may be so bold as to confess that they do not like the preaching. But if he make no mention of the neglect of Sunday worship, while he urge the importance of going to the week-day meeting for prayer, he will prevent the fabrication of some of their excuses, and possibly prepare the way for such an awakening as will lead back these wanderers to all the services of the Church.

CHAPTER III.

CHOICE OF SUBJECTS AND TEXTS FOR REVIVAL SERMONS.

General and special themes—The chief end of a true revival—Preaching on elevating subjects—Combining Law and Gospel—Testimony of Dr. Tholuck—Texts which have been honored by the Spirit—Danger of exclusive attention to the Holy Ghost—A list of common topics—Dr. Kirk's opinion—Doctrine and practice disconnected—Preaching to the brotherhood—Professed readiness may be unreadiness—Future punishment—To be taught Scripturally and in love.

THE evangelist is never able to take thought for the morrow concerning his text or his theme ; and yet he may probably be able to say in general what classes of subjects are best suited to the beginning or middle or end of such a work of grace. Or he may tell us what subjects have been the most manifestly blessed as instruments of the Spirit in his own ministrations.

In considering this question we ought to begin with the postulate that the end of evangelistic preaching is to glorify the triune God, by seeking the reclamation of backsliders, the reformation of professors, and the conversion of the impenitent. Now it is a deplorable fact that a so-called revival may begin, continue, and close with apparent success because of many additions to a church, while, alas ! the triune God has not been exalted in the estimation of the Church. Indeed, the conclusion of the work has been signalized by a revival of irreverence for the Word, for the ministers, and for the house of the Lord. Some evangelists are so fully occupied in describing the nature and wickedness of men, and the various forms or stages of Christian experience, that they find no time to dwell on the attributes and perfections of God. Very strange to these must appear the message borne by the angel once seen flying in the midst of heaven, having the everlasting Gospel to preach. That message is (Rev. 14 : 6): " Fear God and give glory to Him . . . worship Him that made heaven and earth, and the sea, and the fountains of waters." Such, we apprehend, was the spirit and good effect of the preaching. It magnified the supreme excellences of God, and taught all nations that they would best display the fruits of conversion to Christ by obeying and adoring the Maker of heaven and earth, the Saviour of mankind, and the Spirit of all grace. Be it remembered that the Gospel, as first preached by angels, began with the song, " Glory to God in the highest."

We need not wonder, therefore, that such subjects and texts have been most unmistakably and frequently attended with reviving and regnerating grace as have most clearly and vividly exhibited the character, attributes, and works of the Father, Son, and Spirit in their relation to revivals. This kind of preaching is many a time the thunder and lightning that remove the stagnation, miasma, and the oppressive heat that before pervaded the moral atmosphere, and are followed by a cool, bracing, and refreshing breeze from the presence of the Lord. Very numerous are the proofs and illustrations of this statement. Here is one : A Presbyterian minister in Vermont writes to this effect. A powerful revival had just commenced in a manufacturing village in the town of B. A great number were awakened and much alarmed, but there had been but few conversions. In view of this state of things, the church had appointed a day of fasting and prayer.   At the meeting that was held (nearly a thousand persons being present) the deepest solemnity and stillness prevailed, interrupted only by a sigh or a groan from some burdened heart.   A neighboring minister preached in the morning.   Mr. Clark, in the afternoon, to the surprise and grief of many (myself among the rest), preached on the sovereignty of God. But the sermon told on those awakened, guilty hearts, and from that hour the work went on with increased power.*   There are no doubt many congregations and occasions to which this and kindred topics would be ill adapted, but thus much may be said in general, that whenever the preacher is in doubt about the choice of his theme, he may pretty safely rise in soul and select a subject that dwells on the Godward aspects of the work.   When an evangelist visits a church with whose spiritual condition he is not well acquainted, he will often find Mr. Finney's methods suggestive.   He first informed himself on two points : where are his hearers at the time doctrinally, and where are they practically ? If they have been much under the influence of the doctrine of God's sovereignty, he preached responsibility. If he was in an Arminian atmosphere, he would show God on the throne.   But his aim being more particularly to get false professors out of the way, and cold professors into the work of revival, he generally began with a thorough handling of the law and awakening the conscience or raising the thoughts of the people to higher

* The " Complete Works of the Rev. Dr. Daniel A. Clark," vol. i. p. 35.   In the great revival at East Hampton in 1764, the most successful preaching combined the Law and the Gospel.   " Revival in East Hampton," etc., by the Rev. Samuel Buell, D.D. (Sag Harbor, 1808), p. 78.

conceptions of God's requirements and the nature of true holiness, humbling the pride of man, chasing the soul out of every false refuge, and urging an immediate surrender to the Lord's supremacy, and an immediate acceptance of His grace. Mr. Finney somewhere says that the general character of his doctrinal preaching, during his earlier life, was formed by his opposition to the high Calvinism which, as he believed, hindered the progress of revivals in many of the communities in which he was called to labor.

A distinguished and very successful pastor informed the writer that once, when he and his people had determined to invite a certain evangelist to assist him, he commenced a series of sermons on subjects that powerfully appealed to the conscience, in order, as far as possible, to prepare the way for the evangelist, who, as he thought, was too weak in his addresses to the consciences and the fears of his audiences.

"I have observed," says Tholuck, "that wherever in the Roman Catholic Church faithful pastors have preached the way of life, spiritual hunger and thirst have always been excited to a greater extent than in the Lutheran Church. From what other cause does this arise than the fact that our people have been surfeited with the continual preaching of the Gospel, without calls to repentance ; whereas among them the preaching of repentance and of the Law abounds, while there is a dearth of the preaching of the Gospel."

It is a matter of some interest to inquire what texts have been the most highly honored by the Divine Spirit in the conversion of souls. The text used by the celebrated John Livingstone, at the Kirk of Shotts, with such memorable effect, was Ezek. 36 : 25. The words " that every mouth may be stopped "

(Rom. 3 : 19), as preached by President Edwards, produced the most immediate saving fruit that he had ever found as the effect of one discourse. While Whitefield was preaching in Scotland the text that was most blessed to individuals from whom he afterward heard was from Isa. 54 : 5 : "Thy Maker is thy husband." The most of those who were converted through the instrumentality of this sermon were men.

Fifty persons were brought to resolve to seek salvation by the blessing of the Spirit on Nettleton's sermon from the text Gen. 6 : 3. In two instances President Dwight's sermon on Jeremiah 8 : 20 : "The harvest is past," etc., was the beginning of a revival among the students of Yale College. In the first work of grace nearly half of them were united to the college church. Similar effects were ascribed to its delivery on two other occasions in different places.

After considerable observation and some little experience, we are most thoroughly persuaded that Satan's most frequent and most destructive imitations of true revivals are to-day attended with so much preaching, exhortation, and prayer concerning the Holy Spirit as to drown the voice of the Gospel as to salvation through Christ. The end of the Spirit's mission is to convince the world of sin, because they believe not on Him, and to glorify Him (John 16 : 9, 14). Every experience and testimony that does not lead sinners beyond the Spirit and its operations, to an apprehension of and belief in Jesus, is, at best, of doubtful effect ; and is often, we fear, productive of deception and despair. Almost all those who exalt the Spirit at the expense of Jesus (and, alas ! of anxious souls) are loud in professions of wonderful transports and of assured confidence, as well as clamorous in

prayer and uncharitable in reproof. Deplorable in·
deed is the condition of sinners who are exposed to
such delusive or rather diabolic assaults. Jesus stands
at the door and knocks, but He is not heard ; for
Satan has breathed up an infernal wind, which is roar·
ing among the trees, howling in the chimneys, and·
shaking the windows.

The matter of revival sermons is of far greater importance than the manner of their delivery, their style,
or the person who preaches them. The list of topics
on which Nettleton and other revivalists of his day
dwelt were the holiness and immutability of God, the
unchangeable obligations of the divine law, the depravity of the natural heart, the necessity of regener·
ation, the free offers of the Gospel, the fulness and all·
sufficiency of the atonement, the reasonableness and
necessity of immediate repentance and submission,
the variety of the refuges and excuses of sinners, and
the manner, guilt, and danger of slighting, resisting,
and opposing the operations of the Holy Spirit ; the
inability of man to reconcile himself to God by his
own works, the justice of God in the everlasting condemnation of sinners, the sovereignty of God in the
salvation of sinners, and that He is not under any
obligation to save them. These subjects were not
always formally discussed, but the Scriptures of truth
concerning them were freely declared and applied in
an experimental and practical way, as the occasion
demanded. And yet a less strictly Calvinistic kind of
doctrine has often been seemingly successful. " Men
of various theological schools agree in the results of
their preaching, while from local causes, and their individual theological views even, they differ in their
selection of topics. In the hands of some men the

sovereignty of God in election and regeneration is a
Damascus blade to human pride. Others never present
it without a paralyzing effect, awakening resistance
and discouraging the action of the human will. The
Calvinist and the Arminian, Whitefield and Wesley,
are both owned of the Master in the work of converting the soul."*

Facts in the history of revivals indicate that the
extremes alike of Calvinism and Arminianism are
unfriendly to a large and good success in this department of Christian exertion. An aged evangelist, who
was very long and very extensively useful, once told
the writer that the reading of the works of Andrew
Fuller (a moderate Calvinist) had been more profitable
to him than any other human production. Preachers
there are who escape wrong applications of their sermons by combining an equal incapacity for theology
and for logic. They proclaim heresies in abundance,
but being almost always inconsequential in their rea-
sonings, their practical inferences are often excellent,
and of great service in revivals. May not this class
of evangelists be among those of whom it is said,
" Blessed are the poor in spirit, for theirs is the Kingdom of Heaven"? Anyhow, they are made strong
through two weaknesses, which should not, as we are
apt to think, afflict most men of God. But still, as
some " held the truth in unrighteousness," so, by way
of counterpoise, others hold error in righteousness.
There is yet another hopeful class. The fashionable
method of teaching theology, which omits all consideration of practical consequences, and concludes
each part of the system without applications, forms in

* The Rev. Dr. E. N. Kirk, " Lectures on Revivals," p. 264.

the mind of the average student the notion that systematic theology has very little to do with Christian work, experience, and worship. If, therefore, erroneous theories are thus inculcated, they may, happily, in cases not a few, fail to quench the zeal or cripple the activity of the Christian laborers thus mistaught.

An aged revivalist, after a very successful ministry of over fifty years, says that the most of his preaching has been addressed to the active members of the Church, believing that when Zion, has put on her strength mighty works will be accomplished. Hence he has devoted but very few sermons exclusively to the unconverted.

In one instance a pastor whose sermons were very searching and promotive of self-examination, was followed by a preacher who began and continued in strains of hope and benevolent earnestness. He all along took it for granted that the Church were equally prepared for heaven and for work. Large ingatherings followed.

When, however, this hopeful and joyful strain of preaching only serves, like the drum and the fife, to drown the groans of the wounded or to disguise fear, it is but the means of advancing a superficial and evanescent excitement. A certain evangelist was invited to hold a series of meetings in a distant place. On reaching the church he found the brethren engaged in singing the praises of God, and apparently filled with joy and rejoicing. One of the deacons declared to him, "We are all ready to go to work. I do not think you ever met such a church in your life. We are all right." "You have told the truth, my brother," was the preacher's answer, "for it has never yet been my lot to see the church that was all right, just as God would have them." However, the evangelist was assured that he had only to preach to the unconverted, and immediate success would follow. Accordingly he commenced with sermons to the impenitent, who soon filled the place of worship. Many were convicted, but not one was converted. The evangelist now more than suspected that all was not right, and on diligent search found an injured and alienated member of the church. The church met and composed their differences. The fruit of unity was immediate. On the very night of the meeting for reconciliation, five hearts that had been burdened with guilt (although ignorant of the trouble in the church) found freedom and joy. These were the first ingatherings of a harvest of about four hundred souls. In such cases, be it remembered, the Spirit does not wait because of mere matters of opinion or inveterate prejudices, but on account of moral wrongs that destroy fellowship and so quench the Spirit.

As this treatise professedly leans on the past, it may be reasonably expected to ask what is the verdict of revivalists respecting the preaching of future punishment. I have read the history of many revivals, and the biographies of many pastors and evangelists, but have failed to discover any real and lasting work of grace in the course of which the Scripture doctrine of future punishment was either denied or ignored. No fact is more clearly established than this. Nor is it contradicted by antecedent probability. It is obvious that the great Creator knew His own creatures when, in order to move them to secure their eternal safety, he appealed not only to their hopes but to their fears as well. There are caverns in the human soul which will never be visited by the light of Gospel day unless

a path shall have been prepared for it by the lightnings of eternal justice. Let the evangelist, therefore,
set forth this doctrine as he finds it in the oracles of
God. He will indeed find it so admirably coherent
with a sound philosophy that he may in very intelligent communities be tempted to handle it philosophi-
cally ; but let him stoutly resist this temptation. In
like manner, let him withstand every temptation to
touch upon such speculative questions about the future
state as some German theologians venture to discuss.
It speaks volumes against their bold conjectures that
the church of which they are members is forsaken by
the masses of the German people, and that almost all
the Lutheran parishes are candidly considered as
proper missionary fields for American Methodists and
Baptists. ''Christian consciousness'' as an oracle is
deserting those who trusted in its guidance ; ''thy
calf, O Samaria, hath cast thee off.''

Still preach future punishment, but preach it in love
for the people. In looking at the proofs of this Scripture doctrine, we should say, ''I believe, therefore I
speak,'' and in diligently regarding the people we
ought to remember the counsel of the apostle, when
he bids us speak the truth in love ; but this precious
precept should be laid to heart by all winners of souls,
both in revivals and out of them ; as well in the pulpit
as out of the same. Says the late Dr. Tholuck (and
some good things, it may be confessed, do still come
out of Germany), '' A person who had been all over
the world, once told me that he had scarcely ever
fallen into the company of travellers with whom he was
not able to converse pleasantly, and, as he hoped,
with lasting effect, about the journey to the heavenly
country. I expressed my repugnance to talk purposely

commenced with a view to convert, and spoke of the danger of forestalling instead of following in the footsteps of the Holy Spirit, of the snare of pride, and more of the same sort. He meekly answered : ' I endeavored never to speak until I was certain that I loved. I figured to myself, what we too often forget, that we men are all brothers to one another, and all belong to the same Father's house, but are so easily turned aside from the path that leads to it. I thought of the words of Gellert :

> " ' Perchance in heaven one day to me
> 　　Some blessed saint will come and say,
> All hail ! beloved, but for thee
> 　　My soul to death had fallen a prey.
> And oh, what rapture in the thought !
> One soul to glory to have brought.'

" ' This never failed to soften and warm my heart ; and when there was love in mine, I soon found a bridge into that of the stranger. It was as if the breath of God had drawn out a thread from the one and fastened it to the other.' This narrative I have never been able to forget." Solidity and depth of conviction may make us fiercely and destructively earnest, unless it be moderated by compassion for the people.

CHAPTER IV.

THE STYLE MOST SUITABLE FOR REVIVAL PREACHING.

The qualities of this style—Effects of style—Clearness the first requisite—Wesley, Nettleton, Finney, and Moody—Example of brevity from Arnot—The excessive use of climaxes—Sermons hastily prepared—The word " professor."

STYLE stands next to matter, although an appearance of art and finish in such addresses has no proper place.   By style we do not here intend mere diction, or even words, phrases, sentences, and discourses, which meet the requirements of our school rhetorics. We include in our notion of style these excellences of expression which have their source in the inspiration of the Spirit, the best peculiarities of the preacher, and a careful study of the matter of the sermon.   The best revival style is simple, sincere, earnest, and tender, in order that it may give appropriate voice to the thoughts, feelings, and purposes of the true evangelist. The style of a revival sermon is like a tree which is known not by its blossoms, but by its fruit.   It shows internal evidence of its acceptance and success.   A pastor once desired to know the effect of repeating to his people one of Jonathan Edwards's revival sermons. The effect was instant and powerful.   Another pastor made a similar experiment with one of the sermons of Richard Baxter, after a few changes to modernize the style.   He had given previous notice of his intention confidentially to a few friends, in order that the general effect might not be diminished by the novelty of the

proceeding. In this instance also the sermon was
followed by signs of the Lord's returning presence.
There were, says Mr. Finney, two young ministers,
who began to preach at the same time. One of them
had great success in converting sinners, the other
none. Meeting one day, the latter inquired of the
other what was the reason of this difference. " Why,"
replied the other, " the reason is this, that I aim at a
different end. My object is to convert sinners ; but
you aim at no such thing. Here ; take one of my
sermons and preach it to your people, and see what
the effect will be." The man preached the sermon,
and it did produce effect. He was frightened when
sinners began to weep, and when one came to him
after meeting, and asked him what he should do, the
minister apologized to him, and said, " I did not aim
to wound you ; I am sorry I have hurt your feelings."
Let us not be understood as saying that either revival
subject-matter or revival style, or both most wisely
combined, can ever of themselves be sufficient to
secure a gracious visitation of the Spirit. Neither
was the Word without the Spirit, nor the Spirit without the Word, in most of the revivals that have hither
to blessed the Church and the world. True it is that
we cannot always trace every conversion to a particular text, or even to any portion of Scripture. Indeed
there exists some testimony to confirm the opinion
that the works of creation and Providence have been
consecrated as means to the awakening, if not the
conversion, of men. However, these cases must be
regarded as exceptional. Calamities, public and
private, have occasioned such a seriousness and tenderness of heart as have many a time prepared the
people for a special work of grace. But if they come

while the work is in progress, they are often found antagonistic to the advancement of convicting and converting grace. Mr. Nettleton somewhere tells us that the sudden death of a rich man and his great funeral so distracted the attention of a community in which a revival was going forward that it brought the work to a speedy and deplorable end.

But to return. Here we may raise the question, What are the distinctive qualities of the style of the best revival sermons? In answer, we must say that the one essential requisite is clearness. In respect of this excellence all the great revivalists and reformers are as one, while in most other qualities they are dissimilar. Neither Wesley nor Edwards, neither Nettleton nor Moody could be said to be very earnest in style. Indeed Wesley was called by Robert Hall " the quiescence of turbulence," because, while his manner was so calm, it yet seemed to produce commotion all around him. The same might be said of Mr. Finney and Mr. Spurgeon. We must, therefore, distinguish here between what is desirable and what is necessary. Revival preaching, as to style, matter, and spirit, has been forcibly described by the Rev. Dr. Kirk as " enlightening, thought-quickening, heart-searching, heart-quickening, conscience-quickening, and conscience-guiding." To which we may add peace-giving and joy-proclaiming. In treating of mere style, he speaks of a certain moderation as peculiar to its highest forms. " It is," says he, " marked by solemnity, tempered by cheerfulness ; reverence modified by childlike familiarity ; awfulness by tenderness ; profoundness by simplicity ; respectfulness by directness ; self-possession by earnestness."

Even sketches of revival sermons will, in many

cases, be characterized by the same brevity as the general composition. They abound in '' catch-words,'' as the lawyers would call them. A happy instance of this kind may be found among the sermons of the late Rev. William Arnot, of Scotland. The title is, '' Who Knocks ?'' (Rev. 3 : 20). The heads are : 1. Who stands ? 2. How near He comes. 3. How far off he is kept. 4. He knocks for entrance. 5. How many things hinder the hearing. 6. Hear and open. 7. I will come in. True it is, however, that every subject will not admit of such brief indications of the framework of a sermon.

Above all the things that belong to the evangelistic style, the most popular is naturalness. Every great revivalist knows this, and therefore he is content to retain many faults, lest in the attempt to remove them he shall seem to diminish his individuality. It is a mistake, however, to think that in order to be natural we must needs be vulgar or singular or eccentric. But still either of these, or all of them combined, will even be more popular (and so far more useful) than the highest display of manifest art. In proof of this we have only to adduce Messrs. Moody and Sankey, or rather an English clergyman* who witnessed their success in Great Britain. '' While,'' says he, '' mighty masters of music and poetry are studying all the laws of art and threading the myriad mazes of harmony, while bishops and deans, archdeacons and canons, are elaborately endeavoring to consolidate or adorn the edifice of Christianity, behold a common, uncultured, kindly, nasal man, with a single singer of affecting

* '' A Pocket of Pebbles,'' by the Rev. William Philpot, vicar, etc., p. 94 (London, 1877).

doggerel, steps on our shores and becomes the channel of infusing into our English society a new flood of spiritual life, of which princesses and legislators and ministers, both of State and Church, press to drink."

To all such as would study good specimens of the natural, we commend those sermons of Whitefield which were taken down in short-hand. These likewise contain the best examples of his eloquence— examples which are deplorably scarce in modern editions of his sermons. Dr. Dry-as-dust has done Whitefield great damage.

Successful revivalists do not often utter the climax, and never except when it comes unbidden. Why? Because this figure, in its modern form, is very apt to lift our thoughts above the matter in hand, without raising them to God. It is natural for some men of genius to close every paragraph and every subdivision with a mid air explosion of a casket of gems. Others, of more moderate abilities, uniformly indulge in the same figure, with less brilliant effect. When Robert Hall was once asked how he liked a preacher of the last description, he replied, " Not at all, sir ; not at all. Why, sir, he puts me in mind of a little sweep boy, running up a succession of parallel chimneys, and at the top of each crying, Sweep ! sweep !" In his later years Whitefield formed the habit (the ripened fruit of his devotional spirit) of ending some of his divisions with a few fitting words of earnest prayer. But he never allowed this habit to degenerate into formality.

The deepening conviction that sermons which have cost but little study have been instrumental in doing much good has led some evangelists to neglect style, and even method. Such men may learn a lesson from the example of Edward Payson. A sermon of his, which he thought little of, and wrote almost entirely at one sitting, was one of the most effectual that he ever preached. " I could not but wonder," says he, " to see God work by it." And yet facts like these never tempted him to be negligent in his preparations for the pulpit. The very least that the evangelist ought to do is to be ever adding to his matter and revising his sketches or memoranda.

Yet, over and over again, have we to caution ourselves against the delusion that those revival addresses which have cost us little study cannot be of much service. Every evangelist of experience can. recall sermons which rebuke such a delusion. Many of the most successful sermons of a revivalist are intended to meet crises and emergencies. To bring them to the test of the homiletics, falsely so called, now commonly taught in our seminaries, would be impertinent and unjust. Take a specimen from a recent lecture on preaching. There is a text which reads, " They all with one accord began to make excuse." " Shall a man begin to consider the different kinds of excuses ? Of such sermons as that you can make a dozen before breakfast." In spite of such disdainful remarks, almost all the most successful revivalists have in well-studied sermons considered the different kinds of excuses ; they have found them equally necessary and useful ; we also venture to say that not one of them could have been made before breakfast. Another of these venerable professors has no patience with the use of the word professor, in the sense of one who makes a public declaration of his belief in Christ, or in the Christian religion. The unwary student would infer from his remarks that the word is not good English when so employed, whereas its use is authorized by our English Bible, and by the best writers from the days of Bacon and Hammond until now. It expresses a vital distinction ; we have no other to put in its place ; the common people understand it ; and evangelists, one and all, would regret to discover any evidence that it is growing obsolete.*

* In a hand-book like this, the subject of the style which is most serviceable in revival preaching cannot be discussed with due discrimination and thoroughness. The young preacher, so far from indulging the notion that it is a matter of small importance, should read every book that promises to give him a single new ray of light on the subject. Among other works on preaching the writer will perhaps be pardoned for referring to pp. 381-523 of his "System of Christian Rhetoric," where the subject of the oratorical style is discussed with fulness. This volume also attempts to show the relation of style to the inspiration of the Holy Spirit. Some learned critics have ignored the fact that this work is professedly a system of homiletics, while two distinguished professors (having perhaps failed to read the first five pages of the book, or forgotten what they had read of it) have taught that we make the prophetic and apostolic preachers of Scripture our exclusive models, whereas we consider the prophetic matter of the Bible as the only authoritative basis of homiletics, and build on that foundation post apostolical materials of similar kind, including a large quantity of general rhetoric. The volume is divided into four books : I. Inspiration ; II. Invention ; III. Style ; IV. Delivery. Buffon held that " style is of the man ;" we take higher ground, and maintain that a good homiletical style is of the Holy Ghost, first inspiring the man and then assisting him in the study of his subject. It is incontestably true that the evangelist who would really improve his style must relegate and reduce it to the third place in his consideration.

CHAPTER V.

THE IMPORTANCE OF TIMING TEXTS AND SUBJECTS.

Need of discrimination—General and special subjects—Example from Nettleton of the well-timed and the ill-timed—Whitefield's practice in varying parts of his plans—Great sermons often less effective than small ones—Danger of being too nice.

ASIDE from the general question, What are the best subjects for a series of revival sermons? there is this more special one, Is it worth while nicely to study adaptation to the ever-changing phenomena of a genuine work of reviving grace? To this question every true evangelist will make but one emphatic reply. Not more important is it for the farmer to observe the proper time to harvest the different products of his land, than for the evangelist to consider when to address the careless, the ignorant, the sceptical, the anxious, the despairing, the backslidden, and all the other characters that are the subjects of the grace and truth of the Gospel; when to appeal to the young, the mature, the aged; when to reach out after intellect, or conscience, or heart; when to improve the providence of the Spirit as indicated in times, seasons, calamities, and other striking events, as well as in the various forms of opposition that pass in array before the public operations of the Spirit.

A subject may be excellently suitable for revival work in general and yet totally fail to be efficacious, because it was not timeful or opportune. Let us illustrate this by a single example. In the winter of

1821 Mr. Nettleton preached one evening at Farmington, Connecticut, from Gen. 6 : 3. Fifty subsequently dated from that evening their first decided purpose to seek salvation. The same sermon was preached on the following week to two other large and solemn assemblies in adjoining parishes, with no special effect that could afterward be traced. The pastor, the Rev. Dr. Noah Porter, accounts for the difference in this way : " The fact probably was that here it convinced numbers that the Spirit was already striving with them, and that then was their day. ' A word spoken in due season, how good is it ! ' "

The revivalist has often to study not only what themes, but even what propositions, divisions and subdivisions, are most fitted for the next opportunity. The common opinion is that the evangelist possesses a certain number of sermons, which he repeats *verbatim* in every field of labor. None but a novice would do this or believe that others could do it. One who made Whitefield's preaching a study says : " We have some reason to believe that his ordinary practice was to adhere to a common outline, which had been prepared, but to fill it up variously in different places, as his own feelings and sense of duty prompted. It was in this way that he secured regularity in his general methods and trains of reasoning, and yet gave all the freshness of originality, and all the directness of immediate appeal to his addresses. Nearly all the evangelists that have had the largest experience and the most uniform success have, earlier or later, learned the same lesson, and fallen into the same mode of preparation.

Early, therefore, were they compelled to lay aside any ambition they may have had to compose sermons that were, intellectually considered, either graceful or grand. The daily returning necessity of being timely, at short notice and at all hazards, has shut out all attempts at being either profound or sublime, subtle or splendid.

But how can this be obtained? Much daily communion with God and with souls will enable one to decide most doubtful cases. The young evangelist is liable to decide what is the proper subject for the next occasion from insufficient evidence. Some very striking case which he has found in visiting or in the inquiry meeting, or late in the day, in a manner that seems to him providential, or is fresh in his memory or heart, determines his choice at a time, perhaps, when he should have reached his conclusion from a more general survey of the whole field, or from a retrospect of the work from its outset. The veteran revivalist, on the other hand, knowing, as he only can, the importance of timeliness, may be in danger of an anxiety that leads to doubt and hesitation ; so that he may be squandering his precious time in searching for a subject which he should have improved in prayer and study. He, too, equally with his younger brother, is in danger of making more of passing phenomena than of the surer proofs of seed-time and harvest : " He that observeth the wind shall not sow, and he that regardeth the clouds shall not reap" (Eccles. 11 : 4). Here prayer affords the best light. The fisher of men will always see further on his knees than on tip-toe.

The oldest and most skilful evangelists are often taught by results that the Divine Spirit is wiser than they. For He uses the very sermons from which they hoped nothing as instruments of converting many souls, and the sermons which they addressed to one class He makes the power of God to the opposite class. When the people are deeply moved by the Holy Spirit they will apply to themselves almost every subject, but before they are awakened they are much inclined to set their reason and pride against the preacher's arguments and appeals, especially if these are intended for them. The drowning man is not nice in his choice of a plank or spar, while the man who is safe on the shore, waiting for a passage, will perhaps wait weeks or months for a favorite steamer or a desirable state-room, or else, unable to satisfy himself, he will finally abandon all thoughts of a voyage.

CHAPTER VI.

CAN THERE BE TOO MUCH PREACHING IN A REVIVAL?

The question answered—May be too much of some kinds—May be out of proportion to other means of grace—Too much in one strain—Not to make ourselves the standards—Frequency of sermons in the revival at East Hampton—Does emotional preaching create a disrelish for the Bible?—Coaxing and auctioneering—The Salvation Army.

IT is sometimes asserted, rather roundly, that a revival may be checked and even brought to an end by an excess of preaching.   Here we ought to discriminate.

1. A people long accustomed to the pastor's preaching may, when revived, be laid to sleep again, if he continue to preach in his former way, or invite neighboring pastors to preach for the church in their usual manner.

2. The evangelist may often solemnly ask himself, in the midst of a revival, whether the amount of preaching is not too large in comparison of the amount of prayer or praise, short public invitations or personal interviews.

3. Whenever the evangelist finds out that the church or pastor is reposing too much confidence in his preaching, it may well be considered whether it were not safer for himself and all concerned, for him to leave the field, unless he can lead them back to more faith and hope in the Lord of the harvest.

4. There may be too much preaching on particular subjects, to the exclusion of others more timely or

better adapted to contradict the false doctrines or practical errors that are current among the people. There is a time for the plough, a time for the sower, a time for the harrow, a time for the mawkin, a time for the reaper, and a time for the wagon that is to carry the sheaves from the field.

5. There may be too much of certain kinds of feeling and tone. Where the Spirit is really at work awakening, alarming, enlightening, regenerating, etc., there will be a remarkable timeliness, freedom, and variety of thought, feeling, address, means, and measures.

6. If revivals may be preached to death, so they may be sung to death ; but I have never heard of one being prayed to death, especially where the prayers included praise and thanksgiving.

7. However, in judging whether any means of grace are in excess or not, we should beware of making our own experiences the standard. An advanced and tried disciple may not need so much preaching on his own account, as the ignorant and the stupid. But still there are many zealous and self-conceited persons, who fancy that their own exhortations will be more blessed than calmer and more scriptural sermons. They judge too much by their own likings and dislikings. Even the most skilful, vigilant, and prudent pastor may also give way to his prejudices, and consult too little the mental, social, and moral state of the young people. He is not to take it for granted that the present generation is every way like the past. Much allowance, too, must be made for exceptional cases. At any rate, he should exercise toward them much forbearance and indulgence.

8. The question of the amount of preaching can now and then be settled by experiment. The Rev. Dr.

Buell found at East Hampton, in 1764, that frequent preaching appeared to increase the number of converts. So deeply was he impressed with the fact that he longed for the speedy fulfilment of the prophecy (Isa. 62 : 6) when the "watchmen shall never hold their peace, day nor night."

9. It is the opinion of a learned professor in one of our theological seminaries that emotional preaching, aiming always at the hearts and consciences of the people, serves to create an aversion and disgust toward the Scriptures. Whatever may be the cause of this dislike, the true evangelist will do nothing to foster it.

The young evangelist who has been invited to assist a pastor, or to follow another evangelist, should at the outset ascertain what texts and subjects have already been handled, in order that he may avoid them and take up new themes. In this way will he prevent revival preaching from being distasteful and unprofitable to some of that class of zealous laborers who would dispense with all sermons in times of deep religious interest.

It may be well here to distinguish between revivals and ingatherings. By the latter we mean seasons in which many who were converted under the ordinary means of grace, or in former revivals, are persuaded to become members of churches. While great numbers are thus making a public profession, the actual conversions may possibly be as few as in the more quiet days. Whenever there is a movement of this kind, then we do not so much teach as exposulate and exhort. Then the peculiar methods of such a helper as the late "Uncle" John Vassar are found acceptable and effective. But Satan, it is to be feared, often takes advantage of the excitement that attends these ingatherings, to deceive many with a false hope, and so destroy them, and trouble the churches which have received them. Were the excitement confined to such as have an intellectual knowledge of the way of salvation, fewer would be persuaded to make a false profession.

In ignorant communities preaching should never be allowed to sink into mere coaxing, and exhortation to degenerate into auctioneering. Among such the most experienced evangelists and the best educated pastors are needed. As the atonement is sufficient for all, and is to be offered to all, it is but reasonable to suppose that the Divine Spirit will employ such men as are able to teach it to all, and that He will operate by such means as have always and everywhere been found efficient. If it is not so, then the Lord is very partial to those parts of Christendom to which these coaxers are sent, and we ought by all means to raise the cry, " Lo ! here, lo ! there." But certain it is, that the wisdom that is from above is justified of her children. Those who are converted to a sensation will fall away when the sensation has departed, but those who intelligently and deliberately accept the invitations of Christ will choose Him as their Master and pattern. They will obey Him, they will strive for Him, and, if need be, will suffer in His service. Did these coaxers really preach the Gospel, even though they were animated by bad motives in so doing, we might still rejoice ; but as they ignore the Gospel, what remains to us but lamentation, prayer, and hope against hope ? *

* The Methodist Episcopal Church has in probation and the class-meeting safeguards against these evils—evils which have long assailed the purity, peace, and unity of Congregational and Independent churches.

We do well, however, to remember that there is a diversity of gifts and of operations, as there is of conjunctures and emergencies.   Some men evince singular skill in special departments of Christian service.   Nor should we despise it because it may appear to us too much occupied with the merely human, external, and even secular sides of the Divine Kingdom.   Thus Mr. Kimball has manifested very remarkable address and tact in persuading congregations to remove mortgages from church edifices, and Mr. Harrison has acquired uncommon skill in the art and mystery of moving young persons to demonstrate publicly their willingness to enter inquiry meetings and join classes.   Others have an aptitude for processions.   Colonel Booth and his friends of the " Salvation Army" have drawn into the wake of their military movements throngs of rude boys and dissolute men and women, who were not influenced by any existing organizations of Christians. The history of religious processions is a part of the history of Romanism, and is replete with warnings which will ever be heeded by all true Protestants. To construe language literally which was intended to be understood figuratively, is one of the judicial follies of Antichrist.   It is therefore a bad sign that the " Salvation Army" should reduce and debase the military images of Scripture to the actual rank and file of Falstaff's ragged regiment.*   .

---

* As for " the Salvation Army," the best authorities are divided. Some hold that this organization has no support from the history of the primitive churches, that it outrages decency and order, follows the Pharisees in its proselytism, makes no provision for church-membership, and that it imitates the Jesuits by cultivating a military spirit and by centring all authority in one man.   Others maintain that it is reforming a class which no other instrumentalities can reach, is edu-

Among a carefully instructed people revival preaching should not aim so much at growth in knowledge as at immediate practice. The danger ever is, however, in setting too high an estimate on the amount of Christian knowledge possessed by any church, congregation, or community. And then there may be much Scripture knowledge, while there is a deplorable ignorance of all that relates to the progress of the Kingdom of Christ as revealed in the New Testament, and as illustrated by the missionary and evangelistic operations of Christians in all lands, in the past as well as in the present.

One clear and reasonable demand for very frequent preaching in a time of general awakening is when ignorant and fanatical agitators are busy around about us, misleading the young and the unwary. At such a time the true Gospel may need a reaffirmance and defence, while repeated persuasives will perhaps be advisable in order to gather the lambs of the holy flock into the fold of God.

For the rest, we may hope to find the bold preaching of the doctrines of grace of essential service as a test of the reality of many a professed conversion. One young man disputed with his teacher concerning the truth of a Christian doctrine until he was convinced that the trouble was in himself ; and an intelligent lady for a considerable time avowed her inability to

---

cating the reformed for Christian work, chiefly confines its demonstrations to places hitherto the scenes of brawls and riots, and though our sense of decorum may at first be disturbed, we soon lose our aversion in an all-absorbing compassion for the perishing. Hence they say these people are doing a good work in a rough way ; let us forbear to disturb them. Or they say, " Wait : by their fruits we shall know them."

believe a particular doctrine.   Ultimately, however, she found that the difficulty was that she was unwilling that God should be God.   The words of the Spirit will ever be welcome to the works of the Spirit.

CHAPTER VII.

SERVICES FOR READINGS AND EXPOSITIONS.

When and where useful—What portions of Scripture most appropriate
—Should have a practical aim—Revivals resulting from readings
—The practice of Moody, Morehouse, Whittle, and Needham—
Readings in the place of arguments—Whittle's advice—Avoid
one-sidedness.

EXERCISES of this kind are chiefly useful to the
Church, and especially to winners of souls, at mid-day
or afternoon meetings.   They will be found to enlist
the deepest interest in educated communities, where
it has been long neglected, provided only that they
have the leisure to attend them ; and these people
will be most profited by them while the work of conversion is going forward with the greatest activity.
For the preacher and the Christian workers, coming
fresh from their evangelistic labors, now find new
meanings, illustrations, and applications in familiar
passages.   While they are building the tabernacle, the
various parts of the pattern shown on the mount will
become better known to them.

Suitable portions of Scripture to occupy attention in
the earlier stages of a revival will be found in the
character of Noah as a preacher of righteousness ;
in the glimpses given of the awakening in the days of
Enoch, when men began to call upon the name of the
Lord ; the general reformation recorded in the last
chapter of Joshua ; the revival in the time of the
Judges, when Israel " cried unto the Lord," and he
raised up Deborah and Barak to rescue them from

Jabin and Sisera; the awakening in the days of Samuel, when "Israel lamented after the Lord," and He thundered upon the Philistines and discomfited them; the contest of Elijah with the prophets of Baal and his triumph on behalf of the Lord; the revival at Nineveh under the preaching of Jonah; the reformations in the reigns of Hezekiah and Josiah; the awakening in the time of Ezra; the great preparatory movement led by John the Baptist; the ingatherings during the days of the Lord Jesus, and the several revivals recorded in the Acts of the Apostles. The reading of these and other Scripture histories ought to convince the people that revivals are not of modern date, much less of human invention.

Another good series of subjects for reading and exposition may be found in the Scripture accounts of prayers offered and answered, and in instances of the works of faith and labors of love. Readings and expositions of the historical and biographical parts of the Bible will ever be the most effectual. But edification will sometimes be promoted by taking up some important theme of doctrine and commenting on the most significant texts which teach or apply it. Especially ought we to explain the doctrines of grace and the attributes of the triune God in relation to each of them. However, these explanations should all along and finally suggest practical lessons and appeals.

Not less worthy of mention are the reading and explaining of those parts of Scripture which serve to train the members of the Church for the immediate winning of souls, and for such other work as may promise to advance the Church in a career of permanent usefulness. Revivalists can, in the way of exposition, lightly yet effectually touch upon misdoings and shortcomings, which could not be profitably handled in a more formal way.

More than one revival is said to have grown out of Bible readings. Among the most successful readers are Messrs. Moody, Morehouse, Whittle, and Needham. Mr. Moody usually only reads the Bible topically, only reading here and there texts on certain subjects. His readings on the blood of Christ, the Holy Spirit and assurance, have been notably commended and blessed.

These readings have sometimes been of service in inquiry meetings. Mr. Whittle begins his inquiry meetings with an exercise of this description. After an opening prayer he presents three distinct points for the consideration of inquirers :

First, That Christ came to save guilty and condemned sinners. He proves this point from the Bible, and then asks all who accept the doctrine to signify it by holding up their right hand.

Secondly, That all in the room who are thus guilty and condemned need a Saviour. Then Scripture passages in proof of this point are read, and all who assent to this are asked to signify their assent as before.

Thirdly, That we should renounce our sins and accept Christ as our Saviour. These duties are proved to be such from Scripture, and affectionately urged upon the heart and consciences of inquirers. All who can assent to these final lecturings are again requested to hold up their hands. Mr. Whittle then proceeds to the work which usually occupies meetings of this kind.

The apt quotation of Scripture in this way may also

be of great advantage in silencing debaters and gain-
sayers.   In general, it is wisest for all, especially lay-
men, in times of revival to waive all mere argumenta-
tion.   We may here instance a sceptic who had
warded off all exhortations to repentance and all invitations to Christ, by raising objections or making
cynical remarks.   At length the leader of an inquiry
meeting introduced him to a Christian woman.   His
first remark was, " So you have come to interview
me."   The reply was, " No, I do not know enough
for that.   Let us both interview the Bible, and see
what we can learn."   Somewhat disarmed by this
reply, his tone changed, and he said he was very willing to have a conversation.   But his old habit returning upon him, he propounded one after another of
the intellectual difficulties in his way.   The lady met
each one by saying, " I cannot answer you.   I cannot
pretend to do so.   But let us see what the Bible says
about it."   And then opening the Bible she would read
such passages as gave a divine answer to each question.
In this way he was driven back by the sword of the
Spirit from point to point, until, forced to give up
the struggle, he sprang to his feet saying, " This
question must be settled to-night.   Pray for me."
Eventually he was converted, not as the result of
reasoning, but of a judicious use of divine truth.

One caution given by Mr. Whittle to the young
Bible reader is of considerable value, more especially
as it is justified by his own early experience.   It is
this : " Be careful not to make the readings too long.
Better it is to divide your topic into four or six readings, and so bring out the Scripture upon each head to
your own satisfaction, than to crowd too many topics
into one reading.   My first Bible reading on faith con-

tained some sixty Scripture references. Before they were all read the audience grew tired. The same Bible reading for one meeting has now developed into seven for as many successive meetings.*

Evangelists are apt to run to the same extremes in their readings as in their sermons—that is to say, they are tempted to apply every passage with exclusive reference to revival aims and interests. To regard texts with more breadth of view would be more instructive to believers, without being less telling upon the hearts and consciences of unbelievers. Some of the current Scripture readings are so one-sided as to be really inculcations of error.

* Much excellent advice on this subject may be found in " Hand-Book of Bible Readings," by H. B. Chamberlain ; " Hints on Bible Readings," by the Rev. J: C. Hill ; " Notes and Suggestions for Bible Readings," by Messrs. Briggs and Eliott. Specimens of Mr. Moody's Bible readings may be found in the volume " To All People," pp. 191–477.

CHAPTER VIII.

REVIVAL HYMNS AND SINGING.

The minstrel accompanied the Prophet—The rage for novelty—Sacred songs very furthersome—Hymns as means of grace—Testimony of Nettleton and Parker—The abuse of church music—The necessity of choiceness—Advice of Finney and Fish—An occasional substitute for singing recommended.

THE singing of psalms and other sacred songs ought to be considered as a part of the proper ministry of the Word. We do not say that it is a necessary part. But it is important, as appears from the fact that it is authorized by the example of the Hebrew prophets, the preachers of their time, whose utterances were often preceded or followed by minstrelsy. The address of Habakkuk, as it has come down to us, is followed by a psalm of the sublimest description. Indeed, the singing of holy songs, accompanied by the harp or some other "instrument of God," came at length to be called prophesying, and the singers and players prophets or prophetesses.

The most scommon objection, perhaps, to revival singing in our day is that it feeds the rage for novelty at the expense of permanent edification and of good old hymns and music which bear the stamp of devout genius, and have survived the vicissitudes of a century or more. And yet it will not do to refuse a hymn or tune merely for the reason that it is new. Such a reason, if allowed to prevail, would have deprived us of the entire Psalter ; for there must have been occasions when each of these psalms was sung for the first time. But still it must be admitted that a rapid succession of new revival songs of inferior and ephemeral quality has come to be rather a hindrance than a help to revival service. Even those who encourage and patronize it find that, after all, nothing is so helpful in their way as the good old hymns and tunes which have long been familiar to most of the worshippers. No band of singers, however long they may have been trained in novelties, can stand a moment in comparison of a large audience of the common people singing some old hymn to some old music, to which it is married for immortality.

It is, however, a settled question that the revivalist finds a companion or two that are skilled in the best and newest church music very serviceable and profit-able. For many years evangelists or travelling missionaries have often been accompanied by these. We once knew a revivalist whose sister was a very efficient yokefellow in this way. The Rev. Orson Parker gratefully acknowledges the fact that his daughters Georgiana and Cornelia accompanied him on many long campaigns, assisting him with their songs and cheering him in his labors. The fellowship of Messrs. Moody and Sankey, and its blessed results in many cities, need scarcely to be mentioned.

The relative numbers that have been converted through preaching and singing, it would be of much importance to determine. Mr. Moody does not, we learn, regard Mr. Sankey's sheaves as fewer than his own, although it must be remembered that the hymns Mr. Sankey sings the most effectually are ser-mons in verse and melody. Mr. Parker, who held during his long life more than four hundred series of meetings, testifies : '' I believe that there is as much conviction lodged in the mind by singing as by preaching. It keeps the people together more than preaching. The melody softens the feelings, and the sentiment of the hymn leaves its stamp upon the melted heart and ripens into fruit." To the students who stood around his bed in his last illness, Dr. Nettleton said : " If I have ever been of any use as an instrument of spiritual good, it has been, to a great extent, through the reading of sacred poetry ; where I have had my choice of means I have selected it in preference to any other.

But the vital question is not, Shall we have singing? but What kind of singing shall we have ? No singing at all is better than heartless and ill-chosen hymns and music. When, therefore, we cannot be assured upon the point, it is often best to have no singing or playing at the close of the sermon. At the outset of a service a larger liberty may be permitted, with less damage to the final impressions and fruit.

Mr. Finney was opposed to much singing in revivals, on the ground that it is contrary to a spirit of agonizing prayer and deep convictions of sin. He admits that singing a hymn has sometimes produced a powerful effect on sinners who are convicted ; but this, he thinks, is owing to the perfect contrast there is between their feelings and those of the happy souls who sing. He also holds that a revival is often brought to a premature close by the church and minister all giving themselves up to singing with young converts. "Thus, by stopping to rejoice when they ought to feel more and more deeply for sinners, they grieve away the Spirit of God, and they soon find that their agony and travail of soul are all gone." His advice, therefore, is that the hymns should be so selected as to bring out something solemn, and so deepen the feelings of sinners or Christians. This agrees with the experience of one who, amidst the revival at Kilsyth, in Scotland, about the year 1742, testified : " When the notes of the congregation began to swell in a psalm of confession, I felt as if it would have ' hearted' me—as if I must give way altogether." There are some hints given by the late Rev. Dr. Fish,* who made revival music a subject of a good deal of study and experiment. Here are a few of them : " There should not be much singing in the beginning of a revival, because then the meetings are for confession and contrition. A melodeon is better than an organ, as being closer to the audience and more readily handled. As a rule, perhaps, it is better to dispense with instrumental music. Use a given hymn always with the same tune ; use a book in which the hymn and tune are on one page. The connection of the hymn should not be broken by interludes or long pauses. The verses in any one singing should be few, seldom more than two or three. The singing of a familiar hymn will often be more spirited if the reading of it be omitted. Use tunes that are strictly congregational in their structure. If new tunes cannot be learned, use such as are already familiar. Let the sentiment of the hymns, at any given meeting, be uniform from beginning to end. Keep to the ' keynote' in this respect throughout ; otherwise the mind is turned off from the main point of the meeting. Let everything tend to the one object of awakening, edifying, and saving men, and do it heartily as unto the Lord."

We will only add that in case this means of grace

* " Handbook of Revivals, ' pp. 317-319.

is either permanently or temporarily wanting, a good substitute may occasionally be found in exercises of thanksgiving for instances of backsliders restored, doubters obtaining better hopes, or prayers heard in behalf of sinners. In order to vary the exercises and obtain a full blessing, requests for thanksgiving may be made by the grateful persons, orally or written, and sent forward to the leader of the meeting. Readings from the Psalms would properly accompany this service. Such thanksgivings, if blended with adoration, may answer the purposes of the most solemn songs of praise.

CHAPTER IX.

TEMPERANCE WORK IN REVIVALS.

Diversity of opinions about temperance reforms—The Gospel affords a common ground for co-operation—The success of Mr. Moody and others in Christianizing drunkards—Specialists in temperance work not always in sympathy with evangelistic laborers—Christ the Great Physician of diseased souls.

EVERY question that has a tendency to provoke discussion and division among good Christian people should be kept out of revival services, and if admitted it should not for a moment be entertained. In spite of the general disharmony on temperance, one proposal there is, and only one, that can commend itself to the sympathy and co-operation of all Christian laborers. It is this : to work together for the conversion of drunkards and dealers in intoxicating drinks. Here is a basis for unison of action, while any departure from this basis may divert attention from the proper means and objects of revivalistic endeavors, and so disappoint all just expectations.

It should be remembered that even learned men are not agreed respecting the nature and effects of the wines of the East, and that as the study of Christian ethics is more and more neglected from year to year in colleges and seminaries, we cannot at present reasonably expect the common people to obtain clear and distinct notions about their duties either to themselves or their neighbors, or the Church or the state in respect of temperance. Be it remembered, too, that various temperance lecturers, religious, political, and infidel, have, by their activity and push, disseminated a great variety of opinions on the subject. The proposal here recommended is " non-committal" on all points in controversy, but is most pronounced as regards the one question of salvation.

This plan, we scarcely need to say, is to-day exemplified by several evangelists, and in particular by Mr. Moody, who has been instrumental in the conversion of a great number of drunkards in America, England, Ireland, and Scotland. Nor does he despair of bringing to the Saviour the hardest cases. In answer to one who had said he did not think there was any hope for a woman that had been addicted to strong drink, and to another who had said he did not think there was any hope for a confirmed drunkard, he used the following language : " When I look upon the drunkard and think of the pledges he has broken, I might say they are right, but when I read, ' All power is given to Me,' I rejoice to say there is hope for every drunkard on earth. Our God has power to save. I would say to these persons, I would not give a farthing for good resolutions. You must be born again. It is not a reformation, but a new creation you need. You will then hate strong drink as much as you now love it. Thank the Lord, who is stronger than your appetite for strong drink. He is mighty to save ; we want to come boldly to God to ask Him to save the poor drunkard." More recently he has declared that he has more confidence than ever before in the power of divine grace to regenerate the most confirmed drunkard.

His method with the intemperate is to expound the Scriptures to them, and to pray for them. His addresses on Daniel have also proved very useful in reclaiming inebriates. He delivers no " lectures" on the subject, and his fellow-worker, Mr. Sankey, sings no strictly " temperance songs," being content with such as these : " Rescue the perishing," " Take the name of Jesus with you," ' Safe in the arms of Jesus," " Where is my wandering boy to-night ?" After two weeks Mr. Moody begins to hold temperance meetings, one afternoon in each week, and at the conclusion of his labors in any city he devotes a whole day to the cause, when there is commonly a reunion of converted drunkards from his former fields of service.

His practice of devoting certain days to this branch of work enables him to check all such as are always harping on this single string. " Some temperance men," he once observed, " make a great mistake : they lug in the question every time they get a chance. Everything in its own place."

Not a few of these converted tipplers testify that regenerating grace has destroyed in them all craving for strong drink. Some of them say that they can pass among gin-palaces and barrooms without any fear of reviving the old appetite. With the remark of one of this class we were once much pleased. " I am," said he, " a brand plucked from the fire. As such fuel kindles again when brought to the fire much sooner than a fresh piece of wood, I consider my danger, and carefully avoid temptation."*

The signing of the pledge is of great service some- times, especially when it is the serious and deliberate act of a man that is not borne away in a crowd, and when it is invested with the solemnity of a vow to God. The minister should propose prayer as a preliminary.

* " True Path, or Gospel Temperance; Life of Murphy, Reynolds, and Others," by Rev. J. S. Vandersloot (Chicago, 1876).

Without the assistance of the Lord Jesus we can do nothing.

Whenever, during the progress of revival services, a professional lecturer on temperance is introduced or recommended as a helper, he should not be hastily welcomed to share in the work. However high his Christian character, he cannot be expected at once to know his new surroundings, or bring himself into full sympathy with the other workers ; but the chances are that he is a novice, or mayhap a fantical adventurer, who, if he be allowed any opportunity to lecture in the revival meetings, will demand entire control of his time and full liberty to employ his own means and measures ; while, if this be refused, he will organize a series of meetings in opposition, and so draw away thoughtless young people into unbelief and immorality.

The most promising fields for the trustworthy lecturer are in communities among which no revivals are in progress, and to which he may go as a John the Baptist, preparing the way of the Lord. If he do no more than enlighten the people respecting the temporal consequences of tippling, and secure a large number of pledges, he may thereby bring about such lucid intervals of sobriety as will make it possible for many to hearken at least to the Gospel of their salvation.

Great patience and an exhaustless compassion will, in some instances, be requisite to final success. Among the converted tipplers of the revival of 1857 in New York, there was one who signed the pledge twenty-five times before the grace of regeneration came to his rescue. Another inebriate, converted at the same season of refreshing, while seeking the divine remedy, said, with burning earnestness, "I am in a hurry to be a Christian. I must be a Christian to be safe."

Without professing to suggest what the pastor may or may not prudently or lawfully do in the behalf of temperance in the regular discharge of his daily duties, confident we are that for the evangelist or for the pastor in a time of awakening, the Gospel affords the best remedy he can employ in every case of drunkenness, however desperate. Indeed, the revivalist could not recommend any other without creating the suspicion that the grace of the Almighty is not sufficient for the hardest hearts, and that the one divine method of moral renovation is inferior to some means of reformation that are merely human, and for this life alone. Nor does it demand great faith to accept the Gospel method of destroying intemperance. Demonstration here comes to our aid. Facts, figures, and cases passing under daily observation evince the matchless skill of the Great Physician.

CHAPTER X.

THE EVANGELIST IN HIS RELATIONS TO THE PRAYER CURE.

The honesty of the leaders of this movement—Reasons for the revival of these primitive gifts—Romanism, Spiritualism, and Materialism seem to demand its restoration to the churches—Has the age of miracles passed away?—As a question of probability and of testimony—The use of oil in connection with prayer—The laying on of hands—The primitive elder—A caution given—These gifts not bestowed upon all—A churchly rite—Presumption and fanaticism to be guarded against—The Rev. Dr. Gordon's judicious advice—Bengel's discriminating dictum—Physicians and medicine not to be despised—The example of St. Luke, the beloved physician, recommended.

As some evangelists have joined the healing of the body to the cure of the soul, and as there is a growing belief in the power of prayer to remove sickness, it seems necessary that a manual which is designed to be intensely practical and working should contain some information and suggestions on this living question. We propose to regard it partly in its exegetical and historical aspects, but without ignoring it as it appears before us to-day.

It has been the privilege of the present writer to become acquainted with some of the foremost advocates of the " Faith Cure," and he has found them Christians of humility and benevolence, denying themselves for the good of others, and superior to ambition and all idolatrous covetousness. Their simple purpose is to go forth in the light of the New Testament, to give relief to their suffering fellow-creatures, with no secret designs and no ulterior ends. They are, some of them, learned , some of them are of limited intelligence and confined views. I have asked myself, therefore, why they should have been moved by the Divine Spirit to revive the prayer-cure. I may be much mistaken, but the conviction deepens that they have been raised up in these latter days to counteract the demoniac miracle-workers of Romanism and Spiritualism, thus fulfilling the prediction, " When the enemy shall come in like a flood, the Spirit of the Lord shall lift up a standard against him." (Isa. 59 : 19).

Another purpose which the Holy Ghost probably has in reviving His curative power is to silence Materialists. These people loudly and obstinately contend that the violation of every law, whether of matter or of mind, draws after it a sure and unavoidable penalty. They have many analogies in creation and Providence to confirm their claim, and, what is worse, they number some so called preachers of the Gospel among their fellow-doctrinaires. The tendency of this iron philosophy is to do away with all ideas of an atonement, and even of all divine interposition in the affairs of the human race. What must ever make the atonement a matter of universal interest is the fact that it is a divine interference on behalf of the guilty to save them from the punishment of their sins. In the time of Christ's sojourn among the Jews, the popular belief was that all sickness is the consequence of sin, and that the sick ought to bear the penalty of their transgressions. The Saviour, by healing the sick and raising the dead, shook this common superstition to its lowest foundations, and so prepared the way for the belief that his atonement rescued sinners, not only from temporal but from eternal punishment. When, therefore, He healed the sick He performed part of His mission as the Lamb of God, or atoning sin-bearer. And, accordingly, the healing was sometimes coupled with a declaration of the forgiveness of sins (Matt. 9 : 2, 5). In coherence with this is the promise in James 5 : 15. It was only as a sacrifice for sin that Jesus could heal physical disease, as it is only to his pierced hand that we are entitled to look for our daily bread. Hence, we are to put no narrow construction on the words of Isaiah, as quoted by Matthew 8 : 17 : '' Himself took our infirmities and bare our sicknesses.'' Our Saviour bore, among other things, in his own body on the tree, the punishment due to the violation of the laws of man's physical and mental economy.

If it be objected that no other evidences of the divine origin of our religion are demanded than those which we find in the New Testament and the history of Christianty, we reply that the intellectual and moral relation of modern unbelievers, notably in our own country, is much the same as was that of the Roman Empire to Christ and His apostles in the first century of our era. Multitudes are totally indifferent to the New Testament, and multitudes more would not read the Book unless they were hired to do so. Not a few communities among us are essentially heathen as to religion, and as to education barbarous ; while millions from Europe are swarming over our territories to plant colonies, which, unless the grace of God interpose, are to reproduce in the New World the superstition and shameless brutality of the Old. We cannot, therefore, pronounce the revival of the prayer cure as either ill-timed or ill-placed.

Many of us have been taught that the extraordinary gifts which were bestowed upon the primitive churches passed away with the apostles. This we seriously question ; but if it could be demonstrated that they did, it would still remain to be proved that it was the good pleasure of the Lord Jesus that none of them should ever be restored. It is curious to observe into what inconsistencies some learned professors fall in their attempts to make our heavens brass and our earth iron. Thus, they insist that prophesying was confined to the primitive Church, and yet they maintain the duty of upholding the rule of the analogy of the faith, totally regardless of the fact that the apostle applies this rule to prophesying alone (Rom. 12 : 6).

That the prayer of faith should still heal the sick is not improbable beforehand or contrary to our reasonable expectations. What more potent agency could be summoned against disease than the Divine Spirit operating on the human frame through the will and the intellect? Abundant is the proof that the Holy Ghost has often removed forever the drunkard's morbid craving for stimulants—a craving that had long baffled the physician's utmost skill. Nor are we without evidence that regenerating grace has proved friendly to bodily health. We know that the mind can influence every part of the body it inhabits. What, then, can be more demonstrable than that when a divine power enters and takes possession of any mind, it is able, through it, to operate with marvellous effects on the diseases of the body?

The testimony of Dorothea Trudel, of Switzerland ; of Pastor Blumhardt, in Germany ; of Dr. Cullis, of Boston, Massachusetts, and the Rev. Mr. Simpson, of New York City, is not to be impeached. Equally trustworthy is most of the evidence of those who have been healed.*

* " Prayer and its Remarkable Answers," by Rev. Dr. W. W. Patton, chapters xi., xii., and xv.

It is an error, we think, to suppose that any Christian should wait for a peculiar experience before resorting to the prayer of faith. The only incontestable proof that one has this gift is an answer to such a prayer. We are persuaded, therefore, that Pastor Blumhardt was unwise in passing two years in prayers and fastings for an assurance that he should lay hands on the sick for their restoration. We fail to find in the Epistles to the Corinthians, or elsewhere, any intimation that any of those who received the gift of healing either sought or found any inward witness of their call to this ministry, apart from actual experiment. The use of oil has not the support of our Saviour's example. Oil was indeed very often employed by the Jews, Greeks, and Romans as a medicine ; and Meyer is of opinion that St. James here mentions the anointing with oil only in conformity with the general custom of employing it for the refreshing, strengthening, and healing of the body. The fact that the anointing was to be done " in the name of the Lord" does not demonstrate that the act was either a miracle or a sacrament, since all things are to be done in the name of the Lord Jesus (Col. 3 : 17). If this be the import of the words, they teach us to make use of any common household remedy in connection with prayer.

But as it is " the prayer of faith," and not the anointing with oil, that is said to save the sick, some authorities suppose that the anointing was considered a medium through which healing grace was imparted to the sick. This view is also confirmed by the example of Christ and His apostles. Our Lord anointed the eyes of the blind man with clay (John 9 : 6), and the apostles in the life-time of the Messiah anointed with oil many that were sick, and healed them

(Mark 6 : 13). Sometimes, however, no mention is made of anointing, but only of the laying on of hands. Our Lord laid His hands on the sick (Luke 4 : 40 ; 13 : 13). He also touched children (Luke 18 : 15), probably for the purpose of healing them, as he did in other cases (Luke 22 : 51 ; Matt. 8 : 15). In like manner Ananias laid his hands on Saul and restored his sight (Acts 9 : 17), and Paul healed the father of Publius by the imposition of hands (Acts 28 : 8). Indeed, the laying on of hands is mentioned by Paul (Heb. 6 : 1) as one of the seven fundamental principles of Christ. We say seven ; for with the best Greek expositors we consider διδαχῆς (teaching) separately, and place it after βαπτισμῶν, as it stands in the original. It is, perhaps, fair to infer that the gift of healing, as exercised in the Church of Corinth, was accompanied by the laying on of hands (1 Cor. 12 : 9, 30).

It is well worthy of note that " the elders" of the Church are to pray over the sick one, implying, at least, that more than one elder, in cases where they are to be found, should be invited to join in the prayer of faith. Had this direction been followed, the apostate Greek and Latin Churches would not have been tempted to deify their innumerable workers of miracles. In travelling among these churches, and particularly in visiting the shrines and tombs of the most famous saints, how often does one see old pictures of their persons surrounded by a border of smaller pictures, in which are represented the miracles of healing, which, as the legends tell us, they performed. In one case, we are told, a nun only dreamed that her abbess, St. Radagund, anointed her with oil, and awoke healed !

As the " elders" or "presbyters" of the primitive

churches were officers not met with in any modern church or sect, it is important here to ascertain what sort of persons in the churches of to-day most nearly correspond to them in character and standing. According to Mosheim, Neander, Schaff, and others, each church had its band of elders (Acts 14 : 23 ; 20 : 17 ; Titus 1 : 5). They were superintendents, having the general oversight of the church. They were not, at the same time, preachers or teachers by virtue of their office, although some of them (as was the case of some deacons) also preached the Gospel (1 Tim. 3 : 2). Even an apostle might properly style himself an elder (1 Peter 5 : 1 ; 2 John 1 : 1 ; 3 John 1 : 1). The term is employed by some of the apostles sent to the Jews, and hence several learned authors hold that this body of men corresponded to the presbytery of the synagogue. It has been laid down as a general rule that those who are called elders, in speaking of Jewish communities, are called bishops, in speaking of Gentile communities. But, in our humble opinion, this rule does not hold good ; for the apostle to the Gentiles employs the word elder several times. The posture of affairs was this : Almost all the churches planted among the Gentiles were, in great part, composed of converts from Judaism. We have the sole authority of Clemens Romanus for the assertion that the first converts were ordinarily chosen to this office. The case of the household of Stephanas (1 Cor. 16 : 15) has been cited in confirmation of this opinion, but we are nowhere told that any of the family were elders. These Christian officers first appear as the receivers and almoners of the collection made at Antioch, and sent to the churches in Judea (Acts 11 : 30).

To guard against fanaticism, such a body of men

as answers to the eldership of the primitive church should meet and pray for the sick. All the lights we can collect from the office as held both in the synagogues and in the first Christian churches would direct us to send to the sick-room men of mature years, weight of character, Christian knowledge, and faith in the power of prayer. In general, it is seldom wise for the pastor or evangelist, except in cases of necessity, to administer this rite alone.

But are we not told in the First Epistle to the Corinthians (12 : 9, 30) that all have not the gifts of healing : that some were endued with powers to cure many diseases,* while others, we may infer, had no power of this description ? Most assuredly we are ; but it is noticeable that no one man at Corinth stood forth as a great miraculous healer, and if there was any one that gained a temporary distinction of this stamp, it is highly improbable that he went to sick-rooms unattended by some of the brotherhood of Corinth. It is very evidently a part of the meaning of the apostle James that the healing rite should be regarded as a churchly and not a clerical rite.† Whenever, therefore, an evangelist is requested to perform it, he should refer the matter to the church which he is serving, and

---

* Meyer wrongly infers from the plurals in the original that different gifts were needful for different diseases, whereas from 1 Cor. 12 : 9 we learn that one person might possess all these gifts.

† Some authorities are of opinion that this view of the churchly character of the rite is corroborated by the change from the singular number to the plural in Mark 16 : 16, 17. But we are almost all less willing than the Infinite Mind to allow any exceptional cases. Another infirmity of our race is to make a rule out of an exception. Perhaps it would not be far from the truth to recognize as sent of God some few who are endued with special gifts of healing, just as there are at times divine calls given to a few female preachers.

commit to their charge all the responsibilities and privileges of this ministration, and if he is directed to take any part in the prayer cure, he should cause it to be fully understood that he is acting as a messenger of the church (for this is what the Greek word translated elder sometimes imports), and not as one that is individually or officially empowered to discharge this duty.

Too much caution cannot be exercised by the young evangelist in speaking and acting with reference to this subject. " Nothing," says Rev. Dr. Gordon,* " needs to be held with such quietness and reserve as this truth. To press it upon the undevout and uninstructed is to bring it into contempt. Those who have the most wisdom in such matters will be found speaking in very hushed tones, and without presumption or ostentation." The same excellent author likewise admonishes us not to proclaim the doctrine of divine healing in a reckless manner, or to declare that any sick person will surely be restored if we carry the case to God. " We should," he adds, " remember that at one place Paul healed the father of Publius by his prayers, and that at another place he left Trophimus sick."

As for the modern use of oil in this ministry, the judicious Bengel has an important direction coupled with a warning: " Let those use oil who are able by their prayers to obtain recovery for the sick ; let those who cannot do this abstain from the empty sign." Sedulously ought we to guard ourselves and others against the superstition that the oil can or may be made sacred or efficacious by the blessing or benediction of a man of faith or any human being.

---

* " The Ministry of Healing ; or, Miracles of Cure in All Ages" (Boston, 1883).

As early as the ninth century it was decided by the Council of Chalons that the oil with which the sick were anointed was to be blessed by the bishop, and in the Greek Church of to-day, seven priests, if they can be brought together, are to unite in consecrating the oil. The language of the Apostle James knows nothing about any holy or consecrated oil.

And this fact goes to confirm the theory that the oil mentioned by the apostle was a common household remedy, and was recommended to teach us that we are not to neglect medicine, or even the most familiar simples and panaceas. The employment of natural means in connection with the divine power which effects the cure, is, as some hold, also encouraged by Mark 7 : 33 ; 8 : 23 ; John 9 : 6. Certainly no Christian of sound mind can condemn the practice of medicine or the application of scientific prescriptions. There can be no just occasion for discord between a revival of the primitive prayer cure and the most advanced discoveries and methods of medical science. We too commonly speak of the apostles and evangelists as mere ignorant fishermen. The fact is, they were educated for three years in the best theological school that this planet has ever heard of, and one of them was a well-trained physician and a writer of excellent Greek. Just imagine, judicious reader, the evangelist and beloved physician, Luke, discoursing learnedly on the peculiar class of diseases which the Lord Jesus and Peter and Paul could cure ; and setting apart other classes over which, it was very evident, these wonder-workers could not possibly have any dominion. It is an auspicious sign that there are physicians who add prayers to their prescriptions, and so augment human skill by the assistance of divine wisdom and power.

CHAPTER XI.

AWAKENINGS AMONG CHILDREN AND IN SUNDAY-SCHOOLS.

Caution necessary—The proselyting spirit—Blind sympathy and unconscious imitation — Revivalistic formalism and drill—Exceptional cases among the young—Some children are nearer heaven than we think—Parental fondness misjudges sometimes—Testimony of John Todd—Keeping lambs out of the fold—The dream of Myconius—Reaping a harvest from Sunday-school concerts and teachers' prayer-meetings.

THE Gospel is to be preached to all that have the capacity to receive it. The oft-repeated words of the Great Teacher are, "He that hath ears to hear, let him hear." In almost all revivals children make up a majority of the converts, more especially in places where Sunday-schools flourish.

Let us glance at a few of the dangers to which Sunday-schools are exposed. In many of these schools the superintendents and teachers have such "a passion for souls" that the educational function of the schools is kept in undue subordination to the work of conversion. Consequently, the conscience is too often left unenlightened and undisciplined. The law, as enjoined and illustrated in the Old Testament, is the child leader appointed of God to conduct us to Christ. To neglect it, therefore, is to slight that course of moral education, which is as needful to prepare for sound conversion, as it is for the formation of Christian character.

II. The power of sympathy in immature minds is liable to be mistaken for the grace of the Holy Spirit.

This danger is too great and too frequent to be here considered at adequate length.*

III. The principle of imitation is likewise very strong in the young.   So far as words are concerned, some parrots have been very devout so long as they could be kept out of earshot of the profane.

IV. To guard against the peril to which children are greatly exposed, through sympathy and imitativeness in times of revival, it may be difficult and inexpedient to keep them out of the company of other awakened persons ; but it is possible and desirable to save them from the misleading influence of " the drill," in the practice of which children are requested to stand up, to kneel, to come forward, to hold up the hands, etc., in concert and with military punctuality.   Opinions are, we know, divided as to the expediency in any case of this method of expressing anxiety, fear, wishes, purposes, and the like ; but, for the reasons already given, it is among children particularly exposed to abuse.   In the necessary absence of judgment and knowledge, they are unconsciously led into habits of " make-believe" and hypocrisy.

V. Here we are very apt to put exceptional cases in place of the general rule.   Striking and pathetic instances of child-piety, perhaps adorned with precocious wit and wisdom, recur to us whenever the subject is discussed, so that we fail to look at a number of average cases, or else refuse to examine the facts of a bad or doubtful case, which demands immediate attention and scrutiny.

VI. But still it ought to be frankly avowed that we

* The Rev. Dr. John Todd's " Sunday-school Teacher," chap. iii. pp. 98-105.

may err, on the other hand, by ignoring or overlooking exceptional cases of very remarkable piety among children. It is hard for some men to return to childhood in memory and imagination. And if one was not himself converted in childhood he will find it even more difficult to put himself in the place of a converted child. But let such an evangelist or pastor consider that the child brought before him for examination may really be nearer heaven than himself, both in respect of time and preparation. The shepherd sometimes espies a lamb feeding high above himself in a mountain pasture ;

> " And the lark, to meet the morn,
> Soars beyond the shepherd's sight."

The question of the early profession of children and their admission to church-membership is one of very great importance. It may possibly be settled by a few considerations like the following :

1. We are to remember that here the evidence of conversion is to be estimated by the intelligence and the impartiality of the witnesses. It is asked,* " Why be so cautious as to the testimony of a child ? Since it is a question of the validity of evidence, why not weigh the validity of the evidence and act accordingly ? Why give credence to the expression of the adult and reject the experience of a child ?" We ought not, indeed, to refuse the testimony of a child, but we should receive it for what it is worth. Very few children have such a knowledge of the Scripture account of regeneration and repentance as to enable them to decide whether they have been the gracious subjects of either or both. Besides, it should be remembered, as we have

---

* Rev. Dr. Fish's " Handbook," pp. 181, 333.

already said, that they are to an extraordinary degree creatures of sympathy and imitation.

2. But if their parents add their testimony in behalf of the spiritual change, why should others, who have not the same means of knowing a child's changed manner of life, presume to call in question the reality of the change? Here we must not forget that not a few fathers and mothers are in such cases liable to be blinded by the partiality of affection. The late Rev. Dr. John Todd, fond parent though he was, did not allow this fact to mislead him. "I was," says he, "once at the house of a friend, who said he had just received a visit from a gentleman and lady and their child, and was grieved to see that child very uncommonly ill-behaved and disobedient to its parents. Judge of my surprise, a few months after, to read a biography of that child, in which it was described as a paragon of all that is excellent, as having been most dutiful and pious for a year or two . . . I do not say that the child was not really a convert to Christ. I believe it was. But I as fully believe that if an impartial stranger had drawn up the memoir, much, if not all that now interests us would be gone." We would not refuse the testimony of parents in behalf of a child, but its value will ever depend on the degree of partiality that colors and adorns it. Very few are the cases where it could be safely regarded as conclusive.

3. When delay for further inquiry and instruction is recommended, we often hear this pathetic protest : "Why turn them out upon the cold mountains to starve or perish, to see whether they are alive or not?" But this is not a very fair or very reasonable alternative. The children are not deprived of Sunday-school instruction ; in most cases they are not without

Christian teaching in their homes, nor need they be denied the special lessons of the pastor. And what can baptism or the Lord's Supper avail them before they are made to understand the import of these ordinances of the Church?

One of the lesser lights of the Reformation tells us that he once received profitable admonition in a dream. A voice fell from heaven, saying, "Myconius! Myconius! thrust not in thy sickle so near the earth. The Lord of the Harvest needs not the straw, but the wheat." Let us not be misunderstood. Neither are converted children straw nor unconverted adults wheat. All we ask is that children be not admitted to church-membership without clear and sufficient evidence of their conversion.*

We must add a few words concerning the Sunday-school concert or teachers' prayer-meeting. Very great has been the blessing of the Divine Master on these too much neglected meetings. Were we able to enumerate the converts which Sunday-schools have contributed to churches, and to trace the secret means and instruments of their conversion, we would perhaps be surprised at the numbers which owed their awakening to the grace that was sought and found in the Sunday-school prayer-meeting. The great revival in Ireland in 1859 is thought to have had its immediate origin in a prayer-meeting composed of four young men who met in an old school-house near Kells. But its more remote source is supposed to have been a Sabbath-school teachers' prayer-meeting at Tannybrake. It was held in the evening at the close of

---

* "Sabbath-school Teacher," p. 176. An excellent volume on the "Conversion of Children" is by the Rev. Edward Payson Hammond (New York, 1878).

the Sabbath-school. Parents were especially invited. Prayer, praise, and reading the Bible, with plain obser- vations on the portion read, were the regular exercises. The one great and absorbing topic was salvation through faith in Christ.* The returns of about three hundred congregations showed that this revival result- ed in an increase of about eleven thousand persons. Many other congregations were similarly blessed.

* " The Year of Grace," by Rev. Prof. Gibson, pp. 39-41.

CHAPTER XII.

EXPEDIENTS FOR CALLING OUT INQUIRERS.

Fixed ideas and uniform measures unwise—Modes of declaring a resolution or of asking counsel—Advantages of the anxious-seat—Opinions of Jacob Knapp and Orson Parker—Invitations to the anxious should be well-timed—A scriptural illustration: Elijah and the prophets of Baal—Importance of knowing the spiritual mood of the persons invited.

"WHAT expedient, sir, do you prefer for ascertaining who are awakened?" To this question of the writer a veteran in revival work once answered, "I have no favorite method of inducing the anxious to declare themselves. Sometimes I adopt one expedient, sometimes another. Ministers and churches that would not at the beginning of special meetings consent to the 'anxious-seat,' so called, will in the progress of the work propose it of their own accord. I simply study to follow the leadings of the Spirit."

It is of some importance to remove, as far as possible, all obstacles out of the way to a free avowal of religious feelings and purposes. Thus at the close of a large promiscuous meeting it were better to invite the awakened to meet in another room, than to attempt to call them forward or to make some sign in the presence of a crowd of strangers, among whom there are perhaps many triflers and sneerers. Hence, if at any time it be thought necessary to transfer the meetings to the chief audience-room, from a room for lectures or prayers, when the moment shall arrive for calling out the anxious, it will be prudent to dismiss the promiscuous audience, and invite the anxious to retire to the latter place of meeting or to the parsonage. In a more quiet and familiar place of concourse, both the anxious and their Christian friends will be less influenced by fear and whatever distracts attention.

Formerly, the advantages of "the anxious-seat" were set forth in various ways. It served, it was said, as a test of character ; it was a public committal ; it was a very convenient way of making a public acknowledgment of one's need of Christ ; such acknowledgment served to encourage other convicted souls ; the effect of such a step was also an encouragement to the minister and the church.*

The reasons for the gradual disuse of the "anxious-seat" or "penitents' bench" by some revivalists are frankly and fairly stated by the Rev. Orson Parker :† "For about fifteen years I made use of the 'anxious-seat,' till I saw that the people began to trust in it ; and that, although they would go to the 'anxious-seat,' they would not go to Christ. It had been injudiciously used as the 'mourners' bench' and as the 'anxious-seat,' until people generally became prejudiced against it. So that few would come forward when called, unless somebody went and urged them, and almost pulled them forward."

"For a long time I called upon the convicted to rise up for prayers. There is something gained by this, but not as much as is supposed. It brings a man one step forward as an inquirer, and may deepen his conviction, but he often trusts in the prayers of Christians, and hangs upon them until he is shaken off

* "Elder Jacob Knapp's Autobiography.' pp 214-221.
† "The Fire and the Hammer," pp. 48, 49.

and made to feel that Christians cannot save him.   If
a man is convicted enough to ask. the prayers of
Christians, he is convicted enough to go to Christ ;
and there he should be sent, and there he should go.

" Usually, at the close of an evening sermon, I now
let all leave who wish while the people are singing, and
invite all to remain who will, for private conversation,
and so turn the whole house into an inquiry room.
After a few evenings very few will leave, and men
and women will remain to be conversed with, and
many will be converted, who would never get up and
leave their seats and come to what is termed the
'anxious-seat.' And yet in this, as in the case of the
'anxious-seat,' care must be exercised to see that it
helps people toward Christ.   So long as that is the
standard, 'anxious-seats,' rising for prayers, and inquiry meetings may all safely be employed." To the
measures here described we make two objections.   It
appears to us that it is never well to distract the attention of a congregation while the praises of God are
being sung.   To request any class of persons to retire
or to propose taking up a collection during the singing
of hymns is unfriendly to good order and heartfelt and
reverent worship.   This is the rule ; an exceptional
case is that of inviting the anxious to come forward
or pass into the inquiry room while a hymn of invitation or appeal to this very class of persons is being
sung.   Another thing : the attempt to turn a large
audience room into a place for inquiry is not always
successful, because many persons remain from curiosity or from a desire to find matter for criticism or de-
traction.   These will ever, wittingly or unwittingly,
divide the attention both of the inquirers and of those
who are present to give advice to or pray for and with

them. A veteran revivalist of our acquaintance is very firm in the conviction that every inquiry meeting should be restricted to inquirers. He would not admit any unbelievers, however well disposed they might seem. He justifies his practice by a reference to the example of the Divine Healer in Matt. 9 : 25 ; Mark 5 : 37-40 ; Luke 8 : 51-54.

But to return to the question of the "penitents' bench" or "anxious-seat." Several facts are on record to the effect that persons of high self-regard have found peace while on their way to the "anxious-seat." What was required of them was submission to the will of the Lord. As soon as they surrendered pride and wilfulness, they obtained the hope of pardon. Everything depended on a right inclination, and nothing on the "anxious-seat" as such.

The "anxious-seat" and the revival prayer-meeting are sometimes rendered inoperative by a resort to prayer before either the Christian workers or the seekers have learned what are the things that are to be asked of the Lord. Many and various are the delusions of the anxious. These should be found out and removed. The plan of salvation or the nature of repentance may, in some cases, need explanation. "Seekers," says the Rev. Dr. James Porter,[*] "are saved by faith. . . . The suggestions of the devil to one trying to break away from him and turn to Christ are many and diversified, either of which may prevent him from believing unto salvation. Faith is also desirable on the part of those who pray for inquirers, but how can they believe that they will receive an immediate answer, unless they have some definite

[*] "Hints to Self-Educated Ministers," pp. 199-202 (New York, 1879).

understanding of the condition of those for whom they pray?   It is impossible without a special revelation."   The same judicious writer is of opinion that the success of prayer at such times depends much on a Scriptural attitude, spirit, and position, and complains that inquirers are invited forward in an excited and hasty manner.   Very aptly does he illustrate his meaning by the case of Eljiah and the prophets of Baal, in 1 Kings 18 : 30-38.   The prophets of Baal prayed in vain, because in disregard of the law, from morning till noon, saying, " O Baal, hear us."   But Elijah proceeded obediently and with all due preparation. After everything was ready, he delayed prayer until the time of the evening sacrifice, as prescribed by the law of God, and then he urged as one reason for being heard, that it might be known that he had done all these things at God's Word.   " If," says this writer, " we had but fifteen minutes to devote to inquirers, we could spend ten of them in preparing to pray.   We may then accomplish more in five minutes than we could in hours, and even days, while out of position.

One of the common expedients of evangelists, especially in New England, has been to secure a separation of a religious assembly into classes.   By various public demonstrations believers are separated from unbelievers, or professors from non-professors, or the anxious from such as are unconcerned, and the like. In some instances Christian parents have been invited to come forward in the presence of the congregation and unite in praying for their unconverted children. Another form of separation has been exhibited on the occasion of the celebration of the Lord's Supper. Unbelievers or the impenitent have been invited to stay as spectators.   This division is made the subject of appeals to the latter. This kind of demonstration has been recommended as less violent than any other. But an ardent advocate of revivals * has given a judicious opinion on these public separations ; he thinks them suited only to very high states of feeling, and calling for the exercise of the greatest delicacy and prudence.

It is perhaps scarcely necessary to add that no appeal should ever be made to the convicted or the anxious to rise, to lift up their hands, or to come forward, unless the leader of the meeting is assured beforehand that there are some who are willing to do so. Urgent and repeated exhortations, to which there is no response, have a very unhappy effect. Sometimes the leader may place himself in the relation of a public antagonist to the unconverted part of the meeting. " I have seen," says the late Dr. Kirk, " a leader become angry because he was foiled in the attempt to persuade some one to come forward. This can be avoided, however, by simply making the offer and not undertaking to urge the step."

This whole subject is one upon which no prudent man will venture to be very positive. Whenever the Lord commands us to dig ditches, we need not doubt that he will fill them with water (2 Kings 3 : 16-25). Methods that are merely human, although devised with the best intentions, cannot be always and everywhere successful. All things change, and we change with them. But in the use of means and instruments, we may sometimes wisely change without incurring the charge of desiring novelties : we may return to the old, and find it more serviceable than the new.

* " American Revivals," by Rev. Calvin Colton, A.M. London, 1832, pp. 89 106.

CHAPTER XIII.

INQUIRY MEETINGS CONSIDERED.

Objections to seats for inquirers : making a virtue of a public demonstration—No Scripture authority for such seats—Not the mercy-seat—The timid not reached—Time and place of the inquiry meeting—Practice of Edwards Buell, and Humphrey—Instruction to inquirers—Strictures on certain kinds of advice—Moody's method of conducting these meetings.

MANY evangelists adopt some method of finding out who are awakened or anxious at the close of each public service, and then invite all such to a meeting for inquiry. Some, however, depend solely on an inquiry meeting for ascertaining the individuals that need instruction, warning, or encouragement, along with the intercessions of the faithful. The latter are opposed to all expedients for eliciting public manifestations from the awakened, the convicted, or the alarmed. Some of their objections to the "anxious-seat" may be briefly stated as follows :

1. Many awakened sinners feel that by rising and going forward they have publicly committed themselves, and that therefore they have a right to expect regenerating grace—in other words, as they have taken steps toward Christ, they may hope that He will advance to meet them ; whereas they should be taught that Jesus is their first and only refuge, and therefore they are to renounce all ideas of preparation, self-dependence, and even of self-complacency, on the ground that they repose no confidence in themselves, but are

ready to take any step that their pious friends may advise.

2. There is no Scripture authority for this measure, more especially when it is supposed to imply a promise on the part of the unconverted to seek the Lord.

3. The attention of the prayerful is drawn away from the mercy-seat, to secure the success of the " anxious-seat."

4. The persons rising and coming forward are, for the most part, the sanguine, the rash, the self-confident or the self-righteous, while those who are more deeply affected will perhaps keep their seats, and yet will prove to be the modest, the humble, the broken-hearted, and such as are convicted of the deceitfulness of sin, and therefore afraid to take so momentous a step without further consideration.

But still, those who are, for these or like reasons, opposed to the " anxious-seat" do not deny that it is important to call sinners to an immediate decision, and also to an immediate manifestation of that decision. Some of the different methods of accomplishing these objects are the following :

" Sometimes those who are awakened are requested to remain in their places after the congregation have retired, that they may be prayed with and addressed collectively, or conversed with individually by the pastor. Sometimes they are requested to retire from the church to the lecture-room for the same purpose. Sometimes the pastor at the close of the public exercises on Sunday invites all who wish for conversation to come to the parsonage on that evening. At other times, when the number is large, he appoints an inquiry meeting to be held in some convenient place on Monday or Tuesday evening. And sometimes,

for convenience' sake, the inquirers in different neigh-
borhoods are invited to meet the pastor in one of
their own houses.*

The custom of Jonathan Edwards, at Northampton,
Massachusetts, and of Samuel Buell, of East Hampton, Long Island, was to invite the anxious to meet at
the parsonage ; and there are cases not a few where inquirers might profitably go alone, or attended by some
friend, to have a private interview with the pastor or
evangelist.   The bashful and the diffident might often
consent to go to the parsonage when they could not
be induced to appear in a meeting for inquiry.

It is with painful solicitude that many a young pastor asks himself: "How shall I instruct anxious
inquirers?"   Our space will not permit us here to
answer this question in any detail.   There is one general remark, made by the Rev. Jacob Knapp,† which
is worthy of special consideration.   "In the anxious-
room," says he, "I depend more on prayer, on prevailing supplication with God, than all the instruction
that can be given.   Everything is dark to the sinner
until enlightened by the Spirit ; and no coaxing, no
teaching, no driving will compel or induce the devil
to leave his palace in the human soul until the stronger
than the strong man armed comes upon him and binds
him.   Then the work is done, and done effectually.
Hence, I get all on their knees and set them to crying
to God (both saints and sinners) until He sends down
salvation."

---

* The Rev. Dr. Heman Humphrey's "Letters to his Son," pp.
305-6 ; Rev. Dr. Sprague's "Lectures on Revivals," pp. 263, 331, 348.

† Autobiography, p. 221, Rev. Dr. Finney's "Lectures on Revivals," Rev. Dr. Humphrey's "Manual of Revivals," and Hervey's
' Rhetoric of Conversation," contain some counsels on this subject.

But still the question returns, " How shall I instruct inquirers ?   United prayer is indeed the chief instrument of bringing the regenerating Spirit, but how am I to direct those who imagine that they are yet seeking, when they have, in fact, already found their Saviour ?" The wisest advisers are slow to assure such persons in a word that they are regenerate. They choose rather to speak the language of charity and hope. In cases even where the change is unquestionable, there may be such ignorance of the Gospel and of the doctrines of Scripture that the young convert cannot with a good conscience become a member of any church that holds articles of faith. Much trouble results from making evidence of conversion a full qualification for church-membership.

In giving invitations to inquiry meetings, do not make them too general in their terms, otherwise many, perhaps, will come who are not anxious. These last are not likely to derive any benefit from the directions and exhortations given, while they are very liable to give either an air of levity or of cold reserve to the gathering.

In order to break this reserve, and at the same time, avoid distraction and a misleading sympathy and imitation, it is best to speak to each one in a very low tone, and, if possible, while sitting a little apart from the rest.

There are certain phrases which Mr. Finney and others advise ministers to use in these meetings, on the ground that they are always proper or safe. One of these is, " Submit to God."   If the anxious one is depending on his own works or sufferings for salvation, and he has been taught the Gospel doctrine of the Atonement, then submission should be urged.

Scripturally he is now to submit to the righteousness of Christ as a part of God's plan of salvation, and yet many are directed to "submit," when repentance, obedience, or some other duty is more immediately demanded. Another piece of "safe" advice is, "Give your heart to God." But is this advice always safe? To anxious inquirers, who know very little about the excellences and perfections of God the Father, and have, as yet, no heartfelt evidence of the love of Christ to them, cannot give "their hearts to Him," if by that phrase is meant the duty that they should regard Him with a complacent love. They may possibly so love Him as to obey Him. Very carefully should we avoid even Scripture phrases, or words of counsel or exhortation, if they are not suitable for the peculiar state of the inquirer.

Wisely has it been remarked that inquiry meetings cannot be run by rule. Thus Mr. Moody's method is very suitable for his peculiar modes of operation and their results. But still, as something may be learned from those who are not to be followed in most of their ways, we here give a sketch of his method of conducting such a meeting. At the close of the public service he invites the anxious to enter the inquiry room, and at the same time requests the merely curious not to disturb the solemnity of the place by their presence. At the opening of the meeting he assumes that there are only two classes present, the seekers and the "workers." By a call for the inquirers to rise he ascertains their numbers, and at once distributes them in different parts of the room, and assigns a "worker" to each inquirer or each class of inquirers. In a few minutes the whole room presents a hushed and solemn scene. A Bible, without which no worker is welcome in that place, is freely opened, and earnest faces bow together over its pages, as Mr. Moody quotes and explains passages that are appropriate to the matters in hand. In many cases the teacher and inquirer study its promises on their knees, and then engage in prayer. In almost every case the inquirer is urged to pray for himself, and if unable to form the sentences the teacher makes the prayer, which, sentence by sentence, is solemnly repeated. In half an hour, Mr. Moody goes to the platform and asks all to kneel while two or three prayers are offered, to the end that the hour may be one of universal decision. " Now," says the leader, " there are many souls here buffeting the waves ; let us throw out a plank for them. Mr. A., can you tell these people how they can be saved now?" The Christian thus addressed points out in a few brief words or illustrations the path of life. Another, then another, is called upon to throw out some plank from God's Word or his own experience. These testimonies are rapidly given, while eager souls drink in the counsels they contain. Then the leader explains the solemn character of the decision to which he urges the inquirers, and calls on those who are ready to accept Christ to do so at once. One after another they express their purpose to live a Christian life. While some are hesitating between life and death, the leader asks all who can sing the " I will trust Him" or " He will save me," to rise and repeat that chorus. Leading on their faith, he calls for another singing of the same verse, perhaps changing it thus. " I do trust Him" or " He has saved me." At last, the young converts having been earnestly commended to God in prayer, the meeting is promptly closed.*

Some good hints concerning the use of Bible readings in inquiry meetings will be found near the close of the chapter on that branch of our subject. For the sake of variety it may sometimes be well to read one of more sentences or paragraphs in place of singing, after the manner of the offertory in the Book of Common Prayer.

* "Times of Refreshing," by the Rev. Dr. C. L. Thompson, pp. 392, 393.

CHAPTER XIV.

THE AGENCY OF TRACTS AND LETTERS IN REVIVALS.

Evidence on behalf of tracts—Parker, Murphy, and Fish — Correspondence blessed in Scotland—The writing of Christian letters demands prudence—The interest which invests written words and sentences—Letters may be written when the voice is reduced to silence—St. Paul in prison.

THE Reformation in Germany and England was rolled forward not only by great Bibles, but by little tracts as well. The tracts that Luther wrote and circulated, now so highly valued as literary curiosities, did good service in their day. Huss was converted by reading a tract written by Wyckliffe, '' The Morning Star of the Reformation.'' Several of the most successful evangelists or pastors, who have been remarkably blessed with revivals among their people, are very positive in their testimony in behalf of these little adjuvants. The Rev. Orson Parker enumerates them among the means he had found serviceable. The Rev. Dr. Murphy employed them in his parish as one of the preparatives of a work of converting grace. Says he : '' Just before our special meetings commenced, we had a notice of the meetings printed on the backs of one-page tracts, cordially inviting all to attend ; requesting the sympathies and prayers of Christians in our efforts, and kindly urging the unconverted to prepare to meet God. One of these, with a suitable four-page tract, was inclosed in an envelope bearing this printed inscription : ' Please take this home ; read the inclosed carefully ; think about the subject earnestly ; act honestly and promptly. Time is short.' Packages of these were placed in the hands of distributors, with instructions how to give them away. Hundreds were distributed in the city (Salem, New Jersey) and the surrounding country. Frequently a written note was added, and the whole inclosed in another envelope, directed to some friend, and sent through the post-office or by the hand of a messenger. Thus we sought to prepare the way of the Lord." The late Rev. Dr. Fish, of Newark, a pastor who enjoyed more than one special work of grace among the people of his charge, says that " he can safely say that he has known of hundreds of conversions that could be traced to tracts and books. The writer," says he, " well remembers how a youth under his charge (now a distinguished professor in one of our colleges) was finally brought to repentance through the ' Great Inquiry,' which he gave to him, accompanying it with an affectionate letter and many prayers. And in all the revivals among his people he has freely used such tracts as ' Don't put it off,' ' What is it to believe on Christ ? ' ' Come to Jesus ' (by Newman Hall), and his own ' Two Questions,' viz., ' Is your soul safe ?' and ' How can I be saved ?' " He likewise bears witness to their usefulness when given to inquirers, either to awaken or direct, as the case seemed to require. " This," says he, " is of great importance, as reading will tend to fix upon the mind the impression which the conversation may have made, and lead to clearer views of truth and duty."*

Trivial as the hint may appear, yet facts might be

* " Handbook of Revivals," pp. 230-234, 354.

adduced to prove the importance of exacting from the careless and indifferent a promise to read the tract you give them, adding the assurance on your part that you would like to know what they think about its contents.

We have already touched upon the service done by letters. The awakening at Cellardyke, Scotland, in 1860,* was in part occasioned by several letters sent by fishermen at Eyemouth and Ferryden, giving accounts of the work of grace in these fishing towns." "The Christian correspondent," says an anonymous writer,† "may do much for God. A kind letter has often told on the conscience and the heart, when the most affectionate and pointed admonition by word of mouth has proved useless, and even offensive. . . . The station, character, acquirements, joys and sorrows, hopes and fears, both of a writer of a letter on religious topics and of him for whose welfare it is designed, are among a host of things which must be taken into the account, and any of which are sufficient to render a style of communication which in one case would be most appropriate and affecting, in another most impertinent an offensive. The law of kindness in the heart, and the wisdom which cometh from above, will form the best guide in this matter."

There is a persuasiveness in the handwriting of a friend which the most beautiful specimen of typography cannot command. The advantage of the former has been calculated in a pecuniary way by

* "Authentic Records of Revival," by the Rev. William Reid (London, 1860), p. 464.

† "Christian Exertion," pp. 102, 103. This little volume, published by the American Sunday-school Union, explains and enforces the duty of members of churches to labor for the conversion of men.

secretaries of benevolent societies ; and where printed circulars have been addressed by them to individuals, it has been found of much service to add a few words, even in pencil.

The sermons and " Talks" of Mr. Moody contain some facts in proof of the usefulness of letters. Other evangelists whose sermons have not been published also bear witness to the success of this instrumentality. Let the Christian worker rejoice that he may employ this method of reaching souls when all others are forbidden. When the Apostle Paul was manacled, he could still write epistles, and say with joy, " but the word of God is not bound."

CHAPTER XV.

THE MANAGEMENT OF DISTURBERS AND RIOTERS.

The stupidity of mobs—The tact and address of Wesley, Whitefield, Rowland Hill, and others—The text and its unforeseen application—May forcible means be employed?—In every true work of grace heavenly wisdom is given to all such as publicly engage in it—Paroxysms, faintings, and prostrations—The opinions of Wesley, Erskine, and others concerning these seizures.

THE young preacher is sometimes at a loss as to the best way to quell the spirit of disorder and riot which may threaten to invade the meetings, and even to do him personal injury. No city of Christendom is perfectly secure from occasional uprisings of abjects ; and at times a mania for rabbles appears to rage without any sufficient occasion for its prevalence. Mere novelty is then enough to drive it to deeds of lawlessness. The vegetarian, Dr. Graham, was once mobbed in Boston for lecturing against the use of animal food, and Lord Chesterfield in London for obtaining the passage of a bill in Parliament authorizing the New Style in the calendar. But during revivals the malice of Satan is often found opposing the most manifest operations of the Holy Ghost. At such seasons young persons of education and of respectable family are instigated to form conspiracies against the peace of meetings or the reputation and personal safety of the evangelist. Happily, these plots very seldom accomplish the object the Fiend intended ; for the Divine Spirit, who begins and continues every true revival, suggests to the evangelist at the time the best means of detecting and exposing these schemes of satanic wickedness. It was this Spirit of wisdom who came to the aid of Wesley and Whitefield in every emergency of this kind, and inspired them with a courage that was not less astonishing than their prudence. Rowland Hill adroitly put himself under the protection of the very bully that led into one of his assemblies a company of his fellow-roughs. An evangelist equally eccentric, Jabez S. Swan, when challenged to fight, appealed to the " code of honor," and claiming the right to fix the time and place, met his adversary the next day in a public place and began the combat with prayer. The grace of God, coming in answer to the same, broke down the pugilist.

This kind of defence is at once the most scriptural and the most effectual. Very many are the instances of its success ; among the more recent are those which are furnished by the memoirs of " Uncle" John Vassar. " Sometimes," we are told, "a group of reckless young men would come into the evening service, and, by talking and laughing, disturb the meeting. As soon as anything of the kind was commenced, " Uncle" John would quietly move that way, and getting into the group, would drop down and offer such a prayer as would shame them, and sometimes strike every soul with seriousness."

Next to prayer, a sermon or exhortation, suggested by the Holy Spirit for the occasion, has most frequently been of excellent service. A veteran revivalist once, as he told me, was unable to fix on a text. The rebuke in Acts 13 : 10 often occurred to him, and as often was disapproved. It did not appear to him as in any part suitable for the occasion. No Elymas, so far as he knew, was present ; and yet, finding no other text in which he took any interest. and the moment for preaching having come, he rose and began to speak upon it. Receiving more and more liberty and energy as he proceeded, he was at length inwardly assured that he had an application for some person present. The event proved that the subject and the matter of this sermon were given him by the Spirit of all grace. An apostate and an enemy to the revival seeing that a number of young men were growing in anxiety concerning their salvation, he used all his great influence to make them infidels, and went so far as to organize them into a company pledged to one another that they would go to the meeting on that occasion, and by disorder and derision put an end to the work. No sooner did they hear the text than they began to suspect that their plot had been divulged. Fear took the place of foolhardiness, a sense of guilt and danger banished levity, and all, except the apostate, were led to conviction or repentance by that extemporaneous sermon. As the apostles, when brought before kings and governors, were taught by the Spirit what to say, so evangelists, while engaged in the converting work of the Lord, may expect wisdom from above to dictate to them fitting words and measures with which to withstand and attack their enemies.

But are there not places where policemen or constables may justifiably be asked to keep or restore order? Most certainly, and especially where the disturbers are very ignorant young men, animated by the wicked one, or brutish men maddened with drink. Very rarely, indeed, is it prudent for the evangelist, be he ever so skilled in boxing, or stout and active, to resort to "muscular Christianity" in defending himself and the faith. To overcome evil with good, to oppose meekness to violence, to be gentle and patient in intercourse with the rude and the abusive, is often the more Christlike and effectual remedy. Our Divine Master did indeed use violence in driving away profaners from the courts of the Temple. But on these occasions He acted from Divine authority, and with resistless power. On the other hand, He did not always hear cavillings and sophistries with silence and tame forbearance. He ever distinguished between what was intended as an affront to His person and what was due to saving and renewing truth. He was manly in argument, and in Him a devotional spirit was without any evidence of artifice or mental weakness.

Brevity requires us to make an end. We therefore repeat, in the first place, that in all true movements of the Spirit there is commonly given to the preacher and his trusty colaborers such wisdom as each emergency demands. This remark is at once illustrated and proved by the Memoirs and Journals of Wesley, Whitefield, Rowland Hill, and Jacob Knapp. For the prince of darkness and his slaves to outwit and defeat the Holy Spirit and his disciples were to make void the teachings of Scripture, and to break the wheels of eternal Providence.

For the rest, whenever the disorder is incident to the work itself, as where the convicted are deprived of all strength, so as to be quite prostrated, some disorder and confusion may occur while these demonstrations are yet a novelty. When persons thus fall, let them remain. They are in most cases what the grace of God perhaps intended they should be, silent but convincing witnesses of the power of the Holy Ghost.* Such is the

* " Lectures on Revivals by Ministers of Scotland," p. 349. Compare Ralph Erskine's letter in Wesley's Journal.

advice of the closest observers of these seizures and prostrations. They would, however, recommend a different course for all such as are subject to nervous disease, or such as have been repeatedly "stricken down." In such cases it is necessary to separate the individual as much as possible from all exciting causes, to resist the approach of every curious visitor, and by some suitable occupation to draw away the attention from the mind's exercises.*

While in general these "strikings," "seizures," or "prostrations" which attended the revivals led by Wesley and the Erskines, and which appeared in Kentucky in 1804 and Ireland in 1859, were graciously intended to glorify God, by making a direct appeal to the senses of the unbelieving and the careless, yet it seems very probable that in some cases they proceeded from demoniac agency, and had for their object a frustration of the work of grace, and the defence and extension of the kingdom of darkness.

* "Year of Grace," by the Rev. Prof. Gibson, p. 399. This writer devotes a very instructive chapter to the pathological affections or physical manifestations that appeared in Ireland during the revival of 1859.

CHAPTER XVI.

THE INTRUSIONS OF THE FEEBLE-MINDED AND THE INSANE.

What is to be done : resist beginnings—The friends of the feeble-minded may be consulted beforehand—Duty of sextons and ushers—Singing or praying the insane into silence—Advantage taken of the fact that the praying devil is scarce—Order restored by a pleasant remark.

ALMOST every place where the awakened and the recently renewed are wont to assemble seems to attract some insane or feeble-minded person, who occasions disturbance, distraction, and disorder. Few things are more detrimental to the progress of a work of grace than the caricatures and travesties of religion which this kind of mad people are pretty sure to make. The most important question for us to ask here is, What shall we do with them ?

1. Resist the beginnings. In order to effect this object, insist that there shall be no shouting or loud responses during the delivery of the sermons. If we maintain order while preaching, it will be more easy to do so in prayer-meetings. If people of sound mind allow themselves to be noisy, they stir up and embolden the deranged to be much more so.

2. At the beginning of the meetings, the sexton should be consulted about the prospect of any disturbance from persons of this class. He may dissuade some from entering the house, or by giving them a seat near the door, may, if necessary, the more easily obtain their quiet removal.

3. Concerning chronic or incurable cases, their relations or particular friends or a physician may be taken into our confidence. In this way preventive measures may be harmoniously and successfully adopted. It is sadly true that the daily companions of some crazy people grow inattentive to their misbehavior, and hence they are sometimes shocked and offended when any public notice is taken of it.

4. Feeble-minded men may occasionally be induced to promise to take no part in a prayer-meeting. If, therefore, they attempt to do so, they may possibly cease, on being reminded of the promise they made.

5. The interruptions and disturbances caused by monomaniacs and other such persons may, in some cases, be best prevented by adopting the rule of calling on persons by name to pray or exhort.

6. Another less commendable expedient is this : a few persons agree to take part in the meeting in quick succession, or to watch the movements of the deranged for the purpose of getting possession of the floor before him.

7. Forasmuch as mad people very seldom pray, the leader of the meeting may keep them quiet by saying, "Some brother will now pray ; after prayer we will sing this hymn ;" and at the moment the hymn is given out, it may be added, "After singing, another brother will lead us in prayer." If, on such an occasion, an erratic person rises to exhort or expound, the leader may check him with the reminder that prayer or singing is next in order.

8. How can one best arrest a maniac when he has contrived to seize an opportunity to take part ? He is usually sung or prayed down. To attempt to eject him from the meeting is dangerous. As he is very liable to

be censorious or uncharitable or violent, he may expose himself to be called to order. The leader should keep on the lookout for any opportunity to interrupt him and turn aside his attention. As he does not often speak to the point, he can often be told that he is forgetting the object of the meeting. If he be requested to lead in prayer, he will commonly come to a speedy end, for usually he dislikes this kind of religious exercise. Yet, exceptional cases there are. We have known deranged persons to resort to prayer as a shield against the hand of the sexton, while some of this class would hardly be suspected of insanity were it not for the enormous length of their prayers. Happily for us, however, the praying devil is scarce.

9. People should be encouraged to pray for these miserables, especially in their private devotions. The power of Jesus and His disciples over demons ought to embolden our hope that such prayer will be answered.

10. Force must, we are sorry to say, be used sometimes to remove insane persons from a meeting ; hence it is prudent to attend personally to the appointment of ushers to assist the sexton, and they should understand beforehand that a part of their business is to keep out, and, if necessary, to put out all disorderly persons, whether maniacs, drunkards, or unmannerly boys.

11. Needful as force sometimes is, yet '' I show you a more excellent way.'' Cases might be given in which prayer, united and persistent, has done what '' muscular Christianity '' could not do to conquer a peace. In one instance known to us, the leader of a band of young rioters, that had gone so far as to drive all the worshippers out of doors, was converted in answer to the prayers of the very persons who had been thus rudely cast out of the synagogue.

12. Those who are disorderly in sermon time may be the very persons for whose conversion we are praying and preaching. It is therefore desirable to keep them on good terms with ourselves. One day a young man who was very fussy during the sermon was reduced to quiet by the following remark : "The other day I publicly rebuked a hearer for inattention. Judge of my mortification when I learned that the disturber of the peace was an idiot."

CHAPTER XVII.

SOME OF THE EVILS INCIDENT TO TRUE REVIVALS.

Fanaticism—False hopes—Spiritual pride—Want of charity—Exaggeration—Self-confidence—Neglect of the ordinary means of grace—Let the dead bury their dead—Numerical success—Novices—False tests of piety—Party spirit—Vainglory—Resting on means—Changes of feeling—Perpetual ingathering—Examples in England, Scotland, and America—Spiritual discernment of Elisha.

MANY of the most judicious friends of revivals caution us against certain evils and abuses to which revivals are exposed. A few of these we here enumerate :

1. At such times the people are liable to fanaticism. Passion, feeling, extreme opinions, and extravagant measures are very apt to usurp the place that belongs to reason, conscience, sacred reverence, and the fruits of the Spirit. A great excitement may prevail, in connection with religious meetings, which, as results have shown, had its origin neither in the truth nor grace of the Gospel—an excitement that was fruitful in vainglory and self-righteousness.

2. Another evil is the encouragement of false hopes. A true hope is founded on a genuine faith. Some revivalists are content to bring the anxious to "obtain a hope." Others are satisfied if people have an indefinite, aimless, and causeless conviction of sin. Still others demand only and ever "submission," or, it may be, they exact promises and pledges of those who are as yet ignorant of the deceitfulness of their own hearts. "The instrument," says Rev. Dr. Sprague,

" by which every conversion is effected is God's truth. If then ministers during a revival fail to hold up the truth in its distinctive and commanding features, and confine themselves principally to impassioned addresses and earnest hortatory appeals, there is great reason to apprehend many spurious conversions."

3. Spiritual pride is another evil to be avoided. So much is often made of young converts ; they are so often called forward to " bear testimony" to exhort and give their experience, that they are in great danger of self-exaltation and presumption.

4. Nearly related to spiritual pride is another evil—an uncharitable spirit showing itself in talks and exhortations, if not even in sermons. The zealous denounce the inactive and the backslidden in the severest language. They think it enough to speak the truth, whereas they should ever speak it in love. The young censure and rebuke the old, imagining that there are scarcely any other virtues than fervor, activity, and occasional public demonstrations of piety. Nor is it an uncommon thing to see the established and aged disciple, in self-defence, indulging in words of recrimination.

5. Avoid exaggeration. Young converts, while carried away with enthusiasm, are very apt to use extravagant language. The woman of Samaria, transported as she was with the discovery of the Messiah, proclaimed through the streets that Jesus had told her all things that she had ever done. This fault may show itself not only in statements and narratives, but in partial representations of revealed truth. By emphasizing unimportant words or dwelling on trivial incidents ; by putting comparatively small matters in a strong light, while we throw essential doctrines or duties into the

shade, we may produce all the effect of fanaticism in experience, heresy in doctrine, or disobedience in practice.

6. Shun likewise a forward, self-confident spirit. Too often young persons are told that they may all know for certain that they are regenerate or have believed Christ.   Hence they learn to speak of their conversion as if there could be no doubt or mistake, and no room for " the judgment of charity." Some of them will assure us that they can tell the very day and hour when they were converted ; and possibly they can, but in their present ignorance their assurance is little better than conjecture.

7. We are also to beware of the tendency to neglect the ordinary means of grace. In times of revival, regular Sunday observance, the stated meetings of the church, family worship, and secret prayer are frequently allowed to lose their hold on the hearts and habits of the people.   Week-day and evening meetings, with their crowded public engagements, engross attention and occupy every waking hour.   What follows ?   Not a few of the Christian workers, deprived of their daily opportunities of secret or family prayer, ultimately find that while they have been so busy in the harvest field, their garden has been well-nigh destroyed by cattle, and their homes successfully invaded by thieves.   Well aware we are that some grave men of routine are such sturdy defenders of stated appointments and standing rules that they would not hesitate to admit an agent of a benevolent society into the pulpit, and permit him to interrupt a series of revival sermons by long narratives and appeals in behalf of his cause.   We concur, however, with the Rev. Dr. Humphrey, in his letters of advice to his own son, when he writes on the exceeding

importance of a proper timing of subjects : " In certain stages of a revival, anything, any subject, aside from the work which is going on, may do infinite mischief, by being thrust in and crowding out the inquiry, ' What must I do to be saved ? ' Certain subjects must be brought forward immediately. What, now, if an agent were to come and ask you for a Sabbath in the midst of the revival ? Would you not say to him, ' Brother, I am glad to see you, and if you will lay aside your particular object and preach with special reference to the state of my congregation, I shall be glad of your assistance ; but, if not, you must come again.' "

An evangelist of large experience says that he was once called home in the midst of a revival in order to comfort an aged Christian in his dying hours. On his way he met a pious friend, who asked him where he was going. When told, he replied, " Did not your Master say, ' Let the dead bury their dead ? ' There is not another man in the world that can take the work where you leave it ; it will suffer." The evangelist rejoined : " Once I tarried when called home to a funeral, and it gave such offence in the family that had been visited by death, that they were never reconciled to me." Near the close of this life the evangelist comments on this incident as follows : " Yet with the light I now have, if it were my father that desired me, under such circumstances, to leave my work and come to him, I could not do it."

8. Be not wrongly ambitious to add a very large number to the church. Inquire, therefore, what your motive is in seeking the conversion of sinners. Why is it that you are so eagerly desirous to bring certain persons into the church ; why you do so wish that you may be enabled to report a fixed number of converts

on some important occasion. " But may I not err more egregiously by exercising an excessive caution ?" It is difficult to fix the comparative magnitude of the two errors. If we could, they would both be errors still. A very zealous revivalist of our acquaintance was wont to say that over-cautious preachers were like fishermen who refuse to cast forth the net for fear they might catch a devil-fish.

9. Beware of the danger of injuring the reputation or hindering the work of the pastor. Time was when some revivalists were notorious for their hostility to all pastors who would not cheerfully adopt all their measures, and when they left behind them a crowd of professing converts, that were impudent factions and defiant of all authority. The leaders of these were young men of more gifts than graces, who had been injudiciously put forward to conduct prayer-meetings, young people's meetings, and, perhaps, superintend Sunday-schools, although they could not teach and would not learn. Let both pastors and evangelists consider diligently what work can be safely given to new converts. "We ought not," says Bishop McIlvaine, " to take a green sapling and set it up for a pillar in the church. The weight would bend it down and make its branches grow into the earth."

10. Another evil is the judging of piety by unscriptural rules. In cases not a few, persons who have none of those gifts which enable them to shine in revivals namely, boldness, fluency, ardor, demonstrative vivacity—and a loud voice—are suspected of being in an apostate or backslidden state ; while many a person of sanguine-nervous temperament at such seasons passes for an eminent saint dwelling near the gates of the New Jerusalem. As the soldier is ever tempted to despise

every other calling than his own, and all other virtues than those which belong to his vocation, so the new convert is tempted to regard the revival state of the church as its normal one. And, consequently, the man who should be slow to begin and cautious in proceeding during such a work of grace, would run the hazard of being esteemed by him a kind of almost Christian. Sometimes full assurance of faith, suddenly acquired is the standard by which the intending professor is to be tested ; then, again, high feeling or a striking experience is the pass of acceptance.

11. One of the greatest hindrances to a general awakening is the manifestation of the want of candor and justice, truth and charity, which too often attends the prevalence of party spirit. Whether this spirit finds fuel in religious or political matters, or in a combination of both, the result is the same—a quenching of the fires of the Holy Spirit. In one instance, where the house of worship had been opened for a political meeting, an application for the use of the place by the opposite party was refused. This act of palpable unfairness made the church very unpopular in the community, and alienated a minority of its members to such a degree that they did not cordially co-operate in the special services. The evangelist, ignorant of the real trouble, found his exertions very laborious and of little profit. Some forty were reported as converted, but they did not show the spiritual animation which is usually manifested by souls that have risen to newness of life. As the result, not one was added to the church in whose place of worship the meetings were held, although some of the converts resided only a short distance from the house. All the converts sought and found fellowship in other churches. More frequent

and familiar are the effects of a partisan spirit when it is confined to purely religious questions. . As the spread of forest fires is often arrested by digging ditches, so partisan divisions in churches "quench" the advancing flames of the sacred Spirit. They quench them by a demarcation, which serves all at once and extensively to remove their proper fuel.

12. Watch against vainglory in publishing accounts of the character and extent of the work. Very desirable it often is to publish narratives of revivals. There is abundant proof that the divine blessing has many a time attended such reports.. But, as far as may be, avoid every attempt either to flatter the agents or instruments that were employed. The Lord will not give His glory to another.

13. Glide not into a reliance on the means of grace rather than upon grace itself. In the midst of a successful work, in which perhaps the pastor, the evangelist, the singers, and other workers have all been instruments of bringing some to the Saviour, they are liable to indulge in the delusion that the power belongs to the human agents. "Thus," says President Wayland, "reliance on the Spirit of God is forgotten ; a spirit of self-confidence succeeds to a spirit of prayer, and God leaves the work in the hands of men. I need not say that it immediately ceases."

14. We are also admonished to take heed lest we indulge a habit of inconstancy in the religious affections. This danger ever attends revivals. How shall we guard against it? The best answer to this question we have ever found is given by the Rev. Dr. Sprague in these words : "One means of avoiding it is, by endeavoring to keep down animal passion, especially in the height of the revival, when it is most likely to be awakened.

Another means is to keep up spiritual feeling when the general excitement attending a revival begins to pass away ; for that is the critical time when religious languor usually first begins to creep over the soul." The necessity of contending against this pendulum-like tendency will be seen if we consider what will be its effect on the new converts when they shall have been admitted to the fellowship of the church. No doubt one reason why so many of them return to the world or wander into doubt, formality, or worldliness, is that the church itself has relaxed all its energies and gone to sleep. The purpose of all should be to keep up, if not the first fervor of zeal, at least the sense of duty and the exercise of all the Christian graces ; for these, happily, do not depend for their life and energy on physical vigor and activity, but on the Holy Spirit of God. Thus may the gracious visits of Jesus be prolonged—yes, be changed, perhaps, into permanent residence ; or, at any rate, His speedy return may be expected, provided for, and most warmly welcomed.

It has been asked, Why may not the pastor hope for a perpetual ingathering, such as Richard Baxter enjoyed at Kidderminster, John Brown at Haddington, Dr. Romaine in London, and Edward Payson in Portland ? One means of obtaining this blessed state is recommended by the eminent minister last mentioned. He says that from the time of his settlement the church had set apart one day quarterly for the purpose of fasting and prayer. He found no means so much blessed to keep religion alive in the church.*

Some revivals have continued a long time. The work of awakening grace which began at Cambuslang in

* Rev. Dr. Sprague's " Lectures on Revivals," appendix, p. 298.

1742 spread to other parts of Scotland, and prevailed for eight years ; and the revival which appeared at Stewarton in 1625, and ended not until 1630, was, during those five years, according to the testimony of Fleming, like a spreading stream, increasing as it flows, and fertilizing all within its reach.''

But still we need that wisdom which is from above, to apprehend not only when a special work of regeneration has begun, but also when it has come to an end.

Those who quickly find out when the genuine work commences will as readily ascertain when it has finished its course. Elisha evinced his spiritual discernment as clearly when Eljiah first visited him, as when he saw him on fiery wheels ride up behind the clouds. Had he failed to look through the dust of the whirlwind and see the ascension of Eljiah, he would not have inherited his mantle.

CHAPTER XVIII.

FEEDING THE LAMBS OF THE FLOCK.

This duty sometimes neglected—Themes useful for close of special
services—Mere intellectual improvement of secondary importance
—Charles Simeon's testimony—The prejudices of young converts
—The pastor's relation to meetings of young people—Juvenile
influence in ecclesiastical affairs.

BY this we mean the teaching and training of the new
converts, whether young, mature, or aged. Nothing
has of late given us more concern than to observe with
what indifference this duty is often regarded. Instead
of organizing the converts into bands of Christian
workers, converts' Bible-classes, meetings for the study
of the Catechism or Articles of Faith, and other forms
of instruction and service, perhaps the pastor either
returns to his former habit of preaching to advanced
Christians or takes a long vacation, during which, from
motives of economy or benevolence, a variety of cheap
supplies, or else some theological student is engaged ;
consequently both sheep and lambs are for a considerable time poorly fed, or left to wander without a fold
and without an under-shepherd. This, too, is very apt
to happen during those few months following a revival, wherein the lambs are exposed to great temptations and spiritual dangers.

Our space denies us the privilege of treating this
theme with any particularity. But in the selection of
themes, texts, and outlines, we have not omitted any
that appeared profitable either for the close of revival

seasons or for the subsequent instruction of the new converts. We have not thought it worth while here to attempt to give the texts, subjects, and outlines of series of discourses to young converts, the delivery of which would demand a considerable time. Materials for these are, happily, not far to seek. They may be found in the Rev. Dr. Sprague's '' Lectures on Revivals,'' lecture vii. ; '' Revival Sketches and Manual,'' by Rev. Dr. Humphrey, pp. 303-424 ; the Rev. Dr. Kirk's '' Lectures on Revivals,'' pp. 299-322 ; Rev. Dr. J. V. Watson's '' Helps to the Promotion of Revivals,'' chapters vii., xii. ; Rev. Dr. James Porter's '' Revivals of Religion,'' chapter x. ; Rev. Dr. H. C. Fish's '' Handbook of Revivals,'' chapter xvii.; Elder Jacob Knapp's '' Autobiography,'' pp. 222-227.

The various tract and publication societies issue appropriate advice and direction to new converts. The pastor that does not supply them with these, or something better of his own composition, really ought to question whether he be not exposing the lambs of his flock to much needless sin and sorrow.

In cases where the converts are perhaps below the average in intellectual education, the young pastor will be tempted to organize some association whose object is to improve their minds. We say '' tempted ;'' for in all such cases the first real demand will be for direct moral and spiritual training and growth. Let it be his aim, therefore, to form their graces rather than their gifts. If, on the contrary, he aim to make the church a school for the intellect, though he may add to the splendor, he will not increase the inward riches of the church. The windows of the sacred edifice may blaze, not because they are illuminated from within, but because they reflect the cold light of the setting sun.

Even when the real purpose of a young converts' meeting is moral and spiritual improvement, it is still exposed to evils that are alike dangerous to itself and to the church. The object, although a good one, may be defeated by side-issues, ulterior ends, bad management, or other such means. What the Rev. Charles Simeon * said of the "private societies" he set on foot at Cambridge will in part apply to these young people's meetings : "Great care should be taken about the manner of conducting them. The people should never, if it can be avoided, be left to themselves ; the moment they are, there is danger of an unhallowed kind of emulation rising up among them ; and those who by reason of their natural forwardness are most unfit to lead will always obtrude themselves as leaders among them ; while the modest and timid will be discouraged because they cannot exercise those gifts which they behold in others. On such occasions, too, the vain and conceited will be peculiarly gratified, and, mistaking the gratifications of vanity for truly spiritual emotions, they will attach a pre-eminent importance to those opportunities which tend to display their talents, and they will begin to entertain low thoughts of their own minister, whose labors do not afford them the same pleasure." Or, if they have been converted under the ministry of an evangelist, they will perhaps set up his peculiar views, or his sermons, and his methods of procedure as standards by which to test the labors of their pastor, after the season of ingathering has passed away. If the pastor himself

* " Memoirs," chap. xiii., near the end.

has been the instrument of converting them, they will exhibit the same partialities toward him and the same prejudices against his successor in the pastorate, and all other ministers of the Gospel. Mayhap some young man, possessed of more gifts than graces, will put himself forward, and, gaining many admirers, will use his influence against all ministers except his idol, or all the members of the church except the young people. Some of these evils may possibly be avoided by providing a number of leaders, who shall serve in succession, by securing the attendance of the pastor, or other persons of " light and leading." These ought to aim to make the meetings at once more instructive and more sociable, more cheerful and yet more true to the great object of the institution. But if the young people are left to themselves, they forget the allegiance they owe to their pastor and to the church ; they form a party composed of the younger members of the church ; they show a childish and even a babyish petulance whenever their way concerning pastors and teachers does not prevail. Children govern their fathers, well-regulated families vanish from the church, and a proselyting spirit takes the place of Christian morality and evangelical piety.

CHAPTER XIX.

SHALL WE JOIN THE REAPERS OR NOT?

Taking counsel of our fears—First-rate pulpit orators not absolutely
necessary in this kind of service—The example of Wesley, Edwards, and others—Extemporaneous sermons not indispensable
—Example of Davies, Lyman Beecher, and others—Natural ardor
has its drawbacks—Evangelistic success not limited to young
preachers—Youth not always a disadvantage—Waiting for calls
and indications—A general interest in a church or community not
to be expected at the outset—Times of declension and persecution should not discourage pastors and evangelists—A parable.

WE propose in this chapter to address a few words
of cheer and hope to such pastors and evangelists as
are inclined to take counsel of their fears.

More than a few young preachers and pastors are
reluctant to engage in this work from a fear that they
have not such natural or acquired endowments as they
imagine to be necessary to evangelistic usefulness.
Should any such happen to read these pages, let
them remember that in every age it has pleased the
Lord to choose and honor the most unpromising instruments, and often disappoint alike the fears of the
timid and the ardent expectations of the wise. Moses,
Jeremiah, John the Baptist, and the twelve fishermen were, in human judgment, the most unlikely
messengers of the Lord. Man's wisdom would have
said that they were the wrong men in the wrong place.
Look at John Wesley, small of stature, unemotional,
and with no powerful and commanding voice, yet one
of the appointed leaders of the new reformation in
England. Look at Jonathan Edwards, a man of

reserved and scholarly habits, and in preaching tied to
his manuscript, never visiting his people from house to
house, and yet blessed as scarcely any other preacher
in America as a revivalist and an historian of the work
the Lord was pleased to accomplish through him.
Look at Samuel Buell, the humble pastor at East
Hampton, Long Island, New York, a man of great
natural reserve, who spent but little time in social intercourse with his people, preaching very long sermons,
drawing his subjects from the Scriptures rather than
from his observations among his flock, and yet mighty
as a revivalist, and according to the judgment of one
eminent contemporary, Dr. Stiles, President of Yale
College, " he had done more good than any other man
that ever stood on the continent"—a man who has
left a narrative of the awakening of which he was chiefly
instrumental second only to that of President Edwards
in value and attractiveness. The first great revival that
blessed Ulster, in Ireland, began under the ministry of
one of the least gifted of the Scottish preachers, the
Rev. James Glendinning. He was settled at Oldstone,
near Antrim. Previously he was minister at Car-
rickfergus, but acting on the advice of the famous
Robert Blair, he removed to a less conspicuous sphere.
Yet was he the instrument of awakening multitudes,
especially on the banks of the river Six-Mile Water,
and thus of preparing the way for the ingathering of
souls under the preaching of Blair and Livingstone.
" He was," it is said, " a man who never would have
been chosen by a wise assembly of ministers, nor sent
to commence a reformation in Ulster. Yet this was
the Lord's choice to begin with him the admirable
work of God, which I mention on purpose that all may
see how the glory is only the Lord's in making a holy

nation in this profane land, and that it was not by might nor by power, nor by man's wisdom, but by my Spirit, saith the Lord.''*

Look at William McCulloch, of Cambuslang, near Glasgow, in Scotland, whose published sermons are no way distinguished either for eloquence or unction. "He was not," says his son, "a very ready speaker; . . . his manner was slow and cautious—very different from that of popular orators." His parish was small, containing only about nine hundred persons. But still he was greatly honored as a revivalist. During the year 1742 no fewer than four hundred souls were added to the church, and these all continued faithful to the time of their death. True it is that he had the assistance of Whitefield, but the number given does not include such as were awakened under the sermons of this prince of evangelistic preachers.

It is a delusion current in some sections of Christendom that none but extemporaneous preaching is owned by the Divine Spirit. One consequence of this false opinion has been that some young men who cannot extemporize have imagined that they must be powerless in revivals. Let this error be corrected. Edwards and Davies, Buell, Griffin, Lyman Beecher, and not a few other great revivalists, wrote and read their sermons. John Wesley was converted by listening to the reading of Martin Luther's preface to the Epistle to the Romans, in a little meeting of Moravians in London. The writer, while travelling in Virginia many years ago, heard a sermon that had been carefully written by the pastor from beginning to end, and was

* Rev. Prof. William Gibson's " History of the Revival in Ireland in 1859." The work is entitled " The Year of Grace," pp. 21, 22.

read word for word. Though this pastor was surrounded by extemporizers, and the tide of public
opinion ran strongly against written sermons, yet he
had been blessed during the previous year with a
greater number of converts than any other pastor in
that part of the State. Be it kept in mind that we are
not here discussing the general question, but only trying to encourage in the work of the Lord those young
preachers that either cannot preach extempore or
bring their consciences to consent that they may adopt
such a manner of speaking in the cause of the Lord.

Another mistake is that none but men of natural
ardor can achieve any desirable results in revival meetings. Doubtless there is a certain measure of truth in
the Rev. Richard Cecil's maxim that that " the warm
blundering man" will do more than the " cold correct
man." Not seldom are these qualities thus associated
in ministers of the Word ; and yet they may be, and
sometimes are, found apart ; or rather the warm and
correct may be blended in the same character. Now
it seems to us that the man of this latter kind of
composition will, in the long run, be found to be the
most successful evangelist. President Edwards, we
are aware, sets the very highest estimate on zeal and
resolution. Why ? It is because he finds them conspicuous traits in Whitefield, whom he regarded as the
pattern of all evangelists. True it is that these virtues
ought to be strong and active in men that are called
to such public service, but unless they are counter-
balanced, as they were in Whitefield, by prudence and
by that self-command which, as Southey says, he always
possessed in public, they will often do an amount of
mischief which their mere effectiveness and popular attractions fail either to neutralize or to remove.

And this leads us to notice the error of those who, whether pastors or aged evangelists, imagine that they are too far advanced in life to succeed in this kind of ministerial work. The young, say they, have the vigor, push, and enterprise that are here requisite to acceptance and success. This we admit, so far as regards large popularity and immediate and splendid appearances of success. But for real service and thorough work, for sound conversions and full restorations such as do verily build up, unite, and permanently enlarge a church, commend us to men of venerable years and large experience—men that have learned something from the errors of their earlier ministry, as well as from their more extended experience, reading, observation, and reflection. Speed is not always progress. Davenport in New England and Marshall in Kentucky in later years publicly confessed the great errors and wrongs into which the mad and misguided zeal of their earlier years had betrayed them. And neither Wesley nor Whitefield in their later and better years could look back with a smile on the errors in doctrine and transgressions in spirit which sincere piety and a college training could not prevent, while the enthusiasm of youth and the applause of the people drove them forward, as before a favoring gale and tide. Even Jonathan Edwards, a man by nature diffident and cautious, confesses * that the calamities which ultimately came upon the church at Northampton were to be attributed, in part, to his youth and inexperience at the time of the famous awakening in that

---

* Read his remarkable letter to Gillespie of Scotland in 1751, sixteen years after the great revival. It is in " The Great Awakening," by the Rev. Joseph Tracy, p. 403.

town. " Instead of youth," says he, " there was want
of a giant in judgment and discretion among a people
in such an extraordinary state of things." Christian
biography abounds in instances of aged pastors and
evangelists who have, with the help of the Holy Ghost,
achieved their greatest successes near the close of life.
Mr. Robe labored in the parish of Kilsyth thirty years
before he saw the great revival of 1742.

But still the young preacher should not construe
what we have said for the encouragement of the old as
a discouragement for himself. Let him not say with
Jeremiah, " I am a child ; I am small and despised."
Both Wesley and Whitefield began their evangelistic
career very early in life, and although their youth
betrayed them into some blunders, these were as
nothing when compared with what they achieved in
" the new reformation." John Livingstone, who was
so wonderfully assisted in preaching in the churchyard
at Shotts, on Monday, June 21st, 1630, was only
twenty-seven years of age, and not yet ordained.
When he was alone in the fields on the morning
before service, there came upon him, we are told,
such a misgiving, under a sense of unworthiness and
unfitness to speak before so many aged and worthy
ministers and eminent and experienced Christians,
considering also the multitude and expectation of the
people, that he was thinking of stealing away, and had
actually gone to some distance, and was just about to
lose sight of the kirk, when the words, " Was I ever a
barren wilderness, or a land of darkness ?" were
brought to his mind with such an overcoming power as
constrained him to think it his duty to return and
comply with the call to preach. To confirm his reluc-
tance, it had not been customary to have preaching

on Mondays after communions. And yet some five hundred persons were converted, principally by means of this sermon. Nor did the work cease on that day. "It was," says Mr. Fleming, "the sowing of a seed through Clydesdale, so that many of the most eminent Christians in that country could date either their conversion or some remarkable confirmation from it."

Many and various are the excuses of the pastor for delaying the work of reaping and ingathering.

Often he fears that in immediately setting about the work of awakening, he may not be following the leadings of the Spirit and of Providence. "In my early revival efforts," says an aged evangelist, "I used to be accused of getting ahead of God; and was often told that I should wait for God to begin the work; then take hold." His reply to such words was: "My Master always sent men ahead of Him. He sent His disciples two and two into all the cities whither He Himself would come."

Again, he may conclude that he ought not to move toward any service of this kind until there is a very general demand for extra meetings and revival preaching. History proves that almost all great awakenings begin with one or two persons; and that, in no case, does the evangelist have the unanimous co-operation of the church until the time for receiving the new converts into fellowship has arrived. But let him remember that Gideon won a great victory with about a hundredth part of his original army, and that Jabin's host with nine hundred chariots of iron was vanquished by the fighting men of the two tribes of Zebulun and Naphtali.

Some revivalists attempt no new work in the summertime. It can be shown, however, that from the days of Jonah until now there have been mighty works of grace in very warm weather.

There are periods in the life of almost every evangelist when it appears either as if a voice from Heaven bade him retire from the service, or as if, because of the dead-alive state of the 'churches from which he has repeatedly failed to arouse them, it were better for him to abandon the Gospel ministry forever. But let him remember that the seasons which threaten to extinguish hope are almost always brief and apt to be followed by times which call for joy and rejoicing. Just before a storm the heavens often darken, as they do when the sun is in a total eclipse. The dust rising along the streets whirls into the eyes of the travellers, and joins with the darkness in saying to him : Go not forward, but hasten to the nearest shelter.

Mayhap he has seen his exertions in revivals hindered or arrested by local controversies, or the adversaries of revivals. It may be that Satan has stirred up the religious press to calumniate him or misrepresent the nature or extent of his services ; or else rival editors, like Samson's foxes, have dragged torches of discord everywhere, and produced a general conflagration over vast fields that were a little before waving their golden grain in the summer breeze, as if to invite the reapers to cut and bind and stack. Amid such dark days let the evangelist consider that either to leave the ministry or to do the work of an evangelist is not his only alternative. Possibly the Lord would have him for a season do pastoral work. On the other hand, let not a pastor allow himself to leave his flock for any promise of gain. By way of warning to such, the writer makes the following parable : A shepherd boy of small experience was one day leading his little flock near the entrance of a mountain cavern. He had been told that precious stones had often been discovered in such places. He was, therefore, tempted to leave his charge and turn aside to explore the dark recesses of the cavern. He began to crawl in, but as he proceeded his face took on a veil of cobwebs, and his hands mittens of mud. He had not gone far when he saw two gems of a ruby glow lying near each other. He put forth his eager fingers to seize them, when a serpent bit him. In pain and fear he crawled quickly back to the light of day, and ran home to the chief shepherd to obtain some remedy for the bite. The good man, who was also his elder brother, sucked the poison from the wound, and applied to it a healing balm. Never afterward did that shepherd covet the treasures which may lie concealed behind mountain rocks.

CHAPTER XX.

WAITING FOR POWER FROM ON HIGH.

Scripture view of the subject—How this power was manifested—Ministerial success does not depend wholly on Christian experience—Preaching the true Gospel of prime importance— Retreats and ten-day prayer-meetings—St. Paul's weakness in its relation to divine power.

IT is the belief of evangelists not a few that in order to do the most faithful and efficient service, they must needs be invested with the power of the Holy Spirit. By this "power" they understand something very different from sanctifying grace, although some of them consider it as inseparable from Christian faith, love, peace, and joy. If at any time they are conscious that they have it not, they wait for it in prayer, fasting, and study of the Scriptures, believing that, in some sense, they are bound to heed the command of Jesus to His disciples found in Luke 24 : 49. They do not, however, hold that this investiture of power is confined to themselves as evangelists, but is to be sought and obtained by pastors and all Christians who are called to active service in every sphere of usefulness. Nor do they believe that, once endued with this divine energy, it abides with them as a permanent force ; it may forsake them ; and as the scene of Pentecost was, as they think, repeated (see Acts 4 : 31), so they are to seek for themselves and others new investitures of power.

Now, without accepting all the beliefs of all these beloved brethren (for they differ much among themselves), we do certainly learn from Holy Scripture that there is such an enduement or anointing or fulness of the Divine Spirit as prepares Christians for exertion and endeavor (see Luke 24 : 49 ; Acts 1 : 8 ; 1 Cor. 2 : 4 ; 2 Cor. 12 : 9). And this power is said to be not only upon them, but in them (Acts 2 : 4, 4 : 31 ; Col. 1 : 29 ; Eph. 3 : 16). It also enabled holy men not only to act but to speak for Christ (Acts 4 : 33), and to celebrate the praises of the Lord (Acts 2 : 4, 12). Nor was this power or *dynamis* merely the gift of working miracles ; the apostles wrought no miracles, except speaking with tongues on the day of Pentecost, and although John the Baptist is said to have gone before the face of the Lord in the spirit and power of Elijah, and to have been filled with the Holy Ghost from his birth (Luke 1 : 15), yet he did not, like the old Hebrew prophet, perform any miracle (John 10 : 41) ; he was moved by that power to herald the Messiah, to prepare the way for Him by preaching repentance, and to point Him out as the sin-atoning Lamb of God. But still this power is sometimes put in opposition to mere words and forms (1 Cor. 4 : 19, 20 ; 1 Thes. 1 : 5 ; 2 Tim. 3 : 5). It is perhaps best rendered force, a word which is now popularly used to designate power applied and exerted.

The import of the word is not very unlike that which is employed to convey the idea of the fulness of the Divine Spirit. Whenever the primitive disciples are said to be filled with the Holy Ghost, they either say or do something accordingly. The being filled is put, by synecdoche, for overflowing.*

---

* See " System of Christian Rhetoric," by G. W. Hervey, for a more extended discussion of the Greek terms rendered *power*, *authority*, *liberty*, and *fulness*, pp. 52, 54, 55, 57-61.

The evidence, therefore, of this fulness or force is not merely in an inward experience, but in words and actions as well. Some evangelists of high distinction teach that the best proofs of the presence of this power are Christian love, peace, and joy, and maintain that unless the preacher has these he ought not to expect that many conversions will attend his ministry. Our narrow limits forbid us to discuss this opinion with thoroughness. In support of it the 13th chapter of 1 Cor. is cited ; but this only favors the fact that unless a preacher has Christian love his ministrations are totally unprofitable to his own soul. The apostle does not say that the prophesying of the man that is devoid of charity is of necessity unprofitable to his hearers ; if he did say so, he would make it difficult for us to understand how he could rejoice that the Gospel is preached even through envy and strife (Phil. 1 : 15 ; Matt. 23 : 13). Much as the Christian graces must ever enhance the preacher's efficiency, we know of nothing that can prevent souls from being converted through his sermons, but his failure to preach the Gospel as it is given to us in the New Testament. Very deplorable it is that any should perish through the neglect of the heralds of salvation to deliver them proper messages ; but in this case our sadness is lessened by the reflection that it is possible for most hearers to search the Scriptures to ascertain for themselves what the true Gospel is. If, however, the salvation of any large numbers were to depend on the Christian graces of their preachers, it would cast another cloud over the origin of evil, and cause us to wonder how it could be consistent with the divine goodness to permit souls to be lost because they could not ascertain (what no mortal can ascertain to a dead certainty) whether their preacher possessed or not the graces of the Spirit, especially the greatest of these, which is charity. To speak the truth in love is of no small importance ; but to speak the truth is absolutely necessary.

Some of the evangelists whose opinions concerning the power of the Holy Spirit we have just examined, have reduced them to consistent practice by holding prayer-meetings for ten days every year, in supposed imitation of the primitive disciples. Does the reader ask, Shall I join these good brethren in their annual quest of fresh supplies of power? We reply, If you are compelled to serve the Lord publicly throughout the year, it is probable that it would be better for you to spend ten days in prayer and fasting at home in your secret chamber. Besides, the Book of Acts affords no proof that the ten days' prayer-meeting was ever repeated, or that the scenes of the Pentecost were ever fully acted again. The history of the Protestant Reformation is silent on the subject ; but it is well to remember that the Romish priests have their " retreats," and that Jesuitism began in a pretended repetition of the Pentecost. The traveller finds among Papists engravings in which Loyola and his companions are represented as receiving on their heads cloven tongues of fire. Let no one say that we deny the necessity of receiving this power. Nor let us be accused of judging any servant of our common Master. The statements we make are based upon historic facts, without whose lessons this manual would lose its peculiar value. Strong is our attachment to the wise and good brethren who readily observe these annual seasons of prayer ; and we are confident that they will not understand us as intending to make any invidious comparisons, but only to warn them of a possible danger.

To resort to these gatherings is the privilege of but comparatively few. Let not any of these permit themselves to fancy that they have received a power that has been denied to those who have been compelled to confine themselves to the use of the common and old-time means of grace. The disciples of Mahomet have this proverb : " Beware of the man that has been to Mecca." We would rather say, " Let such a man beware of himself." Here the apostle Paul once more comes to our aid. We find (2 Cor. 11 and 12) that the exceeding greatness of the revelations he had received was perilous to his humility ; so much so indeed that a thorn or stake in the flesh must needs be given to him, lest he should be exalted overmuch. Hence he took pleasure, not in his visions and revelations, but gloried rather in the weak points of his character—his doubts, fears, and injuries. Why? Because the Lord had said to him, " My power is made perfect in weakness." " Most gladly, therefore," adds he, " will I rather glory in my weaknesses that the strength of Christ may rest upon me, ... for when I am weak, then am I strong." Less profitable was it to him to remember how he was caught up to Paradise than how he made his escape from Damascus by being let down through a window in a basket by the wall.

CHAPTER XXI.

THE TEMPTATIONS TO WHICH EVANGELISTS ARE EXPOSED.

These temptations enumerated—Safeguards and encouragements—Example of Elijah and Jeremiah—The influence of party spirit—False and true revivals—Historic illustrations—Need of discernment and discrimination—The Lord limits and overrules very imperfect means and instruments.

THE history of revivals proves that evangelists are exposed to peculiar temptations. A few of these it may, for the purposes of self-examination, be here in order mentioned :

1. A tendency to consider evangelistic labors and the conversion of souls as the principal work and object of a church. Very naturally, therefore, the evangelist is inclined more and more to neglect those parts of Scripture which remind him and others of the necessity of glorifying Christ in all things, especially in all the requirements of Christian ethics.

2. A tendency to overvalue, in comparison of other parts of Scripture, those parts which have been found to be the most fruitful in immediate practical results.

3. An inclination to judge rashly of those who do not adopt our views and methods of doing good.

4. The danger of becoming proud, vain, and arrogant. Even Whitefield confesses that he was sometimes " puffed up" with success.

5. Exposure to the sins which attend rivalry, such as intrusiveness and a proselyting spirit. Intense sectarianism is the source of many a spurious revival.

6. A liability to a zeal that makes one blind to the difference between right and wrong as well as good and bad motives.

7. A temptation to gain advantages either by consenting to measures which we ought to condemn, or else by usurping authority that belongs to other men.

8. A leaning toward egotism rather than self-oblivion, so that narratives which are told to illustrate a subject, come to be rather illustrations of our own excellences and achievements.

9. Giving way to an ardor that is ever rising into exaggerations. We paint in fresco, and larger than life ; our flock of geese grows rapidly in numbers, and promises to become all swans.

10. A readiness to live on the popular breath, and to find our happiness the excitements of the '' madding crowd.''

11. A bending toward the general tone and drift in a time of great and prevailing revivals ; taking it for granted that what is commonly thought ''the thing'' is wisest and best ; and so perhaps '' taking the vane for the compass.''

12. An undue reliance on our own experience, judgment, skill, or resources, rather than on that Supreme One, who can, as the old Puritan said, save either by means or without means—yes, and contrary to means.

13. A falling into formality and unfeeling routine. As we cannot first preach this class of subjects to ourselves, except by recalling our early experiences, we are without one of the safeguards which they may have who are occupied in ordinary pastoral preaching.

To these and such-like dangers the evangelist is ever exposed ; and, what is worse, it is necessary to convince him that they exist. His enemies are so false and calumnious that he gives no heed to them, even when they speak the truth. His new-found friends, the converts, the reclaimed, and grateful pastors and flocks think it becomes them to use only words of approval and encouragement. Occasional hearers, however impartial, think their acquaintance with him too slight to allow them the liberty of admonition. What is he to do? His safety is in solitude and self-examination. Let him, therefore, seek occasional retirement, like Elijah by the brook Cherith, or Ezekiel at the river Chebar, or our Lord Himself among the crags and trees of the distant mountain.

In this retirement he should rather foster a spirit of gratitude and thanksgiving, than indulge in vain regrets, brood over disappointments, and murmur at the allotments of his Divine Master. Many an evangelist in his retreat is brought into sympathy with Elijah in his despair as he sat down under the juniper tree, as he journeyed forty days through the desert, and as he lodged in the cave on Mount Horeb; or with Jonah, when, at the end of the great revival in Nineveh, he went and sat down on the east side of the city, repining at that divine mercy which seemed to impeach his own sincerity. In such trials of faith we shall find instruction in the example of Jeremiah, who, in the 119th Psalm,* seeks remedies for all the troubles of his soul and the hardships of his service in prayer to God and in the study of His oracles.

Nor should we overlook, at such seasons, the subtle

---

* This psalm affords much internal evidence of having been written by Jeremiah. We have not space here to discuss this subject with adequate fulness. It is, however, but right that the young student should know that this is still an open question among biblical scholars, most of whom seem to have failed to examine it.

influence of party spirit. It will be well for us if we detect no traces of it in ourselves, or in some of those whom we may have gathered into churches. The church or pastor that has been calumniated or treated with glaring injustice is ever in peril from such a public reaction as will draw too many over to the persecuted cause. It is much to be deplored that party spirit alone may suffice to drive young persons not a few to offer themselves for admission to the church whose cause they have espoused. Not knowing what spirit they are of, they imagine that their new zeal in behalf of justice and fair-dealing is of divine origin. If evangelists do not guard against party spirit, they will only help to fill some churches with mere disputers and anarchists.

There are false revivals as well as true ; and it is astonishing, if not frightful, to trace the close resemblances of the two. Thus, years of national adversity have often been friendly to the work of evangelistic conversion ; but, unhappily, such years have too often been marked by corresponding triumphs of fanaticism and superstition. The far-spreading panic of 1857 in the United States drove many thousands to prayer, and so to the Prince of Peace ; but events proved that, in cases not a few, there was no waking to righteousness, no change of heart, no reformation of life ; while throngs of ignorant but ardent souls were swept by the general excitement into religious error and delusion. The desolation and misery caused by the French Revolution and the wars of the first Napoleon prepared the way for revivals in Switzerland, France, and Spain. The result was that multitudes went back to the idolatries and lies of the dark ages, although a considerable number were really converted, through the preaching of Felix Neff and other Protestant evangelists. To go still farther back, the incalculable loss of life which the wars of Charles V. and Philip II. brought upon Spain drove the mourning survivors to the consolations of religion, and yet in their blind desperation they sought comfort in the false teachings of the Jesuits and the wild raptures and visionary pleasures of Santa Theresa.

In addition to this, it is to be remembered that false men may be used as instruments in a true revival. They may preach with saving effect so long as they preach the veritable Gospel of our salvation. The apostle Paul avowed that in his day some preached the Gospel from bad motives, but he rejoiced that, from whatever motive, the Gospel was still preached.

It must be conceded, moreover, that teachers of false doctrine have been successful in helping to bring about true revivals. How? In this way: they have during the progress of the popular movement held in abeyance their heresies, and urged such motives only as were drawn from true doctrine, or else, confining themselves to those topics of persuasion which do not involve any article of faith, they have reserved for the close of the revival, and the more quiet instruction of the young converts, the inculcation of their unscriqtural opinions.

For the rest, it must likewise be admitted that the most unreasonable and disorderly measures have not always availed to prevent a true awakening. At the call of the Son of God, Lazarus has come forth in spite of every obstacle and impediment.

One of the great fallacies of to-day is to conclude

that because the effect is good, therefore the men and their teachings and their measures are good. We forget that God often causes much good to be done through bad instruments, which He only permits and overrules.

CHAPTER XXII.

THE RELATIONS OF THE PASTOR AND THE EVANGELIST.

The primitive evangelist—The independence of the evangelist—The shepherd's dog—Necessity of fraternal co-operation—Former prejudices disappearing—The ox and the ass—Sowing and reaping—Some know their master, others only his crib—Pastors who have been blessed with great revivals—The shepherd and the Alpine guide.

THE primitive work of the evangelist was that of a travelling missionary, but acting independently of any human authority. Thus the evangelist Philip left Jerusalem and went and preached in Samaria, not because he was commanded by the apostles to do so, but because he was forced out of Jerusalem by persecution ; and when he departed from Samaria and made for the track of the caravans that moved between Jerusalem and Gaza, it was at the bidding, not of an apostle, but of " the angel of the Lord." Likewise, after he had baptized the eunuch he was caught away by the Spirit of the Lord and led to Azotus.

In the list of the officers of the primitive church evangelists are placed in the midst, after " apostles and prophets," and before " pastors and teachers," not, as we suppose, to indicate official rank, but merely order of service ; for one man might hold two or more offices : Philip was deacon as well as evangelist, and Timothy was to do the work of an evangelist, although he was a pastor. But this is not the place to discuss questions which have so often engaged the at-

tention of learned professors. Taking it for granted
that the evangelist of to-day is essentially the evangelist of the first Christian age, we proceed to offer a
few suggestions about his co-operation with pastors.
Some evangelists take no small pains to declare that
they serve in subordination to the pastor as his helper.
Most certainly ought the evangelist to afford assistance
to the pastor, and to act in the light of his peculiar
knowledge and of the wisdom which he has derived
from his own observation and experience. But in respect of his own work, the evangelist cannot safely be
in subjection to any man or body of men. In his own
sphere he must lead, as all candid men will confess.
There are, indeed, Christian workers who are chiefly
useful in exhortation and prayer, and in visiting from
house to house. They sometimes go so far as to
expound the Scriptures, but do not attempt to preach.
Men of this class are in great request among certain
churches, for the reason that they never provoke the
envy or the jealousy of pastors, and seldom wound the
hearts and consciences of their people. One excellent
laborer of this description used to style himself " the
shepherd's dog." And untiringly did he hunt after
the stray sheep over mountains and through valleys.
But such men are not of that class of evangelists which
is now under consideration—men of persuasive gifts—
men " of light and leading" in times of religious excitement—men whose tact and prudence, foresight and in-
sight are never at their best except in seasons of
refreshing from the presence of the Lord. For such
men to surrender their judgment to the pastor in
matters which belong to their own province were to
imperil the most precious interests and to do incalculable damage.

Here the question to be determined is not one of precedence. We commence with the opinion that the evangelist and the pastor are to work together on the footing of fraternal equality. They are to believe in each other ; they are to bear with each other ; they are to be frank to each other ; they will be so cordially intent on helping each other, that they will be very slow to detect any interference, and slower still to desire any. In most cases the danger lies in another direction. The pastor reposes such confidence in the evangelist as to commit to the latter almost all the work. Pastoral visitation, which ought now to be more active than usual, is perhaps totally neglected ; and private interviews with members of his congregation concerning their spiritual welfare are less sought than ever. Indeed, the labors of the evangelist are regarded as a substitute for his own. He considers himself released from customary cares. He is, perhaps, in readiness for an occasional prayer or hymn or exhortation, but from any other service he is apt to excuse himself. We are glad to believe, however, that pastors of this character are few, and that some of these are weary and sick from excessive toil or affliction.

It is a good omen that pastors and evangelists are understanding each other better, and are speaking more charitably of each other than they did in former days. The acrimonious chapters in the history of revivals are not likely to be repeated. Henceforth the sowers and the reapers may be expected to rejoice together. Even Wesley in his Journal deprecates the then too common practice of publicly censuring the Anglican clergy, and declares that he never saw any benefit come of it. And yet the preacher of the Gospel is sustained by the example of his Divine

Master in openly lamenting the conduct of the Pharisees of to-day. On the other hand, evangelists have been calumniated in pretty exact proportion to their activity and usefulness. But there is no good reason why the pastor and the evangelist should be at variance. Difference of work does not necessitate difference of feelings and objects. "Blessed are ye that sow beside all waters, that send forth thither the feet of the ox and the ass" (Isa. 32 : 20). If by the ox is here meant the permanent worker, and by the ass the occasional worker, still both are recognized laborers in planting the religion of Christ. Nor let it be forgotten that when the Messiah made His triumphal entry into Jerusalem it was upon the occasional beast of burden that He rode, and it was under its hoofs that the garments and palm-branches of the jubilant throngs were reverently spread.

It is a promising sign that professors of homiletics are beginning to cease their opposition to revivals and revivalists. Formerly the graduates of our seminaries were kept so ignorant of the subject that when their flocks were blessed with a refreshing from the presence of the Lord, they were, not a few of them, either frightened into the adoption of the most unwise measures or maddened into the most unreasonable antagonism to the work of the Spirit. Now and then the old prejudice finds voice again. Thus, in a recent lecture on preaching, the following language was used : "Evangelists complain that too many sermons are preached that fail to convert. It requires a keen eye, a steady hand, and good judgment to sow seed, but any Irishman can reap the harvest." Here the vocation of the evangelist is unjustly narrowed ; for it should be considered that he often goes before the pastor, clearing the ground of thorns, thistles, and weeds, and then breaking up the fallow ground before the sower can begin to exhibit his sagacity and dexterity. Revival preaching is reacting most favorably on pastoral sermons. Say what you will against it, none can deny that it has contributed much to deepen our belief in the Holy Ghost, and in that homiletical liberty and variety which none but the Holy Ghost can inspire.

Some pastors who are receiving regular incomes from year to year are in the habit of grumbling over the occasional liberality of the church to an evangelist who has labored for it a few weeks. The number of mercenary pastors is small, but in some cases we are tempted to transpose Isa. 1 : 3, and say, '' The ass knoweth his owner, and the ox his master's crib.''

The best gifts for pastoral service are seldom found united with the best gifts for revival work. A good ploughman may not be a good sower, and a good reaper may not be a good thresher. But still, many efficient pastors have proved very successful revivalists. Payson and Griffin, Buell and Colman, Berridge and Simeon, the Erskines and the Tennents, Edwards and Baxter, Bunyan and Fish, Swan and Spurgeon, Romaine, Tyng, and not a few other pastors of distinction, have been blessed with extensive if not repeated revivals among their own people. True it is, however, that many of these earnest pastors were wise enough to appreciate and obtain the assistance of evangelists who were not pastors. Far were they from saying : '' Let neighboring pastors help one another, and it will suffice ; as for evangelists, let them go into regions where there are no churches, and confine their labors to the poor and the ignorant.'' In general, those pastors have not been often or greatly favored with revivals who make it their boast that they have never sought the aid of evangelists.   The shepherd that loves his flock more than he does his own comfort will hearken to the Alpine guide who can lead his sheep to higher and better pastures, although the paths to them may be over ice and snow, while the precipice yawns below and the avalanche threatens above.

INSTRUCTIVE BOOKS ON REVIVALS.

Rev. George Whitefield's Life, Journals, and Sermons (in several forms).

Rev. John Wesley's Life, Journals, and Sermons (in many forms).

President Edwards's Narrative of the Work of God in North ampton, Mass. ; and Thoughts on the Revival of Religion.

The Rev. Dr. Samuel Buell's Narrative of the Revival at East Hampton, L. I.

Dr. Gillies's Historical Collections.

The Rev. Joseph Tracy's Great Awakening.

Revivals of the Eighteenth Century, at Cambuslang and Elsewhere in Scotland, by the Rev. Dr. Macfarlan.

Lectures on Revivals by Ministers of Scotland.

Revivals of Religion in Scotland, Ireland, Wales, and America. (Presbyterian Board of Publication, Philadelphia.)

Duncan's History of Revivals in the British Isles.

Bradley's History of Revivals.

New England Revivals, by the Rev. Dr. Bennett Tyler.

American Revivals, by Rev. Calvin Colton (London, 1832).

Asahel Nettleton's Memoirs and Remains.

Autobiography of Lyman Beecher.

Lorenzo Dow's Life and Journals.

John Leland's Life and Writings.

Christmas Evans's Memoirs and Sermons.

Andrew Fuller's Life and Sermons.

The Rev. William Dawson's Memoirs.

Rev. Peter Cartwright's Memoirs.

Rev. Wm. Taylor's Ten Years' Street Preaching in San Francisco.

Rev. Jas. Canughey's Revival Miscellanies and other works.

Life and Times of the Rev. Thomas S. Sheardown.

The Rev. Emerson Andrews's Life and Sermons.

Rev. Chas. J. Finney's Life, Lectures on Revivals, etc.

Elder Jacob Knapp's Autobiography.

Elder Jabez S. Swan's Autobiography.

Rev. Dr. E. Kirk's Lectures on Revivals and Memoir.

Rev. Dr. H. Humphrey's Revival Sketches and Manual ; also his Letters to his Son in the Ministry.

Rev. Dr. I. Spencer's Pastor's Sketches (2 vols.).

Rev. Dr. Wm. B. Sprague's Lectures on Revivals.

Rev. Albert Barnes's Six Sermons on Revivals (in *National Preacher*, vol. xv.).

Revivals of Religion, by the Rev. Dr. Jas. Porter.

Helps to the Promotion of Revivals, by the Rev. Dr. Jas. B. Watson.

Rev. J. B. Earle's Bringing in Sheaves, and other works.

Rev. Orson Parker's Fire and Hammer; or, Revivals and How to promote them.

Rev. E. P. Hammond's Conversion of Children, and other books.

Mr. Dwight L. Moody's Life, Sermons, and Readings (in many forms).

Rev. George F. Pentecost's Life, Labors, and Bible Studies.

Recollections of Mary Lyon, by Fidelia Fisk.

Harvest and Reaper, by Mrs. Maggie N. Van Cott.

Harvest Work of the Spirit, by the Rev. P. C. Headley.

Harvest and Reapers, by the Rev Dr. H. Newcomb.

Authentic Records of Revival, by Rev. Wm. Reid; Revival in Scotland in 1859.

Year of Grace, by the Rev. Dr. Gibson; Revival in Ireland in 1859.

Boston Revival of 1842, by Martin Moore.

The Revival and its Lessons, by the Rev. Dr. Jas. W. Alexander.

Power of Prayer, by the Rev. Dr. S. I. Prime.

Narrative of Conversions and Revival Incidents, by Wm. C. Conant.

The Rev. A. P. Graves's Life and Sermons.

Hand-Book of Revivals, by the Rev. Dr. H. C. Fish.

The Great Revival in the Southern Army, by the Rev. Dr. Bennett.

The People's Pulpit: Three Series of Sermons by Rev. Dr. Tyng, Jr.

Under Canvas: a Volume of Sermons Preached in a Tent by Rev. Dr. S. H. Tyng, Jr., and others.

The Revival System and the *Paraclete:* a volume made up from articles in the *Church Journal*, in 1858.

Proceedings of the Evangelical Alliance in N. Y., Oct., 1873: a Paper read by the Rev. W. W. Patton, p. 351–356.

Before and After the Revival, by Rev. J. H. Vincent, D.D.

This last little volume should be read in connection with articles by Dr. Vincent and others, in the *Christian Advocate*, N. Y., for Feb. 16th and March 2d and 16th, 1882; also the Autobiography of William Harrison, the "Boy Evangelist."

Revivals: their Place and their Power, by Rev. Herrick Johnson, D.D., pp. 35. (Chicago, 1882.)

Revivals: How and When? by Rev. Dr. W. W. Newell. New York, 1882.

PART II.

THEMES AND TEXTS USED BY
LEADING REVIVALISTS.

FOREWORDS.

OUR first object in making this collection is to suggest to young preachers well-timed texts and themes for revival services. But we have another object, which to many studious preachers will appear not less important : the study of the character of the texts which celebrated revivalists were led to select, the relation of these to the great movements with which these men of God were identified, and of the comparative excellence of the series of texts as employed by different evangelists. To all such as would study the real history of preaching (not the same thing as the biography of preachers, as some writers seem to imagine it is), this collection will impart lessons of considerable value.

Veteran preachers, who have distinguished themselves as sermonizers as well as original thinkers, concur in the opinion that texts, titles, partitions, skeletons, and brief reports of sermons are more suggestive of new lines of thought than are sermons which have been fully composed or printed without condensation.

In this regard the experience of the famous Robert Hall was not unique. While on a short visit to his friend Mr. Greene, he read a volume of the sketches of Beddome's sermons. Though little more than skeletons, he liked them all the better for their compactness ; they supplied him materials for thinking. The result was that the dry and unpopular book suggested to him the subject of one of his most original and useful sermons, preached first at Leicester and afterward at Bristol.*

How far one preacher may borrow from another is still an open question, and promises to remain open for some time to come. One fact is as amusing as it is instructive : those preachers of to-day who have the greatest reputation for independence and originality of mind borrow extensively from British, German, and French rationalists, deists, atheists, and agnostics. These men are much indebted for their reputation to a trick they have of flippantly contradicting or ignoring all scriptural ideas. The effect of this kind of borrowing is very enfeebling to the intellects of the borrowers.

Read President Eliot's article on the Education of Ministers, in the *Princeton Review* for May, 1883. It is valuable as descriptive of the intellectual debility of the Unitarian clergymen of his own circle ; if read as descriptive of the clergy of the United States, as a body, it would amazingly mislead and deceive. Among Dr. Eliot's hallucinations, by the way, one is so dangerous that we must give it a passing mention. It is this : that students of theology do not pursue the same inductive method as modern men of science do, and that therefore the former have lost the confidence of the people ; whereas, the latter are "as candid as a still lake," and "characterized by absolute freedom from the influence of prepossessions or desires as to results. If Dr. Eliot will read for once the history of the achievements of natural science during the past sixty years he will not fail to find a great

* Hall's Works, vol. iv. 54–57, 116.

number of untrustworthy scientists who have been " searching for proofs of foregone conclusions." He will likewise discover that the men of science who have made the greatest discoveries in the same period have carried the philosophy of Lord Bacon with them in their theological as well as their scientific researches, and, like the self-same orthodox Lord Bacon, they have found their " standard of intellectual sincerity" not in the methods of induction, but in the oracles of God. Assuredly, old John Bunyan wrote true prophecy when he said that " Mr. Wrong-thoughts-of-Christ died of a lingering consumption."

But to return to the subject of borrowing. It is not without advantage that we have traced the fact that almost all the Hebrew prophets have repeated (generally with modifications) one or two of the ideas of one or more of his predecessors. This little volume cannot afford room for any adequate illustration of this unquestionable fact. Let one example suffice. David sang : " He maketh my feet like hinds' feet ; and setteth me upon my high places" (2 Sam. 22 : 34). Habakkuk (3 : 19) gives the beautiful simile the form of a prediction, and causes the hind to *walk* on his high places.

We may add that in arranging the list of evangelists we have reversed the alphabetical order, and in designating authors we have, where necessary, given their pseudonyms, and marked as anonymous such examples as we found nameless.

We have arranged this part of the volume in such wise as to make it, in our judgment, the most suggestive. At the expense of a few repetitions, we have thought it, on many accounts, desirable to reproduce each evangelist's texts and themes apart from

those of others.   Even these repetitions are instructive.

In our index of subjects we have made separate references to themes proper to be used before, during,
and after revivals, as well as themes suitable for church
members.

This part of the volume owes much of its value to
the contributions of living evangelists.   Space would
fail us to declare all our obligations ; but special
acknowledgments are due to Messrs. N. Tibbals &
Sons, formerly of 37 Park Row, now of 124 Nassau
Street, New York, who for years generously gave the
writer free access to the vast collection of Christian
literature consumed in the fire that destroyed the
World Building.   Many of those scarce books these
enterprising men will never be able to replace.   May
they soon possess again a stock as extensive, as various, and as rare.

WESLEY'S FIELD PREACHING.

THE reader of the Rev. John Wesley's sermons, as they are published by authority, is liable to form a very inadequate notion of him as a revival preacher. Of these one hundred and forty sermons, not more than forty are noticed in his journals as preached by him during his best years of vast ingathering. Some of his most successful sermons, and oft-repeated, have never been published; indeed, it may well be doubted whether he ever wrote more than their texts and their heads. The present list of his texts is gleaned from his voluminous journals, which have been carefully searched with express reference to this collection. Very few of the one hundred and sixty-six texts here reproduced are to be found at the beginnings of his published sermons, and yet they suggested the themes of almost all the revival sermons which he repeated more or less frequently for fifty years in the circuits he made through England, Ireland, Scotland, and Wales.

In his earlier and more victorious years Wesley preached without much premeditation. Often he selected his texts from the lessons for the day, and once in a while, opening his Bible *ad libitum*, he accepted as final the decision of the Bible lot. Sometimes, however, he would insensibly wander from the text he had chosen, and make another text the foundation of matter more suitable for the audience with which, in a few minutes, he would grow better acquainted. As intellectual productions his later extemporaneous sermons were frequently regarded by his friends as failures; but whoever will consult his journals must be convinced that the Spirit gave them wonderful acceptance and success. Scarcely less wonderful is the skill he evinces in adapting his texts to the intellectual, moral, and spiritual condition of his mixed and ever-changing audiences. He always aimed at immediate fruit, and he sent his missiles in such directions as to bring down to the ground the largest possible quantity all at once. In vain do we regret that we can find out so little about his revival sermons, except from their texts and their overwhelming power. Thus much is certain : his divisions were strictly practical and experimental. One example we give, as it is almost the only one in all his journals. The text is, '' Cast not away your confidence,'' etc. '' Ye who have known and felt your sins forgiven, cast not away your confidence. 1. Though your joy should die away, your love wax cold, and your peace itself be roughly assaulted. Though, 2. You should find doubt or fear, or strong and uninterrupted temptation. Yea, though, 3. You should find a body of sin still in you, and thrusting sore at you that you might fall.'' Could anything be more encouraging to a certain class of young converts ?

Whenever Wesley wrote a sermon he usually completed the task in three days, if he could secure uninterrupted leisure. '' The Great Assize'' he composed in that time. This, with his '' Circumcision of the Heart,'' '' The Use of Money,'' and the '' Good Steward,'' he considered among his very best. The revival sermon which he pronounced his '' favorite'' had for its text : '' Who of God is made unto wisdom,'' etc. It was never published, and probably it was never written in full.

Mr. Wesley's out-door sermons were short, seldom more than half an hour long. His delivery was calm and unimpassioned ; his voice was not loud, but clear and distinct. Very rarely did he depict for the imagination, and he cordially disliked '' prose run mad.'' He much admired the style of St. John, as being at once simple and profound. He always gave a practical turn to his text, and was content '' to open and apply.''

Whoever would know Wesley as a revival preacher should read his journals from beginning to end. He will not find them, in the least, dry and wearisome, but full of the sunbeams and shadows of old English life, with occasional glimpses at wonderland, and not a few foregleams of heaven.

We have not given many outlines or sketches of Wesley's revival addresses, because few are to be found. The subjects and texts of eighteen sermons in this collection were fully developed by him, and may be read in the volumes of his published sermons. The examination of these affords but little knowledge of his general method of handling revival themes. There is ground for the conviction that his field sermons, as he preached them, were more simple in arrangement, more popular in thought, and more familiar in style.

OUTLINES OF SERMONS.

ON THE HOLY SPIRIT.

Now the Lord is that Sp'rit. 2 Cor. 3 : 17.

1. The nature of our fall in Adam : if the Lord were not "that Spirit" he could not be said to redeem us from our fallen condition.

2. Consider the person of Jesus Christ, by which it will appear that "the Lord is that Spirit."

3. The nature and operations of the Holy Spirit as bestowed upon Christians.

ON PUBLIC DIVERSIONS IN A TIME OF CALAMITY.

Shall the trumpet be blown in the city and the people not be afraid ? Shall there be evil in the city and the Lord hath not done it ? Amos 3 : 6.

1. There is no evil in any place but the hand of the Lord is in it.

2. Every uncommon evil is the trumpet of God blown in that place, so that the people may take warning.

3. Consider, whether, after God has blown his trumpet in this place, we have been duly afraid.

SALVATION BY FAITH.

By grace are ye saved, through faith. Eph. 2 : 8.

1. What faith is it through which we are saved ?

2. What is the salvation which is through faith ?

3. Answer some objections.

THE ALMOST CHRISTIAN.

Almost thou persuadest me to be a Christian. Acts 26 : 28.

1. What is implied in being almost a Christian ?

2. What in being altogether a Christian ?

SCRIPTURAL CHRISTIANITY.

And they were all filled with the Holy Ghost. Acts 4 : 31.

Christianity may be considered under three distinct views.

1. As beginning to exist in individuals.
2. As spreading from one to another.
3. As covering the earth.

THE WAY TO THE KINGDOM.

The Kingdom of God is at hand ; repent ye and believe the Gospel. Mark 1 : 15.

1. The nature of true religion or " Kingdom of God."
2. The way thereto : " repent and believe."

THE GOOD STEWARD.

Give an account of thy stewardship, etc. Luke 16 : 2

1. In what respects we are now God's stewards.
2. When he requires our souls of us we can no longer be stewards.
3. It will then only remain to give an account of our stewardship.

THE GREAT ASSIZE.

We shall all stand before the judgment seat of Christ. Rom. 14 : 10.

1. The circumstances which will precede our standing before the judgment-seat of Christ.
2 The judgment itself ; and,
3. A few of the circumstances which will follow it.

THE NATURE OF ENTHUSIASM.

And Festus said with a loud voice, Paul, thou art beside thyself. Acts 26 : 24.

1. Show what enthusiasm is.
2. Describe its various kinds.
3. Draw some practical inferences.

THEMES AND TEXTS.

The Nature of Bigotry and Cautions against it. (Master, we saw one casting out devils in thy name, and he followed not us. . . .) Mark 9 : 38.

The Nature and Necessity of the New Birth. (Marvel not that I said unto thee. . . .) John 3 : 7.

Free Grace and Predestination. (He that spared not his own son . . .) Rom. 8 : 32.

Backsliders encouraged to return to Christ. Ps. 77 : 7–8.

The Nature and Properties of true Zeal. (But it is good to be zealously affected. . . .) Gal. 4 : 18.

The Rich Man and Lazarus. Luke 16 : 31.

The Parable of the Rich Fool explained and applied. Luke 12 : 20.

The Cause and Cure of Earthquakes. Ps. 46 : 8.

Human Life a Dream from which we must awake. Ps. 73 : 20.

Unbelief in refusing the conditions of Salvation. (If I say the truth, why do ye not believe me?) John 8 : 46.

The World overcome by all who are born of God. 1 John 5 : 4.

The Confessor or Martyr nothing without Love. 1 Cor. 13 : 3.

All followers of Christ required to take up their Cross Matt. 16 : 24.

On Hell. Where the worm dieth not. Mark 9 . 48.

All things are ready ; come unto the marriage Matt. 22 : 4.

The Grace of the Lord Jesus Christ and the love of God and the communion of the Holy Ghost.... 2 Cor. 13 : 14.

God hath reconciled us unto himself. 2 Cor. 5 : 18.

The World gained, but the Soul lost. (For what is a man profited if he shall gain the whole world....) Matt. 16 : 26.

A High Priest touched with the feeling of our infirmities. Heb. 4 : 15.

Jesus the Resurrection and the Life. John 11 : 25.

Is there no balm in Gilead? Jer. 8 : 22.

Thou art not far from the Kingdom of God. Mark 12 : 34.

Seek ye the Lord while ye may be found. Isa. 55 : 6.

Blessed are the eyes which see the things which ye see, etc. Luke 10 : 23–24.

Lord, are there few that be saved. Luke 13 : 23.

The foolish took no oil with them. Matt. 25 : 3.

The righteousness of the Scribes and Pharisees. (Except your righteousness shall exceed ...) Matt. 5 : 20.

He hath not dealt so with any nation. Ps. 147 : 20.

It is a fearful thing to fall into the hands of the living God. Heb. 10 : 31.

Harden not your hearts. Heb. 3 : 8.

Justification not by the deeds of the Law, but by Faith. Gal. 3 : 10-11.

The glorified Saints are like the Angels of God. Matt. 22 : 30.

The Harvest past and the Summer ended. Jer. 8 : 20.

The Knowledge of God and of Jesus Christ. (This is life eternal to know thee....) John 17 : 3.

The Word of Faith is in thy Heart, etc. Rom. 10 : 6-8.

The Kingdom of Heaven like a grain of Mustard Seed. Matt. 13 : 31.

Where their worm dieth not, and the fire is not quenched. Mark 9 : 44.

Now is the day of Salvation.　2 Cor. 6 : 2.

One thing is needful.　Luke 10 : 42.

The Good Shepherd giveth his life for the Sheep.　John 10 : 11.

All men commanded to repent.　Acts 17 : 30.

*O that thou hadst known the things that belong to thy peace.　Luke 19 : 42.

Not every one that saith unto me, Lord, Lord, etc.　Matt. 7 : 21.

Will the Lord be favourable no more?　Ps. 77 : 7.

The whole duty of man.　(Fear God and keep his commandments....)　Eccles. 12 : 13.

Behold, I stand at the door and knock.　Rev. 3 : 20.

He is able to save to the uttermost.　Heb. 7 : 25.

Acquaint now thyself with him and be at peace.　Job 22 : 21.

The time is come that judgment must begin at the house of God.　1 Pet. 4 : 17.

"As thou hast believed, so be it done unto thee."　Matt. 8 : 13.

The Kingdom of God is at hand.　Matt. 3 : 2.

How long halt ye between two opinions?　1 Kings 18 : 21.

God, the King, working salvation in the midst of the earth.　Ps. 74 : 12.

[W. used the Psalter's translation of this text ; see Jour., Oct. 11, 1785, and Apr. 22, 1787.]

Lazarus, come forth.　John 11 : 43.

The Lord's throne, glory, and voice.　Ps. 29 : 9–10.

The children are come to the birth, etc.　2 Kings 19 : 3.

Rejoice in the Lord, O ye righteous.　Ps. 33 : 1.

I saw a great white throne and him that sat on it, etc.　Rev. 20 : 11.

Be vigilant, lest we lose a full reward of our labours among you.　2 John 8.

God hath given unto us his Holy Spirit.　1 Thes. 4 : 8.

I will ; be thou clean.　Matt. 8 : 3.

Master, master, we perish, etc.　Luke 8 : 24.

Seek ye first the Kingdom of God, etc.　Matt. 6 : 33.

Receive not the grace of God in vain.　2 Cor. 6 : 1.

Strait is the gate and narrow is the way, etc.　Matt. 7 : 14.

The Vision of Dry Bones.　Ezek. 37 : 1–10.

The Christian believer a fountain full of grace.　(In the last great day of the feast....)　John 7 : 38.

The Promise of healing and love to backsliders.　Hos. 14 : 4.

The Invitation to the Hungry and Thirsty.　Isa. 55 : 1.

Debts forgiven to the destitute.　Luke 7 : 42.

Christ made to us wisdom, etc. [W.'s favourite text.]　1 Cor. 1 : 30.

The blood that cleanses from all sin. 1 John 1 : 7.

The Spiritual Resurrection. (The dead shall hear the voice of God....)· John 5 : 25.

Salvation offered to all men. 1 Tim. 2 : 4.

Christ gave himself a ransom for all. 1 Tim. 2 : 6.

The Prince exalted to give repentance and remission. Acts 5 : 31.

A childlike spirit a preparation for the new Kingdom. Matt. 18 : 3.

The Promise by faith of Jesus Christ given. Gal. 3 : 22.

Not the Righteous but sinners called. Matt. 9 : 13.

Light promised to those who rise from the dead. Eph. 5 : 14.

The Son of Man came not to destroy but to save. Luke 9 : 55-56.

All guilty and silenced. Rom. 3 : 19.

The Scripture concludes all under sin. Gal. 3 : 22.

Sirs, what must I do to be saved? Acts 16 : 30.

All the ends of the earth invited to look and be saved. Isa. 45 : 22.

The word of God compared to rain and snow. Isa. 55 : 10.

Fear of the Pharisees keeps the chief rulers silent. John 12 : 42.

In heaven the wicked cease from troubling. Job 3 17.

Holiness progressive. [To Young Converts] Mark 4 : 25-28.

Christ justifies the ungodly. Rom. 4 : 5.

[The Nature, Cause, and Instrument of justification.]

Looking unto the Author and Finisher of our Faith. Heb. 12 : 2.

As ye have received, so walk. [To Young Converts.] Col. 2 : 6.

The Kingdom of God is not meat and drink, etc. [Often used by W.] Rom. 14 : 17.

Young converts cheered by Christ's victory. (Be of good cheer: I have overcome the world....) John 16 : 33.

In me dwelleth no good thing. Rom. 7 : 18.

The bruised reed and the smoking wick. Isa. 42 : 3.

The atoning blood and the sanctifying water. John 19 : 34.

O ye dry bones, hear the word of the Lord. Ezek. 37 : 4

Stand ye in the ways, and ask for the old paths. Jer. 6 : 16.

Cast not away your confidence, etc. [To Young Converts.] Heb. 10 : 35.

Let him that thinketh he standeth, etc. [To the same.] 1 Cor. 10 : 12.

How shall I give thee up, etc. [To Backsliders.] Hos. 11 : 8.

The Spiritual resurrection. Acts 26 : 8.

O that I had wings like a dove, etc. Ps. 55 : 6.

The believer saved, the unbeliever damned. Mark. 16 : 16.

Stand still and see the salvation of the Lord. Exod. 14 : 13.

All we like sheep have gone astray, etc. Isa. 53 : 6.

Forgiveness and love proportionate. Luke 7 : 47.

Where the Spirit of the Lord is there is liberty. 2 Cor. 3 : 17.

Liberty to enter into the holiest by the blood of Jesus. Heb. 10 : 19.

Perseverance in Prayer illustrated. Luke : 18 : 1.

What is eternal Life? John 17 : 3.

Who art thou, O great mountain? etc. Zech 4 : 7.

Looking unto Jesus. Heb. 12 : 2.

Whom ye ignorantly worship, him declare, etc. Acts 17 : 23.

God is light, and in Him is no darkness at all. 1 John 1 : 5.

The sun and moon standing still. Josh. 10 : 12.

Trust in the God of everlasting strength. Isa. 26 : 4.

He shall save His people from their sins. Matt. 1 : 21.

Perseverance a proof of discipleship. (I will follow thee whithersoever thou goest....let the dead bury their dead.) Matt. 8 : 19-22.

The Son of Man hath power on earth to forgive sins. Matt. 9 : 6.

The righteousness of faith. Rom. 4 : 13.

Why will ye die, O house of Israel? Ezek. 18 : 31.

Abounding in Knowledge and Feeling. (That your love may abound more and more....) Phil. 1 : 9. [See Journal, Sept. 3d, 1742.]

The Lord merciful, gracious, long-suffering, etc. Exod. 34 : 6.

He hath anointed me to preach the Gospel to the poor. Luke 4 : 18.

Say unto Zion, Behold, thy salvation cometh ! etc. Isa. 62 : 11.

None is like the God of Jeshurun, etc. Deut. 33 : 26.

By the blood of thy covenant I have sent forth thy prisoners. Zech. 9 : 11.

Repent ye, and believe the Gospel. Mark 1 : 15.

Who can tell if God will turn and repent? etc. Jonah 3 : 9.

Fear not ye ; for I know that ye seek Jesus, etc. Matt. 28 : 5.

Jacob wrestling with the Angel. Gen. 32 : 24-30.

He healeth the broken in heart. Ps. 147 : 3.

The rescued remnant refusing to repent. (I have overthrown some of you....yet ye have not returned unto me....) Amos 4 : 11.

How shall we escape if we neglect, etc. Heb. 2 : 3.

What doest thou here, Elijah? 1 Kings 19 : 9.

O thou of little faith, wherefore didst thou doubt? Matt. 14 : 31.

The hearer at once and doer builds his house upon a rock. Matt. 7 : 24.

Why tarriest thou? Arise, and be baptized, etc. Acts 22 : 16.

What lack I yet? Matt. 19 : 20.

Him hath God raised up, whereof we are witnesses. Acts 2 · 31.

The Son of God manifested to destroy the works of the devil. I John 3 : 8.

God hath chosen the foolish things of the world, etc. 1 Cor. 1 : 27.

And Gallio cared for none of those things. Acts 18 : 17.

Neither can they die any more, being the children of the resurrection, etc. Luke 20 : 36.

Render into Cæsar the things that are Cæsar's, etc. Matt. 22 : 21.

Dead unto sin, but alive unto God, etc. Rom. 6 : 11.

And some fell among thorns. Matt. 13 : 7.

The one hundred and forty-four thousand, etc. Rev. 14 : 1.

We preach Christ crucified, etc. 1 Cor. 1 : 23.

I will not destroy the city for ten's sake. Gen. 18 : 32.

I saw the dead, small and great, stand before God. Rev. 20 : 12.

The Spirit and the Bride say, Come. Rev. 22 : 17.

Come, Lord Jesus. Rev. 22 : 20.

WHITEFIELD'S SERMONS.

THE revival sermons of the Rev. George Whitefield, unlike those of Wesley, have, many of them, come down to us literally reported by short-hand writers. Even the long and earnest exhortations with which they concluded are, for the most part, carefully reproduced. Consequently we can, even at this late day, obtain a very tolerable idea of the matter and style of his field-preaching. But there is, we are sorry to say, no complete collection of these sermons ; and there never has been, either in England or America. The American octavo edition of his works is sadly defective, being without that famous sermon on the text, "What think ye of Christ?"—the sermon that did so much to form the faith of the Rev. James Hervey. Resolved to make out a full if not complete list of his revival texts, we have for years taken every opportunity to find out notices of the themes of his ministrations, or any separate and forgotten sermon of his, bound up, mayhap, among old pamphlets or the discourses or tracts of other authors. Whitefield's habit of preparing for the pulpit was to write a skeleton, and trust more or less in the inspiration of the Spirit and the suggestions of the hour for suitable and telling amplifications. Each repetition of the sermon demanded new adaptations ; for, like Wesley, he exercised admirable skill in the selection of his materials, and in the fitting and forcible application of his subject. The sermons which he fully wrote were chiefly composed while he was at sea, and were published by his good friend Benjamin Franklin, of Philadelphia. They want the vivacity, the ease, the brilliance of his extemporaneous addresses. Neither Whitefield nor Wesley did himself justice when he attempted to write out a volume of sermons for the press.

Occasionally Whitefield, like Wesley, wandered away from his text in trying to arrest the attention and convert the souls of his auditors. As he was once preaching, all of a sudden his heart led him into a digression, in which he talked at some length, against depending on our natural reason. His friends were astonished, and so was he, that he should have so far turned aside from his theme. Afterward, however, he found out that a group of rationalists were in the congregation, and that his digression was graciously made for their benefit.

Highly as Whitefield valued the guidance of the Spirit, he did not hold cheap the advantages of a thorough training in oratory. He repeatedly acknowledges his early obligations to it, and makes provision for rhetorical instruction in his " Bethesda." According to Southey, his delivery was perfect. He commenced his ministry by writing his sermons and reading them to his audiences ; but in the year 1738 he was convinced by observation that it was better for him to preach extemporaneously. His earlier attempts to preach in the fields, if Wesley's judgment is to be trusted, betrayed many inaccuracies of language. But as he often repeated his sermons, he continually improved them in style and delivery. The sermons which he confessedly wrote out after preaching, and the volumes of his letters, were composed in excellent English. The latter are fuller of heart than even those of John Newton.

His journals will reward careful study. Indeed, they demand it; for in his haste Whitefield did not diligently compare one day's experiences with those of another. One day he exults in the abundance of God's help, and declares rather presumptuously that "it is *more than* sufficient for him." Soon he sinks almost into despair, but does not seem to suspect that it was the fruit of his presumption.

In preaching he gave way to a soul full of generous passions. With a sensibility so tender that he could cry as easily as a child, his appeals were irresistibly pathetic and affecting. Yet was he simple, natural, and honest-in all his tears, exclamations, and lamentations. He had, on principle, exercised as parts of the new man, those powers of feeling which were in him natural endowments. Finding Christian people everywhere dry, formal, and lukewarm, he would often say, " Let us be all heart." . . . " The world wants more heat than light." . . . " Lord, make us all flames of fire." While preaching one day at Cambuslang to twenty thousand people, he saw a universal thrill : " the motion fled as swift as lightning from one end of the congregation to the other."

His audiences were very large—the numbers were perhaps exaggerated. Once he had eight thousand ; on two occasions he is said to have had nine thousand hearers ; at two other open-air services he had twenty thousand. Sometimes his pulpit was a pile of turf. His voice, when exerted according to its natural capacity, could be heard a great way, but when surrounded by multitudes he sometimes strained his throat until it bled again. In a ministry of thirty-four years he preached about eighteen thousand sermons. One day he preached seven times. He gradually acquired peaceful and gentle habits of feeling and delivery. The sum of his wisdom on this point is found in the following : " The further we go in the spiritual life, the more cool and rational shall we be, and yet more truly zealous. I speak from experience."

OUTLINES OF SERMONS.

THE KINGDOM OF GOD.

For the kingdom of God is not meat and drink.... Rom. 14 : 17.

The Introduction explains the context.

1. Explain what we are to understand by the Kingdom of God.
2. Show that the Kingdom of God is not meat and drink.
3. Show what the Kingdom positively is.

THE METHOD OF GRACE.

Saying, Peace, peace ; when there is no peace.... Jer. 6 : 14.

The Introduction reviews Jeremiah's account of the false prophets of his day.

How far must we go, and what must be wrought in us before we can speak peace to our hearts?

Here give me leave to premise a caution or two.

a. I take it for granted that religion is a work of the heart wrought in the soul by the power of the Spirit of God.

b. I would by no means say that God is confined to one way of acting, or that all persons, before they can have a settled peace, are obliged to undergo the same degrees of conviction.

1. Before you can speak peace to your hearts, you must be made to see, made to feel, made to bewail *your actual transgressions of the law of God.*

2. Before you can speak peace to your hearts, conviction must go deeper. You must be convinced of the foundation of all your transgressions—that is to say, *original sin,* that original corruption each of us brings into the world.

3. Further : before you can speak peace to your hearts, you must not only be troubled for the sins of your life and the sin of your nature, but likewise for the sins of your best duties and performances.

4. Before you can speak peace to your hearts, you must be troubled on account of *the sin of unbelief.* This is the reigning damning sin of the Christian world, and yet the Christian world seldom or never think of it. We are not to be satisfied with an historical faith.

5. Once more : before you can speak peace to your heart, you must also lay hold by faith of the perfect and all-sufficient righteousness of Jesus Christ.

The application consists of a long and animated address to several sorts of persons—congratulations to those who have found peace ; cautions to such as are in danger of resting on their first conversion ; lamentation over those who have no peace with God ; warning to the self-secure ; directions to those who are partly awakened ; to backsliders.

THE DUTY OF A GOSPEL MINISTER.

The Spirit of the Lord is upon me....to preach the acceptable year of the Lord.
Luke 4 : 18, 19.

Introduction drawn from the context.

1. Every minister ought to be able to say, " The Spirit of the Lord is upon me," etc.

2. I shall show what the Gospel is, which ministers, thus qualified, are to preach.

3. To whom this Gospel is to be preached—the poor, the broken-hearted, the captives, etc.

5. A general application.*

DOST THOU BELIEVE IN THE SON OF GOD ?

John 9 : 35.

1. Some marks of those who believe on Christ.

2. The happiness of such as truly believe on Him.

EXHORTATION TO UNITY, ZEAL, AND OTHER BECOMING VIRTUES.

(A farewell sermon.)   Phil. 1 : 27-28.

I take the words in their order.

1. " Let your conversation be as becometh the Gospel of Christ." He would have them keep a Gospel walk with God.

2. " Stand fast in one spirit, in one mind."   He recommends unity and love.

3. " Striving together," etc.   He recommends zeal.

4. " And in nothing terrified by your adversaries."   A caution not to be afraid of your enemies.

PERSECUTION EVERY CHRISTIAN'S LOT.

2 Tim. 3 : 12.

1. What it is to live godly in Christ Jesus.

2. The different kinds of persecution to which the godly are exposed.

3. Why is it that the godly must expect to suffer persecution ?

4. Application.

EXHORTATION TO CLEAVE TO THE LORD.

Acts 11 : 23.

---

* The three sermons outlined above were preached in the High Church yard of Glasgow, in September, 1741.

ABRAHAM OFFERING UP HIS SON ISAAC.

Gen. 22 : 12.

1. The narrative. 2. Practical inferences.*

THE LORD OUR RIGHTEOUSNESS.

Jer. 23 : 6.

1. Consider who we are to understand by the word *Lord*.

2. How the Lord is man's righteousness.

3. Consider some of the objections that are urged against this doctrine.

4. Show some of the ill consequences that flow from denying this doctrine.

5. Conclude with an exhortation to all to come to Christ by faith, that they may be enabled to say with the prophet in the text, " The Lord our righteousness."

CHRIST THE BELIEVER'S HUSBAND.

For thy Maker is thy husband.... Isa. 54 : 5.

1. Show what must pass between Jesus Christ and our souls before we can say our Maker is our husband.

2. The duties of love which we owe to our Lord, who stands in so near a relation to Him.

3. The miserable condition of such as cannot yet say their Maker is their husband.

4. Exhortation to the class last mentioned.

THE POTTER AND THE CLAY.

Arise and go down to the potter's house.... Jer. 18 : 1-6.

1. Prove that every man by nature is, in the sight of God, only " a piece of marred clay."

2. That, being thus marred, he must necessarily be renewed.

3. Point out by whose agency this change is to be brought about.

THE POWER OF CHRIST'S RESURRECTION.

Philip. 3 : 10.

1. Show that Christ is indeed risen from the dead, and that it was necessary for Him so to do.

2. Show that it highly concerns us to know and experience the power of His resurrection.

---

* This sermon, like all others on the subject with which we are acquainted, passes without due notice Heb 11 : 17-19, which affords a key to the mystery of the apparently stoical conduct of the patriarch during the trial of his faith.

THE INDWELLING SPIRIT THE PRIVILEGE OF ALL BELIEVERS.

If any man thirst, let him come unto me and drink.... John 7 : 37-39.

1. Show what is meant by the word Spirit.
2. That this Spirit is the privilege of all believers.
3. The reason on which this doctrine is founded.
4. Conclude with a general exhortation to believe on Jesus Christ, whereby alone we can receive this Spirit.

THIS IS LIFE ETERNAL.

John 17 : 3.

1. I shall show that there is one true God.
2. What is the knowledge you must have of Jesus Christ.
3. An exhortation to all classes to seek this knowledge.

WHAT THINK YE OF CHRIST?

Matt. 22 : 42.

1. What think ye about the person of Christ? Whose son is He?
2. What think ye of the incarnation of Christ?
3. What think ye about being justified by Christ?
4. What think ye of Christ being formed within you ?*

THEMES AND TEXTS.

Christ's Transfiguration. Luke 9 : 28-36.

✓ A penitent heart the best New Year's gift. (Except ye repent....) Luke 13 : 3.

The Gospel Supper. An exposition. (Go out unto the highways....) Luke 14 : 22-24.

The Marriage of Cana. John 2 : 11.

The Duty of searching the Scriptures. John 5 : 3-9.

The Resurrection of Lazarus. John 11 : 43, 44.

Marks of having received the Holy Ghost. (Have ye received the Holy Ghost?) Acts 19 : 2.

The Almost Christian. Acts 26 : 28.

The Knowledge of Christ the best Knowledge. (Not to know anything.) 1 Cor. 2 : 2.

Of Justification by Christ. (Ye are justified in the name of the Lord Jesus. ..) 1 Cor. 6 : 11.

The Duty of Charity recommended. 1 Cor. 13 : 8.

Satan's Devices. 1 Cor. 2 : 11.

---

* The Rev. James Hervey set a high value on this sermon: it was the means of correcting his errors concerning the method of salvation. Whitefield became his friend, and recommended from the pulpit his " Theron and Aspasio."

Of Regeneration. (If any man be in Christ, he is a new creature....) 2 Cor. 5 : 17.

Christians' Temples of the Living God. 2 Cor. 6 : 16.

The Sin of Drunkenness. (And be not drunk with wine....) Eph. 5 : 18.

Christ the only preservative against a Reprobate Spirit. (....Jesus is in you, except ye be....) 2 Cor. 13 : 5.

Peter's Denial of his Lord. Matt. 26 : 75.

The true way of beholding the Lamb of God. John 1 : 35, 56.

Great is Diana of the Ephesians. Acts 19 : 28.

The Serpent lifted up a type of Christ crucified. John 3 : 14.

Not ashamed of the Gospel of Christ. Rom. 1 : 16.

Self-inquiry concerning the Work of God. (....What hath God wrought?...) Num. 23 : 23.

Neglect of Christ the killing sin. (...Ye will not come ...) John 5 : 40.

The Righteousness of Christ an everlasting righteousness. Dan. 9 : 24.

The true way of keeping Christmas. (And she shall bring forth a son ...) Matt. 1 : 21.

The Temptation of Christ. Matt. 4 : 1–11.

The sin of Profane Swearing. (Swear not at all....) Matt. 5 : 34.

Christ the support of the tempted. (Lead us not....for thine is the Kingdom....) Matt. 6 : 13.

Worldly business no plea for the neglect of religion. (Follow me, and let the dead bury their dead ...) Matt. 8 : 22.

Christ the only rest for the weary and heavy laden. Matt. 11 : 28.

The Danger of parting with Christ for the pleasures of Life. Matt. 8 : 23–34. [An exposition.]

A childlike Spirit a mark of true Conversion. (Except ye be converted and become as little children....) Matt. 10 : 3.

Blind Bartimeus. Mark 10 : 52.

Directions how to hear sermons. (Take heed how ye hear....) Luke 8 : 18.

The Nature and Reasonableness of Self-Denial. Luke 9 : 23.

Intercession every Christian's duty. 1 Thess. 5 : 25.

The eternity of Hell torments. Matt. 25 : 46.

Go out into the highways and hedges. Luke 14 : 22.

The great duty of Family Religion. Joshua 24 : 15.

The Wise and the Foolish Virgins. Matt. 25 : 13.

We do not corrupt the word of God. 2 Cor. 2 : 17.

Christ the Believer's Refuge. Ps. 46 : 1–6.

Soul Prosperity. 3 John 2.

Soul Dejection. Ps. 43 : 5.

The Gospel a dying saint's triumph. (Go ye into all the world....
he that believeth not shall be damned.) Mark 16 : 15,16.

God the believer's Glory. Isa. 60 : 19.

The Burning Bush. Exod. 3 : 2, 3.

The Lord our Light. Isa. 60 : 19, 20.

Present discouragement and future rest. (There remaineth therefore a rest....) Heb. 4 : 9.

The Duty of going directly to Jesus for spiritual food. (Go unto
Joseph ; what he saith to you, do) Gen. 41 : 53. [The sermon from
this text was preached at Cambuslang in 1742. It was never reported.]

Ignorance of the New Birth. (Art thou a master in Israel?....)
John 3 : 10.

Saul's Conversion. Acts 9 : 22.

Christ the believer's wisdom, righteousness, sanctification, and redemption. 1 Cor. 1 : 30.

The Pharisee and the Publican. Luke 18 : 14.

This is my beloved ; this is my friend. Canticles 5 : 16.

The Holy Spirit convincing the world of sin, righteousness, and
judgment. John 16 : 8.

The Marriage in Cana. John 2 : 2.

The Conversion of Zaccheus. Luke 19 : 9,10.

The Conversion of the Eunuch. Acts 8 : 26-39.

The Penitent Thief. Luke 23 : 42.

Noah a preacher of Righteousness. 2 Pet. 2 : 5.

The cave Adullam a refuge. 1 Sam. 22 : 2.

The Seed of the Woman and the Seed of the Serpent. Gen. 3 : 45.
[This sermon is chiefly an exposition of the first fifteen verses of the
3d chapter of Genesis.]

A sermon addressed to soldiers. Luke 3 : 14.

Walking with God. Gen. 5 : 24.

Christ the best husband. (Hearken, O daughter.... worship thou
him.) Ps. 45 : 10, 11.

Thanksgiving a necessary duty. Ps. 107 : 30, 31.

The Folly and Danger of not being righteous enough. Eccles.
7 : 16.

The Benefits of Early Piety. Eccles. 12 : 1.

Mourning sinners comforted. Matt. 5 : 4.

The Necessity of Regeneration. John 3 : 3.

The Unbeliever Convinced. (Thomas, because thou hast seen ....)
John 20 : 29.

The Balm of Gilead, or Christ the Physician of souls. Jer. 8 : 20, 21.

The remnant that is left. Isa. 1 : 9.

Jacob's Ladder. Gen. 28 : 12-15. [A farewell sermon.]

The Good Shepherd John 10 : 27, 28. [A farewell sermon.]

Paul's parting speech to the elders of Ephesus. Acts 20 : 17-35. [A farewell sermon.]

A minister's parting blessing. Rev. 22 : 21. [A farewell sermon.]

SERMONS BY REV. JOHN WELCH,

Of Ayr, Scotland.

OUTLINES.

EIGHT SERMONS ON REPENTANCE.

SERMON I. Rev. 2 : 2-5.

1. The testimony in behalf of Ephesus. "I know thy works," etc.

2. The charge against them. "Nevertheless I have somewhat," etc.

3. Christ bids her do the first works of love, zeal, and patience.

SERMON II. (Same subject continued.) Rev. 2 : 5.

1. The names the Holy Spirit gives to repentance in Scripture·

2. How many ways repentance is taken in the Scripture.

SERMON III. (Same subject continued.) Rev. 2 : 5.

1. What true repentance is.

SERMON IV. (Same subject continued.) Rev. 2 : 5.

1. What true repentance is.

2. Objections answered.

SERMON V. (Same subject continued.) Rev. 2 : 5.

1. Who is the Author of true repentance.

2. Reasons why we should not delay repentance.

3. Motives to repentance.

4. The persons who ought to repent.

5. Means used by the Lord to bring His own to repentance.

SERMON VI. (Same subject continued.) Rev. 2 . 5.

1. What are the fruits of true repentance.

2. Why God gives repentance to some and denies it to others.

3. The parts of true repentance.

SERMON VII. (Same subject continued.) Rev. 2 : 5

1. The parts of repentance in respect of *times and manners.*

2. Degrees of repentance.

3. What are the contraries of true repentance.

4. The means to be used by us to get repentance.

SERMON VIII. (Same subject continued.) Rev. 2 : 5.

1. How to renew and recover repentance after we have abandoned it and can with difficulty renew it.

2. Motives to use the means of renewing repentance.

ON FAITH.

Now faith is the substance.... Heb. 11 : 1.

Three properties of Faith.

1. The ground of things hoped for, etc.

2. It causes us to be well reported of both with God and man, as Enoch.

3. It makes all the mysteries of God credible.

4. All the good saints ever received or did was through faith.

The just shall live by faith.... Rom. 1 : 17.

1. The just man lives—that is, the man that is covered with the righteousness of Christ is blessed. Ps. 32 : 1.

2. The just man lives—that is, makes the law of God his delight.

3. How does he live? By faith.

ON THE LAST JUDGMENT.

Rev. 20 : 11.

1. The throne is great.

2. It is white.

Same subject continued. (Same text.)

1. The Judge.

2. The manner of the judgment.

3. The execution of the judgment.

THEMES AND TEXTS.

Paul lives, or rather Christ lives in him. Gal. 2 : 20.

God's love to the world the ground of faith. (God so loved the world....that the world through him might be saved....) John 3 : 16–17.

The Benefits of Faith in Christ. (Same text.)

Same subject continued. (Same text.)

The Unbeliever condemned. John 3 : 17.

On the causes of condemnation. John 3 : 18.

Mr. Welch has left nine sermons on Eph. 6 : 10-21. These were probably preached to the new converts. Ever do they need to know the Christian Armor.

SERMONS* BY REV. G. W. WOODHOUSE,

Vicar of Albrighton, England.

THEMES AND TEXTS.

The Christian accountable for his privileges. (Consider how great things he hath done for you....) 1 Sam. 12 : 24.

Present Impunity. (They consider not in their hearts that I remember all their wickedness....) Hosea 7 : 2.

False Confidences. (For the Lord hath rejected thy confidences and thou shalt not prosper in them....) Jer. 2 : 37.

Vain Excuses. (Bring forth your strong reasons, saith the King of Jacob....) Isa. 41 : 21.

The Retrospect. (And Jacob awaked out of his sleep, and he said, Surely the Lord is in this place ; and I knew it not....) Gen. 28 : 16.

Pardon for the Penitent. (Because he considereth and turneth away from all his transgressions that he hath committed ; he shall surely live, he shall not die....) Ezek. 18 : 28.

The only safe state. (Who shall ascend into the hill of the Lord....) Ps. 24 : 3.

The Danger of Delay. (Give glory to the Lord before He causes darkness, and before your feet stumble upon the dark mountains....) Jer. 13 : 16.

The Judgment to Come. 2 Cor. 5 : 10.

SERMONS BY REV. GILBERT TENNENT.

THEMES AND TEXTS.

Christ's Invitation to Rest. (Come unto me all ye that labor....) Matt. 11 : 28.

Prayer to the Breath of God. (Come, O breath....) Ezek. 37 : 9.

* Addressed to careless Christians.

The Prodigal Son. Luke 15.

The Law reviving sin. Rom. 7 : 9.

The Lord's call to Adam. Gen. 3 : 9.

Words of rejoicing and exhortation. (Was glad and exhorted....)
Acts 11 : 23.

The Wisdom of God in Redemption. 1 Cor. 1 : 23, 24.

The Benefits of Spiritual Devotions. (No text found.)

SERMONS BY DR. STEPHEN H. TYNG, Sr.

THEMES AND TEXTS.

God's message to Israel [four sermons]. (Prepare to meet thy
God, O Israel....) Amos 4 : 12.

The New Creature [two sermons]. 2 Cor. 5 : 17.

The Lord's Side. (Who is on the Lord's side....) Exod. 32 : 26.

The Protected People. (The man with the inkhorn....set a
mark on the foreheads....go through the city and smite....) Ezek.
9 : 3-6.

The Rescued Brand. (A brand plucked out of the fire....) Zech.
3 : 2.

The Sinner's Choice. (Not this man, but Barabbas....) John
18 : 40.

The Christian's Rock. (Their rock is not as our Rock....) Deut.
32 : 31

A Spiritual Famine. Amos 8 : 11, 12.

The Valley of Decision. (The day of the Lord is near....) Joel
3 : 14.

The Christian's Hindrances. (Hinder me not ...) Gen. 24 : 56.

Difficulties in the way of the conversion of the Aged. Jer. 6 : 4.

The Sorrows of impenitent Old Age. Eccles. 6 : 3.

1. What is the great object of human life.

2. The sorrows of the man that has lived long without attaining it.

Disappointed Procrastination. (And the days of Terah....) Gen.
11 : 32.

Ineffectual Repentance. (And Joab fled and laid hold on the horns
of the altar....) 1 Kings 2 : 28.

The Latter End. (O that they were wise....) Deut. 32 : 29.

SERMONS BY REV. JOHN SUMMERFIELD.

THEMES AND TEXTS.

Spiritual Idolatry. (Ephraim is joined to idols : let him alone....)
Hos. 4 : 17.

Religion First. (But rather seek ye the Kingdom of God....)
Luke 12 : 31.

God's Love to a Perishing World. John 3 : 16.

O that I knew where I might find him. Job 23 : 3, 4.

The Strong Hold. Zech. 9 : 12.

The Nature and Importance of Conversion. James 5 : 19, 20.

Thou art weighed in the Balances. Dan. 5 : 27.

Talents neglected are taken away. Matt. 25 : 29.

Need of Patience. Heb. 10 : 36.

The way of Holiness. Isa. 35 : 8, 10.

1. A high way. 2. A holy way. 3. A plain way. 4. A safe way.
5. A delightful way.

SERMONS BY REV. DR. ICHABOD SPENCER.

THEMES AND TEXTS.

The Depression of Believers. (Make me to hear joy and gladness ;
that the bones which thou hast broken may rejoice....renew a right
spirit within me....) Ps. 51 : 8–10.

The Woman of Canaan in Prayer. Matt.15 : 28.

The Blind led in a way they knew not. Isa. 42 : 16.

Assurance attainable. Rom. 8 : 38, 39.

Sanctification at Death. Heb. 12 : 22, 23.

The Chief of Sinners. 1 Tim. 1 : 15.

1. Delay of Conversion. Argued from the Nature of Man. Ps.
95 : 7, 8.

2. Delay of Conversion. Argued from the Economy of the Holy
Spirit. (Same text.)

3. Delay of Conversion. Argued from Facts. (Same text.)

SERMONS BY REV. C. H. SPURGEON.

OUTLINES.

MOSES LIFTING UP THE SERPENT.

Numbers 9 : 21.

1. The persons in mortal peril for whom the brazen serpent was made and lifted up.

    They had despised God's way and God's bread.

    They had been actually bitten by the serpents.

    The bite of the serpent was painful.

    The bite of these serpents was mortal.

    There is no limit to the stages of poisoning.

2. The remedy provided for them.

    It was purely of divine origin.

    There was but one remedy.

    The healing serpent was bright and lustrous.

    The remedy was an enduring one.

3. The application of the remedy.

    It was very personal.

    It was very instructive.

    It magnified the love of God in Christ.

4. The cure effected.

    They were healed at once.

    This remedy healed again and again.

    It cured all who used it.

    It cured when looked upon by moonlight as well as sunlight.

5. A lesson for all who love the Lord. Publish Christ and His salvation.

THEMES AND TEXTS.

The Carnal mind enmity against God. Rom. 8 : 7. [Vol. I. p. 230.]*

Healing for the Wounded. (He hath smitten my life down to the ground....) Ps. 143 : 3. [Vol. II. 18.]

The Sin of Unbelief. (If the Lord should make windows in heaven....) 2 Kings 7 : 19. [Vol. II. 50.]

Harvest Time. 1 Sam. 12 : 17. [Vol. II. 232.]

The Comer's conflict with Satan. Luke 9 : 42. [Vol. II. 296.]

A Visit to Calvary. John 19 : 5. [Vol. II. 328.]

* The references are to the American edition of these sermons.

Turn or Burn. Ps. 7 : 12. [Vol. II. 426.]

The Fruitless Vine. Ezek. 15 : 1, 2. [Vol. III. 58.]

Spiritual Revival the Want of the Church. Hab. 3 : 2. [Vol. III. 74.]

The Anxious Inquirer. Job 23 : 3. [Vol. III. 90.]

The Sinner's Refuge. Numbers 35 : 11. [Vol. III. 106.]

Secret Sins. Ps. 19 : 12. [Vol. III. 164.]

Elijah's Appeal to the Undecided. 1 Kings 18 : 21. [Vol. III. 179.]

Regeneration. John 3 : 3. [Vol. III. 210.]

Rahab's Faith. Heb. 11 : 31. [Vol. III. 369.]

Manasseh. 2 Chron. 23 : 13. [Vol. III. 311.]

Why are men saved ? (Saved for his name's sake....) Ps. 106 : 8. [Vol.   328.]

A Mighty Saviour. Isa. 63 : 1. [Vol. III. 404.]

The Parable of the Ark. Gen. 7 : 15. [Vol. IV. 1.]

A Time of Finding Lost Sheep. Ezek. 34 : 16. [Vol. IV. 3.]

The Prodigal's Return. Luke 15 : 20. [Vol. IV. 145.]

A Call to the Unconverted. (For as many as are of the works of the law, are under the curse....) Gal. 3 : 10. [Vol. IV. 223.]

The Warning Neglected. Ezek. 33 : 5. [Vol. IV. 240.]

What have I done ? Jer. 8 : 6. [Vol. IV. 258.]

Awake ! Awake ! 1 Thess. 5 : 6. [Vol. IV. 316.]

The Voice of the Blood of Christ. Heb. 12 : 24. [Vol. V. 65.]

The New Heart. Ezek. 36 : 26. [Vol. V. 81.]

Declension from first love. Rev. 2 : 4. [Vol. V. 164.]

Looking unto Jesus. Ps. 34 : 5. [Vol. V. 253.]

The Blood. Exodus 12 : 13. [Vol. V. 303.]

The Great Revival. (The Lord hath made bare his holy arm.... and all the ends of the earth shall see the salvation of our God....) Isa. 52 : 10. [Vol. V. 336.]

The World turned upside down. Acts 17 : 6. [Vol. V. 402.]

Human Responsibility. John 15 : 22. [Vol. V. 420.]

The Outpouring of the Holy Spirit. Acts 10 : 44. [Vol. VI. 31.]

The Sympathy of the Two Worlds. Luke 15 : 10. [Vol. VI. 47.]

The Conversion of Saul of Tarsus. Acts 26 : 14. [Vol. VI. 61.]

The Mission of the Son of Man. Luke 19 : 10. [Vol. VI. 92.]

The Earnest Invitation. Ps. 2 : 12. [Vol. VI. 109.]

How Saints may help the Devil. Ezek. 16 : 54. [Vol. VI. 125.]

The Necessity of the Spirit's Work. Ezek. 36 : 27. [Vol. VI. 186.]

The Meek and Lowly One. Matt. 11 : 28–30. [Vol. VI. 366.]

The Blind Beggar. Mark 10 : 46-52. [Vol. VI. 399.]

Æneas.   Acts 9 : 32-35.   [Vol. X. 379.]
Our cure should be radical.   Jer. 8 : 11.

————

SERMONS BY REV. JABEZ S. SWAN.

OUTLINES.

THE HARVEST OF SOULS.

Matt. 9 : 37, 38.

1. The lordship of Christ over the souls of men.

a. God has given Him power over all flesh.

b. He died and rose again, that he might be Lord, etc.

c. Such lordship reveals His compassion for the multitude.

d. Such lordship indicates his ability to meet the needs of the harvest field, etc.

2. The method devised by Christ to secure sufficient laborers to gather the harvest.

a. He will supply the field in answer to prayer.

b. Thus He throws the responsibility of supplying the field on the disciples.

c. Thus He would teach them that the proper kind of reapers are those alone which Christ Himself sends.

d. Thus all who are sent will be welcomed by those already in the field.

e. Thus they are prepared for greater union with Christ, and for the efforts which the demands of the field excite.

3. Motives by which the disciples are urged to call on the Lord.

a. The plenteousness of the harvest, etc.

b. The scarcity of actual laborers.

c. The ability of Christ to send laborers.

d. If the sickle is not put in, what will be the consequences?

THE EFFECT OF COMMUNION WITH GOD.

Exod. 34 : 29.

1. Communion with God assimilates to His likeness.

2. Likeness to God may exist, though it be obscure to its possessor.

FIXING OUR MINDS ON CHRIST.

Matt. 14 : 30.

1. Attention diverted from Christ forebodes evil.

2. The remedy found in reclaimed attention.

EVANGELISTIC INDUSTRY.

Mark 26 : 20.

Doctrine : Industry in Religion secures corresponding success.
1. The industry which the religion of Christ demands.
2. The manner in which God has secured its success.

FISHERS OF MEN MUST BE OBEDIENT TO CHRIST.

Luke 5 : 5.

1. The commands of Christ the law of Christian action.
2. Obedience to His commands secures large success.

THE DANGER OF MAKING EXCUSES.

Luke 14 : 19.

1. The nature of the excuses for refusing the Gospel invitations.
2. These excuses liable to exclude those who make them from the happiness of heaven.

SELF-EXAMINATION.

John 21 : 17.

1. The necessity of such questions among professors.
2. The reply which true religion will furnish.

THE POWER OF THE HOLY GHOST.

Acts 1 : 8.

1. The proper preparation for an interest in revivals.
2. The object to be accomplished by those who are thus qualified.

CHRISTIANS BOUGHT WITH A PRICE.

1 Cor. 6 : 20.

1. Ye belong to God by purchase, both body and spirit.
2. The object of God in this purchase.
3. The purchase paid is the motive to action.

THE CONCOMITANTS OF SALVATION.

Heb. 6 : 9.

1. Things which accompany salvation in its attainment.
2. Things which accompany its enjoyment.

WORKS THAT SHOW LUKEWARMNESS.

Rev. 3 : 16.

Doctrine : Religious Indifference.
1. Its criminality.
2. Its offensiveness to God.
3. Its danger.

SPIRITUAL DEATH AND LIFE.

2 Cor. 6 : 9.

Doctrine : In the Kingdom of God, death the harbinger of life.

1. The death which is the harbinger of life.

2. The life which follows death.

TEMPORAL HINDRANCES.

Regard not your stuff.... Gen. 45 : 20.

Doctrine : Lesser good should be sacrificed to the greater.

THE HOLY ROD CAST UPON THE GROUND.

Exod. 4 : 2–4.

The dreadful results of casting down holy things. Among holy things are :

1. Fallen vows.

2. Prostration of secret, family and public altars.

3. The only way to get out of this danger is to take hold of the serpent.

EXHORTATION TO LAY HOLD OF CHRIST BY FAITH.

"Lay hold on eternal life."

PUTTING ON STRENGTH.

Awake, awake, put on thy strength, O Zion.... Isa. 52 : 1.

1. What Christian strength is. God is our strength. "The Lord is thy strength and shield." Suppose that the shield is laid aside, etc.

2. Importance of obtaining this strength.

a. Without this strength no man is able to do anything. We may resolve, but without this strength we cannot carry out our resolutions.

b. Without it we have no ability to prevail with our brethren.

c. Nor with the unconverted.

d. Nor with God.

3. How to obtain it.

a. We must prevail with God.

b. Jacob had power with God and with man, etc.

4. Decision of action is demanded. Why?

THE RELATIONS OF COURAGE AND STRENGTH.

Be of good courage, and He shall strengthen your heart, all ye that hope in the Lord.

Ps. 31 : 24.

1. Fearlessness in religious life.

a. The timidity of human hearts must be overcome.

b. This timidity baffles all attempts to glorify God.

2. The strength which is accumulated by fearlessness in religion.

a. Every department of religious life demands a high and commanding fortitude.

(*a*) It is needed to endure hardships and severe toil.

(*β*) To meet frowning aspects and events.

b. The promises of God are made for the exigencies of Christian life.

(*a*) For the renewal of fortitude in labor. " He that reapeth receiveth wages."

(*β*) The soul that is utterly disabled may fall back upon the promise : He giveth power to the faint.

c. This strengthens the heart.

(*a*) The heart without this strength palsies all the powers of the soul.

(*β*) With it the heart is mighty in working the work of God.

(*γ*) Inspires high hopes of success : " Ye that hope in the Lord."

Conclusion.

1. Be courageous and strong, for the time is short.

2. For the enemy is alert.

3. For your divine Leader is worthy.

SERMONS BY EDWARD PAYSON, D.D.

OUTLINE.

THE OLD WAY WHICH WICKED MEN HAVE TRODDEN.

Job 22 : 15-17.

1. Let us consider the way itself.

2. The termination of this way.

Application.

1. Are any of you walking in this way ?

2. If you are walking therein, forsake it without delay.

SINS ESTIMATED IN THE LIGHT OF HEAVEN.

Ps. 90 : 8.

Introduction : If we would know what our sins really are we must regard them in the same light that God does.

1. Bring forward *our iniquities*, or our more open and gross sins, and see how they appear in the light of God's countenance.

2. Bring our *secret sins*, the sins of the heart, into heaven, and see how they will appear in that world of unclouded light.

3. Let us take a similar view of our sins of *omission*.

Conclusion.

You perceive the reason why your sins appear more numerous and more criminal in the sight of God than they do in your own.

THEMES AND TEXTS.

Men tried and found defective. Dan. 5 : 27.

Our sins infinite in number and enormity. (Is not thy wickedness great....) Job 22 : 5.

The wicked, from pride, refuse to seek God. Ps. 10 : 4.

Recollections of God painful to the wicked. Ps. 77 : 3.

Sinners wilful and perverse. (They are like children sitting in the market place....) (Luke 7 : 31-35.

Amiable instincts not holiness. (The God of peace sanctify you wholly....) 1 Thes. 5 : 23.

The Final Judgment. 2 Cor. 15 : 10.

The sinner entreated to hear God's voice. Heb. 3 : 7-8.

The difficulty of escaping the damnation of hell. Matt. 23 : 33.

The Mark of Deliverance. Ezek. 9 : 4-6.

The punishment of the wicked dreadful and interminable. Mark 9 : 44.

Sinners in Zion described and doomed. Amos 6 : 1.

A class of sinners excluded from mercy. (When the boughs are withered, they are broken off ; the women came and set them on fire....) Isa. 27 : 11.

Punishment of the impenitent inevitable and justifiable. Jer. 22 : 24.

The guilt of indifference to divine threatenings. Jer. 26 : 24.

The sin, danger, and unreasonableness of despair. Jer. 18 : 12.

The stubborn sinner submitting to God. (As a bullock unaccustomed to the yoke....) Jer. 31 : 18-20.

Christ rejects none who come unto him. John 6 : 37.

Christ's special tenderness toward penitent disciples. Mark 16 : 7.

Christ the Saviour of the lost. Luke 19 : 10.

Man's treatment of Christ. (They will reverence my son....) Mark 12 : 6.

An assembly convoked against sinners. Neh. 5 : 7.

Why the wicked are spared for a season. Gen. 15 : 16.

The sleeper awakened. (What meanest thou, O sleeper....) Jonah 1 : 6.

Joy in heaven over repenting sinners. Luke 15 : 10.

How little children are prevented from coming to Christ. Mark 10 : 14.

How to prolong the gracious visits of Christ.   Luke 4 : 42.

An early interest in God's mercy essential to a happy life.   Ps. 90 : 14.

SERMONS BY REV. ORSON PARKER.

THEMES AND TEXTS.

Self-Examination.   (Search me, and know my heart. . . .) Ps. 139 : 23, 24.

Building up the Walls of the Church.   Neh. 2 : 17, 18.

The conditions God requires before blessing His people.   2 Chron. 7 : 14.

Do you really believe your Articles of Faith?   (Any man upon whom is the mark. . . .and begin at my sanctuary. . . .) Ezek. 9 : 6.

"Their strength is to sit still."   Isa. 30 : 7.   Idleness and neglect of professors reproved.

Prayer of the Church for Help.   2 Chron. 20 : 4.

The Settlement of Difficulties.   Rom. 12 : 1.

Providence calls upon us to seek the conversion of our relatives. ("Who knoweth whether Thou art come to the Kingdom for such a time as this?"   Esther 4 : 14.)

Religion all-important.   "Is it not so?"   Judges 14 : 15.

How long wilt thou sleep?   Prov. 6 : 9.

Ye must be born again.   John 3 : 3.

Is it nothing to you?   Lam. 1 : 12.

The one thing needful.   Luke 10 : 41.

The sinners' excuses.   Luke 9 : 61.

Repentance.   (Repent ye, and believe the gospel. . . .) Mark 1 : 15.

How sinners fail to become Christians.   Mark 5 : 26.

Morality alone saves no one.   Rom. 3 : 20.

The way to be saved.   Acts 16 : 30.

The early conversion of children.   Prov. 22 : 6.

Is it well with thee?   2 Kings 4 : 26.

Joshua's resolution.   Josh. 24 : 15.

I will pay my vows.   Ps. 66 : 13, 14.

Now is the accepted time.   2 Cor. 6 : 2.

The Jailer and Felix contrasted.   Acts 16 : 30; 24 : 25.

As the will is, so is the man.   (I will arise and go to my father, and will say. . . .)   Luke 15 : 18.

The almost Christian is lost.   Acts 26 : 28.

The sinner crossing the line. (I gave her space to repent, and she repented not.) Rev. 2 : 21.

The danger of halting half way. (Remember Lot's wi e.) Luke 17 : 32.

Private fasting for friends. (This kind goeth not out but by prayer and fasting....) Matt. 17 : 20.

God will send His blessings as long as the people will receive them. (And the oil stayed.) 2 Kings 4 : 6.

Why should the work cease? Neh. 6 : 3.

Farewell address to young converts. Josh. 24 : 22.

SERMONS BY REV. G. F. PENTECOST.

THEMES AND TEXTS.

The Gospel coming in power. (Not in word only, but in power.) 1 Thess. 1 : 5.

Keeping ourselves in the love of God. Jude 20, 21.

Helpers and Hinderers. (One sick of the palsy borne of four.... they could not come nigh unto him for the press....) Mark 2 : 1–12.

The Genius of the Gospel the Germ of Foreign Missions. Mark 16 : 15.

Words to young converts. Exod. 14 : 15.

The Christian and the Ball-room. Isa. 47 : 7, 8.

Christ and Christian. Acts 11 : 26.

Pharisaism. Matt. 5 : 20.

Bible Readings.

1. Old Testament.
2. Genesis.
3. Exodus.
4. New Testament.
5. Parable of the Sower.
6. The Good Seed and the Tares.
7. The Leaven.
8. Christ the Hidden Treasure.
9. Simon and the Sinful Woman.
10. The Vine.
11. The Sixth of Romans.

12. The Taking of Jericho. (Joshua, chap. 6.)
13. Christ's Resurrection.
14. Eternal Redemption.

———

SERMONS BY ASAHEL NETTLETON, D.D.

OUTLINES.

CHRISTIANS URGED TO AWAKE OUT OF SLEEP.
Rom. 13 : 11.

1. When the Christian may be said to be asleep.
2. Offer some motives which ought to induce him to awake.

SINNERS AFFECTIONATELY ENTREATED TO BEGIN THE CHRISTIAN PILGRIMAGE.
Num. 10 : 29.

1. Christians are journeying.
2. Christians desire others, and especially their kindred, to journey with them.
3. Those whom they cannot persuade to go with them they must give the parting hand.

THE SIN AND CONSEQUENCES OF BEING ASHAMED OF CHRIST.
Luke 9 : 26.

1. Who are ashamed of Christ.
2. The greatness of this sin.
3. The consequences of it.

THE PARABLE OF THE LOST SHEEP.
Luke 15 : 3-7.

Introduction : The nature of Christ's parables—When the parable was spoken—For what purpose—Who are the just persons here mentioned ? The subject suggests the following reflections :

1. Sinners are lost.
2. Christ knows His own sheep. If one of them be gone astray, He knows it.
3. Christ seeks and finds the sinner.
4. How great must be the joy occasioned by the repentance of one sinner.
5. The repentance of every sinner when first discovered, is the cause of new joy.

6. What must have been the hearts of the scribes and Pharisees who murmured because publicans and sinners were converted.

THE PARABLE OF THE PRODIGAL SON.

Luke 15 : 11-25.

An Exposition :

1. The Departing Prodigal.
2. The Returning Prodigal.

INDECISION IN RELIGION.

1 Kings 18 : 21.

1. Why you have hitherto neglected to come to a decided choice.
2. How long do you purpose to halt ?

THE FEARFUL CONDITION OF APOSTATES.

Matt. 12 : 43-45.

We shall consider the parable as applicable—

1. To the Jews.
2. To sinners under the Gospel.

THE DANGER OF HYPOCRISY.

Parable of the Virgins. Matt. 25 : 1-8.

From this parable we learn :

1. That many professors of religion will finally be lost.
2. Persons who appear alike now may possess characters widely different in the sight of God.
3. It should be our great and constant purpose to be prepared for the coming of Christ.
4. Real Christians, even the best of them, are never too much engaged in religion.
5. We see in what lies the distinction between true and false professors of religion—not in the head, but in the heart.
6. We learn from this subject the true reason why so many professors of religion will be lost. *They do not begin right.*

THE GREAT SALVATION.

Heb. 2 : 3.

1. In what the greatness of this salvation consists.
2. Who are guilty of neglecting this salvation.
3. The import of the language, " How shall we escape ?"

SELF-EXAMINATION.

2 Cor. 13 : 5.

1. A person may be a Christian without certainly knowing it.
2. He who is a true Christian may know it.

CHRIST COMING TO JUDGMENT.
Matt. 25 : 31, 32.

1. The certainty of Christ's coming as Judge.
2. The time of His coming.
3. The manner of His coming. (Two sermons.)

THE RICH MAN AND LAZARUS.
Luke 16 : 19-31.

The occasion and matter of the parable.

Remarks.

1. Those who die Christians go immediately to heaven.
2. Those who die sinners go immediately to hell.
3. All sinners will pray sooner or later.
4. Those who lose their souls will remember what took place on earth.
5. We see what the damned would say, were they to come back to this world.
6. We learn that sinners in hell are not yet convinced of the awful depravity of the heart. The rich man thought that moral suasion, if increased to a certain amount, would be sufficient to bring sinners to repéntance.
7. Finally learn from this subject that our Saviour was a very plain preacher.

MORTIFICATION OF SIN.
Gal. 5 : 24.

1. What it implies.
2. Wherein it resembles crucifixion. Under the second head he gives four points of resemblance.
    a. The death of the cross was a violent death.
    b. The death of the cross was a shameful death.
    c. It was a lingering death.
    d. It was a painful death.
3. The means of promoting it.

SAME SUBJECT CONTINUED.

1. Evidence that the work is begun and is in progress.
2. Inferences from the whole subject.
3. Motives to engage immediately in the duty.

SINNERS ENTREATED TO BE RECONCILED TO GOD.
2 Cor. 5 : 20.

1. What is implied in being reconciled to God.
2. To beseech impenitent hearers to be thus reconciled.

THE FOLLY OF MAKING A HYPOCRITICAL PROFESSION OF RELIGION.

Matt. 25 : 2.

1. What is required in a wise profession of religion ?
2. Why some profess religion without possessing it.
3. Why they are called foolish.

CHRIST STANDING AT THE DOOR.

Rev. 3 : 20.

An exposition, concluding with reflections. The text is introduced with a note of admiration —" Behold !"

1. " Behold " the greatness of our Redeemer.
2. "Behold " the depth of Christ's condescension.
3. " Behold " his willingness to receive sinners.
4. " Behold " your danger.

THE SINNER SLAIN BY THE LAW.

Rom. 7 : 9.

1. The life which Paul lives.
2. The death which he died.
3. Reflections.

a. Many think themselves to be Christians when they are not. They have not been under conviction of sin.

b. We see the importance of preaching the law.

c. Sinners that are under conviction realize that they are becoming worse and worse.

d. The preaching of the gospel will distress sinners more and more, while unreconciled to God.

e. The sooner sinners die in the sense of the text, the better.

THE NECESSITY OF REGENERATION NO MATTER OF WONDER.

John 3 : 7.

Sinners would not be happy if taken to heaven without a change of heart. Object is to prove this declaration.

1. It is a holy place.
2. A place of ineffable glory.
3. The inhabitants of heaven are holy.
4. The employments of heaven are holy.

GOD'S SPIRIT WILL NOT ALWAYS STRIVE.

Gen. 6 : 3.

1. The fact that the Spirit does strive with men.
2. The fact that He will not always strive.
3. The consequences of His ceasing to strive.

THE TWO THIEVES.

Luke 23 : 39-43.

1. In what respects they were alike.
2. In what respects they differed.
3. What made the difference.

THEMES AND TEXTS.

Preaching to the conviction of sinners.   John 4 : 29.

The wrath of man praising God.   Ps. 73 : 10.

Men mistake their own character.   Matt. 23 : 30.

Whose prayer is it that is not answered.   James 1 : 7.

They all with one consent began to make excuse.   Luke 14 : 18.

True repentance not antecedent to regeneration.   (Surely after that I turned, I repented ...)   Jer. 31 : 19.

The Perseverance of the Saints.   (He that hath begun a good work in you....)   Philip. 1 : 6.

Death (a sermon preached on the last Sunday in the year).   (O that they were wise, that they understood this....)   Deut. 32 : 29.

The duty of fasting, and the manner of its observance.   Neh. 1 : 4.

The ruin of all such as do not seek salvation.   Luke 13 : 24.

Some now alive greater sinners than some who are in hell. (Suppose ye that all these Galileans were sinners above all the Galileans....)   Luke 13 : 1-5.

The government of God matter of rejoicing.   Ps. 97 : 1.

Religion the source of true happiness (addressed to youth).   Prov. 3 : 13.

The backslider restored.   Ps. 51 : 12, 13.

Total Depravity.   Gen. 6 : 5.

Sins covered.   (He that covereth his sins shall not prosper....)   Prov. 28 : 13.

The example of Esau.   Heb. 12 : 16.

Causes of alarm.   (Men and brethren, what shall we do ?)   Acts 2 : 37.

Come to Christ for rest.   Matt. 11 : 28-30.

The Nature and Reasonableness of Repentance.   Acts 17 : 30.

The Remembered Prediction.   (After three days I will rise again.)   Matt. 27 : 63.

Salvation for the Lost.   Luke 19 : 10.

Judicial Credulity.   (God shall send them strong delusion....)   2 Thess. 2 : 11, 12.

The sovereignty of God in conversion.   Rom. 9 : 16.

Ye know not what spirit ye are of.   Luke 9 : 54, 55.

Affliction preventing a sinner from following Christ. (Suffer me first to go and bury my father.) Luke 9 : 59.

Different Experiences of Converts   1 Cor. 12 : 6.

Thinking on our ways, and making haste to find God's way. Ps. 119 : 59, 60.

Christ's appeal to us to rise up against evil-doers. Ps. 94 : 16.

Shut in, or shut out of the house. (When once the master of the house he is risen up, and hath shut to the door....) Luke 13 : 25.

Agree with thine adversary quickly. Matt. 5 : 25.

Many die eternally because they will not give up some sin. Ezek. 33 : 11.

———

SERMONS AND READINGS BY D. L. MOODY.

THEMES AND TEXTS.

Courage in the Work of the Lord.   Joshua 1 : 6.

His own Brother.   John 1 : 41.

Stones to be rolled away.   John 11 : 39.

Power of Faith.   (And when he saw their faith....)   Luke 5 : 20.

Compassion and Sympathy.   (Who is my neighbor? ...)   Luke 10 : 29.

A Solemn Question.   (And the Lord God called unto Adam....) Gen. 3 : 9.

What Christ is to us.   (Unto you is born this day in the city of David....)   Luke 2 : 11.

Enthusiasm in the work of the Lord.   (For the zeal of thine house hath....)   Ps. 69 : 9.

Our first Duty.   Matt. 6 : 33.

Walking with God.   Gen. 5 : 24.

Our Lord's Return.   2 Tim. 3 : 16.

Reaping and Gathering Fruit.   John 4 : 36.

Laying up Treasures in Heaven.   Matt. 6 : 20.

SERM. I. The Holy Spirit and his Work.   Acts 19 : 2.

SERM. II. Man's relations to the Holy Spirit.   John 14 : 17.

SERM. III. By it we are made free from the Law.   (No text.)

SERM. IV. The Power of the Holy Spirit.   (No text.)

The Prophet Daniel.   Dan. 1 : 8.

Christian Work.   Dan. 11 : 32.

Responsibilities of Parents.   Deut. 5 : 29 and 6 : 7.

The Lost seeking Christ.   Isa. 55 : 6.

Christ seeking the Lost.   Luke 19 : 10.

Lost and Saved.   (Same text.)

Heaven, and who are there.   (No text.)

Grace.   (No text.)

Same subject continued.   (No text.)

On being born again.   John 3 : 3.

The Brazen Serpent.   John 3 : 14, 15.

Faith, and how to get it.   (O woman great is thy faith....)   Matt.
15 : 28.

Two Sermons on the Blood of Christ.

SERM. I. Tracing the Scarlet Thread.   Heb. 9 : 22.

SERM. II. The Blood of the New Testament.   Matt. 26 : 28.

How God loves Men.   1 John 4 : 16.

God hates sin and loves the sinner.   (Same text.)

Jesus died for our sins.   1 Cor. 15 : 3.

The Sinner's Excuses.   Luke 14 : 19.

SERM. I. The Glorious Gospel.   Luke 4 : 18.

SERM. II. The Friend of the Sorrowing.   (Same text.)

SERM. III. Deliverance for Captives.   (Same text.)

SERM. IV. The Blind Cured.   (Same text.)

Seeking and Finding the Lord.   Isa. 55 : 6, 7.

Repentance.   (The times of this ignorance.... but now commandeth
all men everywhere to repent....)   Acts 17 : 30.

Universality of the Gospel offer.   Mark 16 : 15, 16.

The Prodigal Son.   Luke 15 : 36.

Lessons from Paul's Conversion.   (No text.)

Confessing Christ.   Rom. 10 : 9–11.

Naaman.   2 Kings 5.

How memory torments the lost soul.   Luke 16 : 25.

How to study the Bible.   Acts 8 : 30.

The five ONE THINGS of Scripture.   (Five texts.)

Regeneration instantaneous.   (No text.)

The BEHOLDS of the Bible.   (Many texts.)

The best methods with Inquirers.   (No text.)

Christ Jesus the God-Man.   Matt. 22 : 42.

Young Men should decide for God.   1 Kings 18 : 21.

Praise an element of power.   (The joy of the Lord is your
strength....   Neh. 8 : 10.

Weighed in the balances of the Law.   Dan. 5 : 27.

The Eight I WILLS of Christ.   (Eight texts.)

Lot in Sodom.   Gen. 13 : 12.

Their rock not equal to ours.   Deut. 32 : 31.

Christ either received or rejected. Matt. 27 : 22.

The Rich Fool. Luke 12 : 20.

The Pharisee and the Publican. Luke 18 : 9-14.

What shall the harvest be? (For whatever a man soweth, that shall he also reap....) Gal. 6 : 7-9.

Sermon to erring women. Luke 5 : 32.

The Ten COMES of Scripture. (Ten texts.)

How to be saved. Acts 16 : 30.

The Resurrection of Christ. (No text.)

Jesus in Prophecy. (The testimony of Jesus is the spirit of prophecy....) Rev. 19 : 10.

Christ the Wonderful. Isa. 9 : 6.

Christ working for us, and we working for others. (Now our Lord Jesus Christ himself....stablish you in every good word and work. 2 Thes. 2 : 16-17.

Who are Christians? 1 John 3 : 14.

Instant salvation. (No text.)

Jesus and John the Baptist. Matt. 3 : 13.

The miracle of the Conversion of Saul of Tarsus. Acts 9 : 11.

Address to Reformed Men. (No text.)

The faith of Caleb and Joshua. (Let us go up at once and possess it ; for we are able to overcome it....) Num. 13 : 30.

Saved or Lost. (No text.)

Perseverance, or Be not weary in well doing. Gal. 6 : 9.

Life and Character of Jacob. (No text.)

Life and Character of Joshua. (No text.)

Life and Character of Ahab. (No text.)

Life and Character of Peter. (No text.)

God's love to the sinner. (No text.)

One thing thou lackest. Luke 18 : 22.

Christ in the Old Testament. (Several texts.)

Christ in the New Testament. (Several texts.)

Christ as a Shepherd. (Several texts.)

God's despised instruments. (But God hath chosen the foolish things of the world....) 1 Cor. 1 : 27.

Salvation, addressed to Women. (Several texts.)

The Second Coming of Christ. (Several texts.)

Farewell sermon : God able to keep the Converts. Rom. 14 : 4.

BIBLE READINGS.

I. The Divinity of Christ. 1st chap. of John.

Christ's Miracle at Cana. 2d chap. of John.

The New Birth. 3d chap. of John.
Christ the Water of Life. 4th chap. of John.
Christ the Physician. 5th chap of John.
Christ the Bread of Life. 6th chap. of John.
Christ the Fountain of Living Waters. 7th chap. of John.
II. Christ, His Divinity. 8th chap. of John.
Christ restoring the Blind. 9th chap. of John.
Christ the Good Shepherd. 10th chap. of John.
III. Christ, His Divinity. 11th chap. of John.
The Miracle wrought through Peter. Acts, 3d chap.
Confession the Key to Salvation. Rom., 10th chap.

SERMONS BY REV. JOHN NEWLAND MAFFITT.*

THEMES AND TEXTS.

Moses' Choice. Heb. 11 : 4-25.
Search the Scriptures. John 5 : 39.
The Sufferings of Christ. Matt. 26 : 38.
The Messiah's Reign. 1 Cor. 15 : 25.
Pure and undefiled religion. Jas. 1 : 27.
Jacob's Ladder. Gen. 2 : 17.
The Angel flying in the midst of heaven preaching the Gospel.
Rev. 14 : 6.
Paul's review of his conflicts. 2 Tim. 4 : 7.
Despisers that wonder and perish. Acts 13 : 41.
The fall of Nebuchadnezzar. Dan. 4 : 13, 14.
The Vision of the Dry Bones. Ezek. 37 : 4.
The Judgment Day. (No text.)

SERMONS BY REV. W. J. KNOX LITTLE, M.A.,

Rector of St. Alban's, Manchester, England.

Mr. Little, along with Canon Reynolds Hole, has been very active in preaching "missions." He excels as an extem-

---

* There are two other existing sermons of Mr. Maffitt—a fast day sermon from Isa. 5 : 4, 5; another entitled The Christian's Encouragement in the Way to the Heavenly Canaan, 1 Tim. 1 : 15. See *Methodist Preacher*, edited by D. Holmes, Auburn, N. Y., 1852.

porizer, and not a few of his sermons have been reported by phonographers. A considerable number of these have been revised by himself and published in volumes. The present list is derived from three books published in 1880 and 1881, entitled, "Characteristics and Motives of the Christian Life," Sermons Preached at Manchester; "The Mystery of the Passion of our Most Holy Redeemer."

THEMES AND TEXTS.

CHRISTIAN WORK.

I must work the work of him.... John 9 : 4.

1. The Nature of the Christian's Work.
2. The Solemnity of his Work.

THE CHRISTIAN ADVANCE.

If ye be risen with Christ. Col. 3 : 1.

CHRISTIAN WATCHING.

Watch therefore ; for ye know not what hour your Lord doth come. Matt. 24 : 42.

CHRISTIAN BATTLE.

Now therefore endure hardness as a good soldier of Jesus Christ. 2 Tim. 2 : 3.

CHRISTIAN SUFFERING.

To make the Captain of their salvation perfect through suffering. Heb. 2 : 10.

CHRISTIAN JOY.

Who for the joy that was set before him.... Heb. 12 : 2.

FOR THE SAKE OF JESUS.

Blessed are ye when men shall revile you.... Matt. 5 : 11.

THE CLAIMS OF CHRIST.

Come unto me, all ye that labor.... Matt. 11 : 28.

THE SOUL INSTRUCTED OF GOD.

Come now, and let us reason together. Isa. 1 : 18.

THE CLAIMS OF GOD UPON THE SOUL.

Behold, all souls are mine. Ezek. 17 : 4.

THE SUPERNATURAL POWERS OF THE SOUL.

What is man that thou art mindful of him....and hast crowned him with glory and honor. Ps. 8 : 4, 5.

THE SOUL IN THE WORLD AND AT THE JUDGMENT.

1 Cor. 7 : 31 ; Rom. 14 : 10.

THE LAW OF PREPARATION.

And at midnight there was a cry.... Matt. 25 : 6.

THE PRINCIPLE OF PREPARATION.

Thou desirest truth in the inward parts.... Ps. 51 : 6.

THE TEMPER OF PREPARATION.

While we were yet sinners, Christ died for us. Rom. 5 : 8.

THE ENERGY OF PREPARATION.

Seeing that ye look for such things, be diligent. 2 Pet. 3 : 14.

THE SOUL'S NEED AND GOD'S NATURE.

My soul thirsteth for God... Ps. 42 : 2.

SERMONS ON THE MYSTERY OF THE PASSION OF THE REDEEMER.

1. The Mystery of Humiliation. Phil. 2 : 7, 8.
2. The Mystery of Sorrow. Isa. 53 : 3.
3. The Mystery of Suffering. Phil. 3 : 10.
4. The Mystery of Sacrifice. 1 Pet. 1 : 18, 19.
5. The Mystery of Power. 1 Cor. 1 : 23, 24.
6. The Mystery of Death. 1 Cor. 15 : 3.
7. The Mystery of the Grave. 1 Cor. 1 : 3, 4.
8 The Mystery of Loyalty—The Master and Slave—Paul a slave of Jesus Christ. Rom. 1 : 1.
9. The Mystery of Peace. John 16 : 33.
10. The Revelation of the Mystery. Rev. 1 : 7.

———

SERMONS BY REV. JACOB KNAPP.

OUTLINES.

BALAAM'S PRAYER.

Let me die the death of the righteous.... Num. 23 : 10.

Introduction : Balaam's Character.

1. Some reasons why the death of the righteous is preferable to that of the wicked.

a. Because the sting of death is taken away from the hearts of the righteous, while it remains in the hearts of the wicked.

Illustrations : Payson and a Christian mother dying calmly and joy-fully. Contrasted with death of Voltaire, Hobbs, Thomas Paine.

b. Because angels will attend the dying bed of the one, while devils will wait at the bedside of the other.

c. Because the one is put in possession of his real treasures, while the other leaves all his fancied treasures behind.

d. The righteous will join their departed friends, while the wicked will be shut out from theirs.

e. The righteous will at death be delivered from their last enemy, but the wicked will be delivered into the power of their worst enemies.

f. The righteous will look forward to the morning of the resurrection with delight. Not so with the wicked ; they will regard that day with dark forebodings.

g. The desires of the one will be more than realized ; but the fears of the other will be exceeded by the evils that shall come upon them.

h. The one will cease from his labors ; the other will just commence his.

i. All the attainments of the good in this world have laid the foundation of future glory and blessedness ; but all the attainments of the wicked have only laid the foundation of eternal misery.

Inferences.

1. There are many who pray like Balaam, '' Let me die the death of the righteous,'' but die as the fool dieth.

2. If you would die the death of the righteous, you must be born again.

3. Thus will you live the life of the righteous.

THE NEW BIRTH.

Marvel not that I said unto thee, Ye must be born again. John 3 : 7.

Introduction from the context.

1. The necessity of the New Birth.

a. From positive Bible testimony.

(*υ*) There is a repetition in the context three times.

(*β*) '' Which were born not of the will of man... ''

(*γ*) '' Born from above....''

b. Man cannot be saved without it, while the government of God is maintained. Saul of Tarsus could not have been saved while persecuting the Church.

c. Without this change man cannot be pardoned.

d. Cannot see the Kingdom of God.

e. Cannot understand the language of Canaan.

f. Absolutely necessary for the enjoyment or Heaven.

2. How is regeneration produced ?

a. Not by a change of purpose.

b. Not by baptism.

c. But by the Holy Ghost.

d. Hence the work of sovereign grace.

Remarks.

1. The doctrine of the text is at the very foundation of the Gospel.

2. Seek this change without delay. Possibly God's mercy may bestow upon you this great blessing.

AGAINST INFIDELITY.

For the invisible ... Rom. 1 : 20.

1. The existence of a God proved.

a. From testimony. Certain kinds of testimony are of little value in this case.

(*a*) The testimony of a witness who has an interest in the matter pending is not considered good evidence. How much more difficult it is to lead a man to believe that slavery is a sin, that has $10,000 invested in slaves, than the man that has none. Hence the infidel is not a good witness.

(*β*) But we ought to admit good testimony. We daily receive testimony, and act on it. You date a letter 1838. This implies that Christ died so many years ago. But how do you know that? From testimony you celebrate the Fourth of July. Why? Because on that day, 1776, the Declaration of Independence was signed. How do you know that? Were you there?

b. This world either existed from all eternity, or else there was a point in that eternity when it was created.

c. Is it reasonable to suppose that this world came by *chance?* What would you say of the man who should say of this Church edifice, It did not owe its existence to an intelligent mind? You would say, He is either a fool, or he is insane. And you, infidel, who deny the existence of God Almighty, you are a fool ; for God says by David, " The fool hath said," etc.

d. We may argue the existence of God from the order of the planetary system. The sun is placed at the right distance from the earth, and other planets by which it is surrounded. If its relations were altered, it would produce infinite mischief. It would either burn us up or freeze us to death. Did blind chance arrange all this?

e. From the atmosphere which surrounds the earth.

f. From the marks of design in different species of animals—man, the bird, the bee, the ant.

g. From the Providence of God. But some man will say, These results are produced by the laws of Nature. Where did the laws of Nature come from?

h. Hear the confessions of infidels—Voltaire, Hobbs, Bolingbroke, Paine.

i. The testimony of Christians everywhere.

Remarks.

1. According to the Word of God, every infidel is a fool.

2. Those who deny the divinity of Christ are the same.

3. Universalism is next door to infidelity. The devil was the first Universalist preacher.

4. The Lord Jesus came to seek and to save the lost.

THE JUSTICE OF GOD IN THE DAMNATION OF THE SINNER.

Rom. 3 : 8.

Proof : 1. You have broken the law of God, and therefore you must suffer its penalty.

The character of the law of God : Contrast God's government with human governments. The more virtuous a community is, the more strict it will be in the maintenance of law and order. Justice demands the execution of the penalties of law. So the sinner is under the curse of God's law. The penalty is damnation.

2. God has made an atonement through the death of Christ, whereby salvation is offered to the sinner.

3. The sinner is guilty of rejecting this Gospel. Here is a man that to-night breaks open a store and steals $10,000. The officers arrest him ; he is tried, and convicted, and sent to the State Prison for seven years. Now, suppose the very man from whom he stole goes to work and draws up a petition to the Governor for his pardon, signs it, and goes round among his friends and obtains their names. He then goes to the prisoner and asks him to sign the petition. But he refuses his signature ; but the merchant perseveres ; he goes to the Governor to obtain a pardon ; the Governor signs it, and the merchant returns to the prison with the pardon in his hand, exclaiming, "I have been successful, here is the pardon, signed by the Governor !" He hands it to the prisoner. He coolly takes it in his hands and tears it in pieces, saying, "I wish you would mind your own business ; I can take care of myself" and stamps under his feet the pieces of the torn pardon. Now, what would you say of that man ?

4. Your damnation will be great because you have been guilty of rejecting God's provision for making you holy and happy forever.

Suppose a man a hundred miles away, surrounded by deep snow, and dying of starvation. The Governor hears of it, and despatches his son with provisions, and men to dig their way through the snow. After much exertion and fatigue, he reaches the cabin. What do they find ? The starving man has seen him coming, and barred and bolted the door and fastened the windows. The son tries every means to gain admission, but in vain. The starving man says, " I know who you are ; you are the Governor's son. I will not be indebted to you. I do not want your provision."

5. You have treated God's method of salvation with perfect contempt. Jesus says that there is only one way of salvation. Yet here is a man who tries to save himself by his own morality. See him building a ladder. He gives twenty-five cents to some poor person, or does some other act of kindness, which he regards as a round in his ladder. Thus he adds round to round, then he climbs up, and hopes in this way to get to heaven. At length he reaches the top of the ladder, and looks up ; but, to his dismay, finds an infinite distance between him and heaven. He sees the very lightnings of heaven writing his doom in the dark clouds. " He that climbeth up some other way, the same is a thief and a robber."

Another expects to go to hell and suffer for his sins. Well, suppose this were so. What would you do when you got to heaven ? You could not sing the new song which the Bible puts into the mouths of the redeemed. You have not been redeemed by the Lamb according to your theory. You have been redeemed by the fires of hell—burned out like an old pipe. Your proper song would be, " Glory to God who made hell. Glory to the flames of damnation, for they have purified my soul and made me happy forever."

But here is another ; he says he is going to be punished as he goes along through this life. His own conscience is punishment enough for him. Then all he has to do is to continue in sin, for the more he sins the less will his conscience trouble him.

6. This career of rebellion and refusal of mercy is unprovoked. What has God done that you should treat Him so ?

7. God has given you the day and the means of grace. Angels that rebelled were immediately cast down to hell, etc.

8. The terms are as easy as they can be.

IMMEDIATE CHOICE.

Choose you this day whom ye will serve. Joshua 24 : 15.

History of Joshua in the context.

Two classes in the world, saints and sinners.

Two masters, Christ and Satan.

Look at these two masters by way of contrast.

1. The Christian's Master is the Lord of all.

2. The sinner's master, the devil, is a created being.

3. Our Master is the origin of all light, natural and spiritual.

4. Your master is the origin of all evil, natural and moral.

5. Our Master feeds His people with the bread of life, and gives them unlimited happiness hereafter.

6. Your master deceives you, leads you into sin, and consequently into remorse an l misery.

7. All the promises held out by our Master are more than realized.

8. All the hopes raised by the devil end in disappointment.

9. Christ clothes His people with white robes, and puts crowns on their heads.

10. Your master, the devil, leads you in such a course that you are finally clothed with shame and everlasting contempt.

11. Christ comforts His people in a dying hour.

12. The devil leads you to that hour, and then either forsakes you or only remains to aid in exciting your fears of the wrath to come.

Remark.

God commands you to choose this day.

THE CHOICE OF MOSES.

Heb. 11 : 25.

Introduction : The biography of Moses.

1. The afflictions of Christians, which are peculiar to them. Let us look at some of the sources of these :

a. One source is the remaining depravity of the human heart.

b. Another is found in backsliders and hypocrites. Moses had more affliction from this source than all others.

c. The desolations of Zion.

d. The prevalence of crime.

e. The persecution of the wicked. The effect of persecution is the same in every age. Water thrown upon lime eighteen hundred years ago produced the same effect that it does to day. If you live godly in Christ Jesus, you must suffer persecution.

2. Notice the pleasures of sin.

There is pleasure in the amusements and fantastic joys of the world. Describe them. But God says that they are only for a season.

a. There is pleasure in riches, from the love of money and ambition to make it—but only for a season.

b. There is pleasure in the honors of the world—but only for a season.

c. There is a pleasure in propagating false doctrine—but it is only for a season.

3. Contrast the pleasures of sin and the afflictions of God's people.

a. The pleasures of sin tend to strengthen the malignant passions of the heart, while the afflictions of Christians tend, by God's grace, to wean them from the world.

b. The one tends to the extension of an aching void, while the other fills it with joy unspeakable.

c. The one quickens our pace toward heaven, while the other quickens our steps toward hell.

d. The one tends to make a happy death-bed, while the other makes a miserable one.

Remarks.

1. Which will you choose—the affliction of God's people, or the pleasures of sin?

2. Both you cannot have.

STRIVE TO ENTER IN AT THE STRAIT GATE.

Luke 13 : 24.

Introduction : An account of the context, illustrated by a case supposed. Suppose this assembly were met to discuss the question of universal salvation, and one half believed that doctrine, and the other half did not. Brother —— is appointed moderator. Now suppose that, after we had debated the question for an hour, all of a sudden the Lord Jesus Christ should appear in this pulpit, and the moderator should say, "The Lord Jesus is present, and we will submit this question to Him." All agree to this. He then asks, "Lord, are there few that be saved?" Jesus replies, "Strive," etc., verse 24. But up jumps one and says, "Lord, that does not satisfy me." Jesus replies by repeating verse 25.

"And yet, Lord," says another, "is it not written, As in Adam all die, so in Christ shall all be made alive?" Jesus replies by repeating verses 27 and 28.

But, says another, "I have taken the Universalist newspapers a long time, and they teach a different doctrine." Jesus answers by repeating Matt. 7 : 14, 15, 21.

Up jumps another, and says, "My father died in the full belief of universal salvation, and if he was mistaken I want proof of the fact in black and white." The Lord turns to him, and simply says, "These shall go away into everlasting punishment. He that believeth not shall not see life, but the wrath of God abideth on him."

1. What is this gate? Being born again. Every man is by nature in the broad road.

2. Why is this gate called strait?

a. Because every man, previous to his conversion, is in great distress of mind. Ask Saul of Tarsus ; ask all these Christians.

b. Because it will admit of nothing crooked. The hearts of sinners are like the hearts of those trees which are crooked. Take, for example, the man that overreaches, or that uses or sells rum, or makes merchandise of the souls and bodies of his fellow-men ; he cannot get within gunshot of this gate until he stops this business, which comes from the devil.

3. Why is it necessary to go through this gate?

a. Because there is no other way to heaven.

b. Because the sinner, if admitted, could not enjoy heaven without this change. Suppose there were two hundred warm-hearted Holy Ghost Christians on a steamboat which they have chartered to go to a certain place to pray and labor for the salvation of the people. As the boat is casting loose from the wharf, a man rushes on board with a carpet-bag in his hand. He enters the cabin, and finds the passengers either reading or engaged in conversation. He sits down by a table on which there is a backgammon board, and invites a gentleman to play with him. The man looks at him a moment with surprise, and then begins to preach Jesus unto him. Presently he hears a song of Zion from a group at the other end of the cabin, and then they begin to pray. Then the man by his side exclaims, "My dear sir, you are lost! You are out of Christ! Come, kneel down and pray for salvation," and so drops down by his side and begins to pray. The ungodly passenger now starts up, and thinks this is rather singular. Just then he hears the voice of song from one of the state-rooms. He walks toward the office, and is met by another, who says, "Brother, is your calling and election sure?" He breaks away, and rushes to the office and exclaims, "Captain, for God's sake, what kind of people have you on board?" "Why," says the captain, "I have some two hundred live Christians ; what shall I do ?" " Put me ashore at the first landing."

4. Why necessary for the sinners to strive or agonize to enter in ?

a. Because he has to go contrary to all his sinful passions.

b. Because his ungodly companions and associates will do all they can to prevent him from entering. Parents prevent children, husbands wives, etc.

c. Because he must break away from the strong grasp of the devil.

5. Why are many not " able" to enter?

a. One is not able because he cannot carry his riches through the gate.

b. Another cannot carry his honors through with him.

c. Yet another cannot carry with him his unlawful business.

6. Exhortation. " But he said, Lord, suffer me first to go bury my father." Luke 9 : 59.

NO MAN CARED FOR MY SOUL.

Ps. 142 : 4.

Introduction : Souls may be saved by the right use of means.

1. The worth of the soul.

a. The soul will continue to improve forever.

b. The righteous will grow more happy, and the wicked more miserable throughout eternity.

c. The value of the soul is proved by the price paid for it.

2. Contrast the care man takes for his soul and the souls of his fellow-men and the care he takes for worldly objects.

a. The solicitude manifested for riches.

b. Our care in educating our children.

c. A great many little things—dress, honors, business.

d. Anxiety for human life. Describe a child lost.

e. Contrast our care for souls and Christ's care. Paul. Primitive Christians. Luther, Whitefield, Edwards.

f. Contrast our care now with what it was once.

3. Some few things which show that this care does not exist.

a. If you do not statedly observe secret prayer.

b. If your souls are not burdened with the souls of others.

c. If you neglect family prayer.

d. If you do not attend prayer-meetings.

Remarks.

The great responsibility resting on every Christian.

AGREE WITH THINE ADVERSARY.

Matt. 5 : 25, 26.

An account of the context. God is the adversary of every impenitent sinner. There is a rebellion against His government and He is bound to put it down. Now to the law and to the testimony : "The carnal mind," etc. "God is angry with the wicked every day." "As though God did beseech you by us, be ye reconciled," etc. Impenitent men know that they are in opposition to God's Word.

1. Notice what you must agree to, if you would effect a settlement or reconciliation with God.

a. You must agree that God is right, and you entirely wrong in this controversy.

b. You must agree that if God's charges against you are true, that you deserve damnation.

(*a*). God charges you with hating Him.

(*b*). With rebellion.

c. You must agree to surrender unconditionally.

d. You must agree to renounce the world, the flesh, and the devil.

e. You must agree to be saved by sovereign grace alone.

2. Notice when you are to agree with thine adversary—quickly, "while thou art in the way with him." Why?

a. Because you are certain of losing your case.

b. Because you will have no witnesses.

c. No advocate.

3. Now, because it may be that to-day thou art in the way with him.

SAUL'S CONVERSION.

And he said, Who art thou, Lord? Acts 9 : 5.

Introduction : Saul's conversion narrated. The devil had to pay Paul's passage to Rome ; God had some work for him to do there. The disciples were poor, and God compelled the wicked to carry him to Rome. Sinners are good for nothing in all God's universe, but to serve God and fulfil His purposes.

1. Some of the obstructions God puts in the way of sinners.

a. That which arises from the voice of nature.

b. His Holy Word.

c. A preached Gospel.

d. The admonition of faithful Christians.

e. The prayers of God's people.

f. The sickness and death of friends.

g. Threatening danger by the bellowing thunders and the forked lightnings of God in a storm.

h. The strivings of the Holy Spirit.

2. Notice some of the ways in which sinners kick against the goads.

a. While you attempt to conceal your feelings.

b. While giving yourself to the amusments of the world.

c. By clinging to some form of error.

d. By keeping away from the people of God.

Remarks.

1. It costs a man more to go to hell than to go to heaven.

2. God will be just in the eternal damnation of your soul.

3. Those who oppose God until death claims them will find it hard to kick against the spikes.

HOW TO SEEK GOD.

The wicked, through the pride of his countenance...., Ps. 10 : 4.

The word countenance is supposed to represent the moral character of the sinner. At all events, I shall take it for the present in that sense.

Now, understand that God must be sought, or the soul damned.   No two ways about this.   "Seek ye the Lord," etc.

How God must be sought.

a. Diligently, as the woman in the parable swept the house for the lost piece of silver.   Diligence in worldly business.

b. Boldly.   Blind Bartimeus.   He did not study his prayers.   Was not afraid of noise, but boldly pressed his cry.   Some of you would like to have religion softly, others covertly ; but I tell you, Jesus Christ will have the open avowal, or you will be damned.   No corners in God's kingdom to creep into.   No secret hopes or concealed religion.

c. Timely.   There is a special time.

d. Perseveringly.   Woman with the bloody issue.   If your only son were lost in a dense forest, would you stop to hear the birds sing their sweet songs ?   The sinner is cross-grained ; the grains run one way *inside*, and the other way *outside*.

If you could buy religion, you would have it before morning.   But being what you are, if you went to heaven, you would not stay there, unless God locked you in ; you would be out of your element.

You say that you do not like to seek religion in a time of excitement.   Ah ! yes, you have had a calm time the most of your days, but you did not go to Christ then.   The truth is, you do not want it at all—this is the difficulty.   The devil lost three thousand souls during the first protracted meeting after the Ascension.

e. You must seek God penitently.   This point illustrated by examples in the New Testament.   Exhortation to seek God *now*.

WHY THE WICKED LIVE.

Their foot shall sl'de in due time.   Deut. 32 : 35.

The Psalmist saw the wicked standing on slippery places.   The position of mankind.   All standing on a plain—all moving on together.   At the head of this plain all is beautiful and delightful.   Fields, flowers, etc.   But at the foot rolls a lake of fire.   And those who do not seek the bower above will slide in due time.   The Lord Jesus has entered this plain, and will save, etc.

What is meant by "due time."   There is a seeming delay.   Why ?

1. That the wheat may not be rooted up with the tares.

2. To give time and space for repentance.   Barren fig-tree.

3. To test character.

4. To show the long-suffering of God in Christ.   Not slack concerning his promises.   Days of Noah.

5. For the benefit of the righteous.   Uses the wicked as a furnace. Illustration : a man ascending Mt. Blanc.*

SINNERS HARDENING THEMSELVES AGAINST GOD.

Job 9: 4.

It is strange that man should contend with God ; strange that he should stir up Leviathan.

1. Notice some of the ways in which men harden themselves against God.

a. It is the effect of sin.   The pirate once a different man.

b. By setting up the same plea that Adam did.   I did not make sin.

c. Some contend with God when He takes away their friends, their health, or their money.

d. Others, when they complain of the law of God as too strict.

e. When we neglect the plan of salvation and depend on our morality.   This insults God.

f. Others say, We are going to heaven : perhaps first to hell, then to heaven. The Deluge and its lessons.

g. Again, many find fault with plain, pointed preaching.   But they do not like the truth ; they harden themselves against God.

h. Some do this by violating resolutions and promises.

i. Others by neglecting the means of grace.

2. Now, who that has done this has prospered ?

a. Did the rebel angels ?

b. Did Adam prosper ?

c. Did Cain ?

d. Antediluvians ?

e. City of Sodom ?

f. Pharaoh ?

g. Saul of Tarsus ?

h. The Jews ?

i. Ananias and his wife ?

j. Who has prospered ?

THEMES AND TEXTS.

The calls of the Gospel (the Hen Sermon).   Matt. 23 : 37.
The New Birth (two texts).   Ezek. 18 : 31 ; Ps. 51 : 10.
The Ox Sermon.   Isa. 1 : 3.
Enthusiasm.†   Acts 26 : 24.

* This sermon has been published in full with his Autobiography.
† This and the three preceding sermons are published in his Autobiography.

SERMONS BY HALSEY W. KNAPP, D.D.

OUTLINES.

HALTING BETWEEN TWO OPINIONS.

1 Kings 18 : 21.

Elijah addressed double-minded men—some for God, some for Baal ; some for both.

1. Describe this class.

a. They live between two thoughts—God and the world ; righteousness and sin ; salvation and damnation.

b. They live two lives—outwardly Christian, practically worldlings ; sometimes very warm, then very cold ; religious at one moment, devilish the next.

c. They live between two fears—God's penalty and the world's frown ; the soul's loss, the loss of Heaven.

2. The folly of halting between two opinions.

a. You are not deceiving God.

b. You are not deceiving the devil.

c. You are simply deceiving yourself.

3. How long will you continue the controversy?

a. What does reason say ? " If God be God, serve him," etc.

b. What does your soul say ? " Save me ; save me."

c. What does God say ? " To day, if ye will hear," " Look unto me," etc.

THE GOD THAT ANSWERETH BY FIRE.

1 Kings 18 : 24.

1. God has manifested Himself by fire before. A flaming sword in Eden ; a rain of fire upon Sodom ; the fire on Mt. Sinai ; fire from the Lord destroyed Korah. . . . Elijah knew this : hence his appeal.

2. What Elijah did to secure the result.

a. He firmly believed that God would vindicate Himself.

b. He laid every obstacle to the miracle upon and around the altar ; water on and around the sacrifice.

c. He called on God in believing prayer (verses 36, 37), and the fire came.

3. God will answer by prayer *now.*

a. He will quicken His people by the Holy Spirit ; warm them ; inspire them ; enthuse them.

b. He will send burning arrows of conviction.

c. He will give a baptism of the Holy Spirit.

Conclusion : God requires our firm faith ; our entire consecration ; our active co-operation.

THE CLOUD AS A MAN'S HAND.

1 Kings 18 : 44.

Theme : The beginnings of a work of grace.

1. It begins in the heart of God's people. Felt before seen in the soul, in the closet, in prayer ; a deep conviction.

2. It manifests itself in a solemn interest among the unsaved. Men begin to think—to hear the Word—to lose their taste for the world—to think on God and salvation.

3. Conversions follow, but with feeble experiences. Converts are feeble when the Church is weak.

4. But as we take hold on God, the cloud enlarges and gives rain.

WHAT DOEST THOU HERE, ELIJAH ?

1 Kings 19 : 19.

1. Elijah was where the Lord did not want him.

2. Elijah was where the Lord could not bless him.

3. Elijah compelled God's rebuke.

THE PRICE IN THE HAND OF A FOOL TO GET WISDOM.

Prov. 17 : 16.

We have here two facts stated, and an interrogation.

1. *First Fact :* that wisdom is within the reach of man.

a. We have God's revelation concerning true wisdom.

b. We have intellectual ability to consider this question.

c. We have divine grace to help us.

d. We have time and opportunity to secure it.

2. *Second Fact :* that men have no heart to secure this wisdom.

a. Their heart-treasure is elsewhere.

b. The subject is entirely distasteful.

c. The need seems not a present one, but entirely a future one.

3. *The Interrogation :* Why has God put this price into the hand of those who will not use it ?

a. Because he loves man.

b. Because he would save man.

c. That every mouth may be silent in final condemnation.

STRIVING WITH OUR MAKER.

Isa. 45 : 9.

Theme : The sin and folly of contending with God about His plan for our salvation.

1. When do men contend with God?

a. When He interferes with their social and secular affairs.

b. When the Gospel comes home to them.

c. When convicted of their sins.

d. When they see that faith in Christ is their only hope.

2. The folly and sin of their course.

a. The folly :

(*a*) You cannot prevail over God's will.

(*β*) You only add to your sorrow.

b. The sin :

(*a*) You are trampling on the blood of redemption.

(*β*) You are sealing your own doom.

THE MEANS TO SECURE SALVATION.

Isa. 55 : 2.

What are these means?

1. God must be heard.

a. To enlighten—to convince—to draw.

b. He must be heard attentively and anxiously.

2. God must be approached.

a. In order to do this you must abandon sin.

b. You must come as you are.

c. You must come by the Lord Jesus.

d. You must come in faith.

3. God will bless.

a. Your soul shall live.

b. Guilt and condemnation shall be taken away.

c. Pardon will be vouchsafed.

d. God declares this ; will you prove it?

SEEKING THE LORD WHILE HE MAY BE FOUND.

Isa. 55 : 6.

1. We are to seek God.

2. The time to seek Him is while He may be found.

THE WARNING OF THE TRUMPET UNHEEDED.

Ezek. 33: 5.

1. A time of peril.

2. A warning trumpet.

3. The alarm despised.

4. A doom pronounced.

GOD'S METHOD OF REVEALING HIS BLESSINGS TO HIS PEOPLE.

Hosea 10: 12.

1. What will be the effect of seeking the Lord ?

a. We shall be restored to His favor and fellowship.

b. We shall have full possession of divine grace.

c. We shall have an enduring and conquering faith.

2. We are to seek Him until He come.

a. If it take your life-time, give it.

b. You will know that He has come by the blessing conferred. Then only can you be truly of service to Him.

GOD DELIGHTS IN MERCY.

Micah 7 : 18.

1. Why God's anger is turned away from men.

a. Not because it exhausts itself.

b. Not because men cannot help sinning.

c. Not for any penalty that men may endure.

d. But because of the propitiation that His mercy has provided.

2. Wherein God's mercy is still manifest to us.

a. In preserving our lives in spite of our rebellion.

b. In repeated calls to salvation.

c. In the opportunities of this hour.

THE LABORERS ARE FEW.

Matt. 9 : 37.

1. All Christians are not laborers. Some are idle or careless or unwilling.

2. All willing to work are not qualified.

3. The Lord requires of laborers those things which but few possess.

a. Heartfelt piety before God.

b. Willingness to sacrifice self.

c. Compassion for souls.

d. Power with God in prayer.

e. Dependence on the Holy Spirit.

f. Strong faith.

THE PEARL OF GREAT PRICE.

1. This man was seeking pearls.

a. How to free himself from sin.

b. How to come before God.

c. How to obtain salvation.

2. The man discovered a pearl of great price.

a. He knew where it was.

b. He knew what it was.

c. He knew what it could do.

3. To possess this great pearl required a great sacrifice.

a. To be of benefit to him, he must possess it.

b. To possess it, he must part with all he had.

c. He did this, and the pearl was his.

CHRISTIAN FAITH CAN BE SEEN.

Mark 2 : 5.

What is faith? What its manifestation?

1. Christian faith can be seen.

a. Seen laying hold of the helpless.

b. Seen carrying them to Jesus.

c. Leaving them with Jesus.

2. Christian faith will be rewarded.

a. As it honors Christ, He will honor us.

b. The object sought will be gained.

c. Your faith will be strengthened by exercise.

d. One victory of faith will assure it of many.

Conclusion.

1. What has your faith done for you?

2. What has it done for Jesus and men in this field.

I WILL ARISE AND GO TO MY FATHER.

Luke 15 : 18.

1. There is an awakened consciousness of moral destitution.

2. An energetic determination to escape from destruction.

3. The right and only course to secure freedom and salvation.

DIVINE TESTIMONY AND HUMAN INSTRUMENTALITY IN CONVERSION.

John 4 : 42.

What Jesus saw, knew, and said.   John 5 : 6.

Without me ye can do nothing.   John 15 : 5.

Pentecost the beginning of revival power.   Acts 2 : 37.

Fellowship with devils.   1 Cor. 10 : 20.

Almost persuaded.   Acts 26 : 28.

Who gave Himself for our sins.   Gal. 1 : 4.

The enemies of the cross of Christ.   Philip. 3 : 18.

For all men have not faith.   2 Thess. 3 : 2.

Hearing God's voice to-day.   Heb. 3 : 7–8.

Falling into the hands of the living God.   Heb. 10 : 31.

Going forth to Christ without the camp.   Heb. 13 : 13.

How is it that ye have no faith?   Mark 4 : 40.

Confessing Christ at home.   Mark 5 : 19.

SERMONS BY REV. E. N. KIRK.

OUTLINE.

MAN'S NATURAL ENMITY TO GOD.

Rom. 8 : 7.

The introduction defines the " enmity" negatively and positively.
Proof of the declaration of the text.

1. Man hates the character of God as a Lawgiver.
2. Man hates the sovereignty of God.
3. The carnal mind hates the mercy of God.

Remarks.

1. The supreme love of the creature is a dreadful evil.
a. It makes it impossible to enter heaven.
b. It arrays us against the will of God, and exposes us to His condemnation.
2. Regeneration is necessary to salvation.
3. The carnal mind must be put away.   But where must we begin ?
At the cross of Christ ; renounce the world, and cast thyself on Christ.
4. The conquest of the carnal mind is not the work of a moment ;
it is the labor of life. · But there must be a moment in which it
begins ; that moment should be *now.*   There is a spot of earth where
you should give yourself for healing into the hands of the great Physician ; that spot you occupy *now.*

THEMES AND TEXTS.

Sermon to Children.   Ps. 24 : 11.
Agreement with God.   Amos 3 : 3.
ADDRESSES TO PROMOTE THE REVIVAL OF RELIGION.
1. The Philosophy of Revivals.
2. The Lord's controversy with His people.
3. The Desirableness of Prayer for the Outpouring of the Spirit.
4. Address on the Origin of Foreign Missions.

A SERMON BY F. W. KRUMMACHER, D.D.

OUTLINE.

Canticles 2 : 12.

1. *Take a nearer view of the Turtle Dove.*

As the Son of God chooses the lamb for his symbol, so the Holy Spirit selects the dove for His.

a. In order to discover the full meaning of the symbol, take Sacred History as your guide. Three times does it present this image.

(α) The Spirit of God moved (literally rendered, brooded) upon the face of the void and formless deep. The Spirit is here compared to a bird (beyond a doubt the dove) with her wings expanded as if brooding on her eggs.

(β) Again she moves over the waters—those of the deluge.

(γ) Once more she moves over the waters—those of Jordan.

b. Why was the dove chosen as the symbol of the Holy Ghost?

(α) The dove is a tender and faithful bird, hence an emblem of constant love.

(β) Of all birds, the dove is the most clean and delicate. In filthy places she will not abide at rest.

(γ) The dove is gentle.

(δ) As the Spirit like a dove brooded upon the face of the waters at the Creation, so the Holy Spirit is the life-giving, formative, and beautifying power in the new creation.

(ε) As the dove of Noah was the wished-for messenger of peace and joy, so the Holy Spirit assures us of mercy, reconciliation, and causes rejoicing and rest.

(ζ) As the olive branch is a symbol of honor, and Noah a type of Christ, so the Holy Spirit crowns Jesus Lord of All, and glorifies Him.

2. *Listen to its voice in the land.*

a. Her notes are wonderful and enchanting.

b. This Turtle Dove has always been heard, in gentle strains at least, in some part of the world. Scripture history cited in proof.

c. She is also heard in the land of our hearts.

d. Her melodious voice reverberates from our hearts in confessions, exhortations, in prayer and praises. True, the raven voice of the old man sometimes tries to imitate the voice of the dove. But there is a difference between "Shibboleth" and "Sibboleth" to the ear of those who hold the ford of Jordan. The apparent trifle marks the friendly Gileadite from the rebellious Ephraimite.

e. The Dove speaks through the children of God, but not always in the same notes. Sometimes its strains are sorrowful or complaining, sometimes joyful or persuasive.

f. The Turtle Dove is heard in *our* land. God be praised, a period has already dawned in which these words have a delightful application to the land in which we dwell. The drooping and expiring Church of Christ begins to revive and put forth blossoms.

SERMONS BY REV. S. REYNOLDS HOLE,

Canon of Lincoln. *

THEMES AND TEXTS.

The Warnings of God. (Knowing, therefore, the terrors of the Lord....) 2 Cor. 5 : 11.

The Lord's Beacons of War and Victory. Isa. 30 : 17.

Sleeping and Waking. Eph. 5 : 14.

The History of the Prodigal. Luke 15 : 11–24.

How the slave of sin may become free. (That thou shouldest receive him forever.) Philemon 15.

The Covetousness of Balaam. Num. 31 : 8.

The ten following sermons were preached at the Manchester, Reading, and Grimsby Missions :

The Missioner's Motive. (His spirit was stirred....) Acts 17 : 16.

The Missioner's Message. (Therefore disputed he....) Acts 17 : 17.

The Missioner's Difficulties : Unbelief. Acts 17 : 32.

The Missioner's Difficulties : Excuses. Acts 17 : 32.

The Missioner's Difficulties : Fatal Delay. Acts 17 : 33.

The Missioner's Hopes : of a true Repentance. Acts 17 : 34.

The Missioner's Hopes : of a dutiful Repentance. Micah 6 : 8.

---

* These subjects are given from a volume of his, entitled "Hints to Preachers, illustrated by Sermons and Addresses," Parker & Co., Oxford, 1881. The volume is dedicated to Right Hon. W. E. Gladstone. Mr. H., with Mr. Knox Little and others, is doing the work of "Missioners" in the Anglican parishes. The book gives one a good idea of this new and significant movement.

The Missioner's Hopes : of a Charitable Repentance. (We are verily guilty concerning our brother....) Gen. 42 : 21.

The Missioner's Hopes : of a Generous, Prayerful, Self-denying Repentance (on the duties of Almsgiving, Prayer, and Fasting). Matt. 6 : 2, 6, 17.

The Missioner's Hopes : of increasing the number of True Worshippers. (And Abraham said unto his young men, Abide ye here with the ass, and I and the lad will go yonder....) Gen. 22 : 5.

SERMONS BY HEMAN HUMPHREY, D.D.

THEMES AND TEXTS.

Prepare the Way of the Lord. Isa. 40 : 3.

O Lord, revive thy Work. Heb. 3 : 2.

O Lord, increase our faith. Luke 17 : 5.

Take up the stumbling-blocks out of the way. Isa. 57 : 14.

Waiting for the Saviour's Return. Luke 8 : 40.

Come down ere my child die. John 4 : 49.

And he did not many mighty works there, because of their unbelief. Matt. 13 : 58.

Sirs, what must I do to be saved ? Acts 16 : 30.

Come unto me, and I will give you rest. Matt. 11 : 28.

The carnal mind is enmity against God. Rom. 8 : 7.

Strive to enter in at the strait gate. Luke 13 : 24.

She was nothing bettered, but rather grew worse. Mark 5 : 26.

Go thy way for this time : when I have a convenient season.... Acts 24 : 25.

Almost thou persuadest me to be a Christian. Acts 26 : 28.

Commune with your own heart, and be still. Ps. 4 : 4.

Quench not the Spirit. 1 Thes. 5 : 19.

The Wiles of the Devil (to young converts). Eph. 6 : 11.

He that endureth to the end shall be saved (to young converts). Matt. 10 : 22.

SERMONS BY EDWARD D. GRIFFIN, D.D.

OUTLINES.

JESUS OF NAZARETH PASSING BY.

Matt. 20 : 29–34.

The historical incidents of the miracle.

The bodily cures wrought by Christ were designed to announce him to the world as the Great Physician of the soul, and to teach sinners how to apply to Him for healing. I am therefore authorized to employ this piece of history for such a purpose.

1. It was necessary for the blind man to be by the wayside *while* Jesus was passing by. So anxious sinners should attend to the means of grace.

2. It was not enough for these men to sit *idly* by the wayside without faith and without application to Him.

3. These unhappy men, knowing themselves to be wholly unworthy of the Saviour's notice, *made no demands*, but only sued for mercy.

4. In the *earnestness* of these men we see an opportunity for us.

5. *Nor could they be silenced* by the frowns of the multitude.

6. The *difference* between the conduct of our Saviour and that of the multitude.

7. The blind men asked Jesus, not for riches or honors, but for sight.

8. They were not denied.

9. Some one that is spiritually blind will say, O that I had lived in that day, or, O that it were as easy to find relief now. Jesus of Nazareth is present now, and is now ready to afford relief.

10. It was the last time that Jesus ever passed that way before He left the world.

THE BRAZEN SERPENT.

John 3 : 14, 15.

Introduction : An account of the Brazen Serpent.

Let us trace the resemblance between this type and the antitype.

1. It was provided for people in a condition somewhat resembling that of the race to whom the Saviour was sent.

2. The Brazen Serpent had the *form* of the fiery serpents, but not their poison. So Christ came in the likeness of sinful flesh, etc.

3. The bite of the serpents must be cured by the *lifting up*, not of an eagle, but of a *serpent*. So Christ must take upon Himself, not

"the nature of angels," but the seed of Abraham. It must be the Son of *man* that is *lifted up* to atone for the sins of man.

4. The serpent being erected in full view of the camp, the people, when bitten, had only to *fix their eyes* upon it in order to live. So sinners are to fix a believing eye on the crucified Saviour.

5. On what *easy terms* might the poor distressed Hebrews live. They had not to search the world for physicians.

6. And in this way *must* man be pardoned, if pardoned at all.

THE FRUITLESS FIG TREE.

Luke 13 : 6-8.

(Parable explained by way of introduction.)

1. Men are placed in this world for no other end than to bring forth fruit to God.

2. God has an absolute right to all the fruit we can bear, just as the owner of a vineyard has a right to all the grapes it brings forth.

3. God has appointed one to dress His vineyard.

4. God attentively watches to see whether His vineyard be fruitful or not.

5. There are some trees in God's vineyard on which, when He comes, year after year, seeking fruit, He finds none.

6. Such trees the Lord, weary of waiting, would cast down, did not the Mediator step in and plead, "Spare it a little longer."

7. The trial is short, and precisely limited. The request was, "Let it alone this year."

Subject Applied.

a. To any present who have resisted the calls of God all their days, and are now exercised with affliction.

b. Are there any present under the special calls of the Spirit?

c. Are there any present who in former revivals were unmoved or mockers, but are now awakened?

d. Are there here any who were formerly awakened, and then returned to insensibility, but are now awakened again.

e. Those who were formerly awakened but cannot now be moved by all that is passing before ther eyes.

f. Those who were unmoved in former revivals, and remain unmoved in this.

g. Such as have an uncertain hope without acknowledging Christ before the world.

h. Are there present any unfruitful professors?

i. Finally, all who are out of Christ, and have not passed their last trial.

EXCUSES.

And they all with one consent began to make excuse. Luke 14 : 18.

Parable described.   It presents these three ideas :

1. That all rejecters of the Gospel are prone to make excuses.

2. That in the view of God these excuses are frivolous.

3. That they arise from aversion to the Gospel and an unwillingness to bear the blame of rejecting it.

From what has been said—

a. We see the wickedness, the folly, and the bad reflex influence of all these excuses.

b. We see that the unconverted are in a most guilty, forlorn, and dangerous state.

c. Let impenitent hearers never make another excuse.

d. Here then you stand, without one excuse for rejecting the Gospel another moment.

RETURNING FROM THE CRUCIFIXION.

Luke 23 47, 48.

Five kinds of people at the cross described.

Lessons : 1. A sudden discovery of the claims of Christ connected with a sense of having rejected and crucified Him, will cause men to tremble and smite their breasts.

2. There are some whom no wonders can subdue or convince.

ABRAHAM'S STEWARD.

Gen. 24 : 49.

Historical introduction.   Let us apply this piece of history to illustrate Gospel truth.

The marriage of Isaac and Rebekah may be considered as an emblem of the union of Christ and believers.   The embassy of Abraham's steward may also illustrate the work of Gospel ministers. These ought to imitate the frank and honest zeal of Eleazer, saying to sinners, "And now, if ye will deal kindly," etc.

Jesus asks sincere love   Had Rebekah feigned consent, but married another, she would not have dealt " kindly and truly."

But you who are not wedded to Christ will have many objections to all this.   And that these objections may appear in all their strangeness, let us put them into the mouth of Rebekah on the occasion before us.

a. Suppose her to say, " You describe indeed the attractions of the country and the virtues of your master ; but I have never seen either" *b.* Suppose her further to object : " How shall I forsake the favorite walks of my youth, my relatives, my dearest friends?"......

c. "Ay,' she replies ; " you say I shall never wish to return, and this is the very reason why I am unwilling to go"......

d. Suppose her still to object. " The way is long and obstructed by rivers and sandy deserts, and exposed to robbers and savage beasts"......

e. Do I hear her say, " I fear I shall grow weary of the way, and have longings after home, and to return, and be a derision to my acquaintance"......

f. But I hear her say, " I am unworthy of so great and good a man, and it is impossible that he is sincere."

g. None of these objections did Rebekah make. The duty and the interest of Rebekah are here amplified. " But greater reasons urge you to an alliance with the spiritual Isaac."

(α) I come to espouse you to Christ. It is your duty, etc.

(β) Great are the pains he has taken to obtain you.

(γ) I come in the name of a Master who will not brook delay.

WHERE IS THE LORD GOD OF ELIJAH ?

2 Kings 2 : 14.

This inquiry Elisha made when he smote the waters of Jordan with Elijah's mantle and opened a passage for himself to return on dry ground. We may *suppose* that he made the same inquiry when he wrought all his other miracles.

The particular point in which I wish to view the prophet as inquiring for the Lord God of Elijah is in the act of raising the son of the Shunammite.

a. Our dear children are dead. Many parents among us have not a living child in the world : all are spiritually dead.

b. To whom can we apply ? Only to the Lord God of Elijah.

c. When Elisha smote the waters of Jordan and cried, " Where," etc. he looked back on a season of divine wonders. So may we while making the same appeal. Accounts of former and recent revivals.

d. Where is the Lord God of all revivals ?

THE DOVE.

Gen. 8 : 8, 9.

The pigeon or dove is held up in Scripture as an emblem of the Church.... The dove may also be considered as the emblem of the Christian. I employ the text, not in its original historic sense, nor in a typical import, but as an illustration of the wanderings of Christians, their uneasiness in their absence from the Church, and their glad return.

1. The dove wandered from the ark ; and Christians, alas, are too prone to wander from Christ.

2. It was not without an *object* that the dove left the ark ; she went to seek *another rest.*

3. " But the dove found no rest for the sole of her foot."

4. The dove at length returned, forced back by the prevalence of the waters.

5. When the dove returned and mourned at the window, did the patriarch shut the heart of his compassion against her ?

THE HEART OF GOD AFFECTED BY PRAYER.

Gen. 32 : 28.

Jacob's importunity and its success.

a. The Scriptures of the Old Testament speak of God as really affected by prayer.

b. Christ teaches us that our Heavenly Father is as truly affected by our prayers as parents are by the petitions of their children.

c. " But is not God unchangeable ?"

d. A motive to *union* in prayer. If Jacob *alone* was invincible, etc.

TOKENS OF PERDITION.

Now learn ye the parable of the fig tree.... Matt. 24 : 32, 33.

1. The first token of perdition which I shall mention is vicious habits.

2. Infidelity or universalism.

3. A false hope and a false profession.

4. The approach of age without religion.

5. A state of carnal security.

6. A satisfaction with worldly good.

7. A presumptuous confidence in God's mercy.

8. Profanation of the Sabbath and a neglect of the means of grace.

9. A contention against the truth and a demand for smooth prophesyings.

10. The rejection of many calls.

In many instances these tokens cluster. . Half a dozen may be found on the same man ; all may be found on some.

THE HEATH IN THE DESERT, OR STUNTED AND DWARFISH SOULS.

Jer. 18 : 5, 6.

1. Ascertain those against whom this curse is denounced.

a. The worldly who are prayerless and practically atheistic.

b. Those who put their sole trust in means and instruments.

c. Such as cherish false hopes.

2. Show how these resemble the heath in the desert.

a. In their barrenness.

b. In their unblest and forsaken solitariness.

c. In their ignorance and ingratitude concerning "good."

d. In the growth of more of these fruitless and misshapen shrubs when showers come.

e. In their danger of being abandoned to hopeless desolation.

Application addressed to the three classes described in the first part of the sermon.

THE BAND THAT TOOK CHRIST.

John 18 : 6.

The betrayal of our Saviour described.

This piece of history suggests several reflections.

1. The power of Christ and the discoveries of Him to bring down to the ground the stoutest sinner.

2. There are hearts so obstinate that nothing can reclaim them.

3. The strongest impressions may soon pass off and leave nothing but increased stupidity and hardness of heart.

4. If there was so much power and majesty in the voice of Christ, in one of His lowest acts of humiliation, what majesty and power will attend His voice when he shall come in the glory of His Father with the holy angels ?

SERMONS BY REV. A. GRATTAN GUINNESS.

OUTLINES.

REFUGES OF LIES.

Isa. 28 : 17.

An anecdote by way of introduction. A man takes refuge from a storm of wind and hail in a hut upon a barren moor. The wind unroofs it, the man flees from the place affrighted, but is overtaken by lightning and falls dead.

Many thousands are taking refuge from the threatenings of God's wrath beneath the lies of the Evil One.

1. Some say, "I believe in election."

2. Others say "I trust in the mercy of God."

3. Another says, "I do the best I can."

4. Some flatter themselves that they do believe in Christ, when they do not. They do not believe that Jesus is *their own Saviour.*

5. " I must wait God's time."

6. " There is time enough yet."

THE PRODIGAL SON.

Luke 15 : 20.

The parable illustrated by a free rehearsal. Next, its application to wandering and returning sinners.

1. See by this parable how Christ sets forth the sinner as forsaking God.

2. Behold the sinner wasting his substance in riotous living, spending all, and beginning to be in want.

3. See how Christ sets forth the sinner as reduced to servitude and degradation.

4. The sinner coming to himself.

5. The sinner's return to God, and the blessed reception God gives him.

CHRIST PRE-EMINENT.

Col. 1 : 18.

1. Christ is the first.

2. He is the mightiest.

3. The richest.

4. The highest.

5. The loveliest.

6. And the last.

WELCOME TO JESUS.

John 6 : 37.

I wish to speak to you about two things.

1. About coming to Christ—" Him that cometh to me."

2. About the certainty of being received—" I will in no wise cast out."

THE WOMAN OF SAMARIA.

John 4 : 26.

1. How Christ revealed the sinner to herself.

2. How Christ revealed Himself to the sinner.

SIN FORGIVEN AND FORGOTTEN.

Isa. 43 : 25.

In setting precious stones the jeweller often spreads beneath them a dark substance in order to throw out and heighten their brilliancy. So the Lord, in setting this promise, has spread beneath it the blackness of our sins. Read from the 22d verse of this chapter : " But thou hast not called upon me, O Jacob," etc. In meditating on this subject we shall divide the subject into four parts.

1. Free grace blots out our transgressions *from God's book.*

2. Free grace blots out our transgressions *with God's hand.*

3. Free grace blots out our transgressions *for God's sake.*

4. Free grace blots out our transgressions, not only from God's book, with God's hand, and for God's sake, *but from God's memory.*

THE GREEN TREE AND THE DRY.

Luke 23 : 31.

Introduction expository.

1. The glory and destruction of the green tree.

Look first at the natural tree and then at the Saviour, who is represented by it.

a. Out of a barren wilderness sprang up a tree, young, tall, and fair. Christ is that tree of God. He grew out of barren ground, etc.

b. Look at this green tree. How beautiful it is ; it has no twisted branches ; there are no worm-eaten or withered leaves, no weather-beaten blossoms, no bitter or rotten fruit. Behold here a faint picture of Jesus. His birth was as pure as the creation of an angel, His childhood was as spotless as sunshine, etc.

c. Mark the goodness of the green tree. It casts a cool shadow at noontide, etc. So Christ was a refuge, a medicine.

d. A description of the destruction of the green tree as a similitude of the death of Christ.

2 The shame and ruin of the dry tree.

a. Look at that dry tree. It is spring, but not a leaf appears upon it. *Sinner ! thou art that dry tree.*

b. When the summer comes, the dry tree, though surrounded with living trees, remains still dry and dead.

c. When the autumn comes, and other trees round about bear golden fruit, it is fruitless.

d. Each rising sun shines upon it, but finds it more decayed than it was the day before. *Sinner ! thou art that dry tree.*

e. Look again. The dry tree is a nest of reptiles ; lift up the bark and behold the things that crawl beneath. *Sinner! thou art that dry tree.*

f. Look again. Mark the space the dry tree occupies. A living tree might grow upon the very spot where it stands. *Sinner ! thou art that dry tree.*

g. Look again on the dry tree. The showers that soften the folded buds and spread open the tender leaves of the living tree in springtime, rain upon the dry tree with equal abundance, but, alas ! it only decays the faster. *Sinner ! thou art that dry tree.*

h. Look again at the dry tree. There it lies upon the ground, decaying ; how soon it will be gone ! A few more years or months or weeks, and you may seek for it in vain. The little dust it leaves shall be carried away by winds or soaked down into the earth by rains. The fresh grass of the future spring-times shall hide from the sight the spot where it lay. It shall be forgotten forever. *Sinner ! thou art that dry tree.*

Before I conclude I would give a word of warning and a word of encouragement.

SERMONS AND READINGS BY REV. A. P. GRAVES.

THEMES AND TEXTS.

Run, speak to this young man. (To young men.) Zech. 2 : 4.
What is a man profited. (Value of the soul.) Matt. 16 : 26.
A new creature. (Evidence of conversion.) 2 Cor. 5 : 17.
One thing is needful. (Addressed to young ladies.) Luke 10 : 42.
Is it well with thee? (Family religion.) 2 Kings 4 : 26.
Behold, I bring you good tidings. (Good tidings.) Luke 2 : 10.
Now is the day of salvation. (Immediate salvation.) 2 Cor. 6 : 2.
Whosoever speaketh against the Holy Ghost. (The unpardonable sin.) Matt. 12 : 32.
The blood of Jesus Christ, His Son. (The blood of Jesus.) 1 John 1 : 7.

BIBLE READINGS.

Published in his volume " From Earth to Heaven."

" Sheltered by the Blood." Pp 27–47.
" Gethsemane." Pp. 80-95.
A Faith that God accepts. Pp. 111–123.
Eighteenth chapter of Matthew. Pp. 148–156.
Assurance. Pp. 176–192.
The Holy Spirit. Pp. 291–307.
Heaven. Pp. 324–341.

ADDRESSES.

Bible Work. Pp. 72–79.
The Higher Christian Life. Pp. 193–200.

United Efforts in Revival.   Pp. 215–225.
Secret Societies and their Evils.   Pp. 244–248.
Social Amusements and their Temptations.   Pp. 264–270.

SERMONS BY REV. JOHN FLETCHER,

Of Madeley.

THEMES AND TEXTS.

The New Birth.   John 3 : 3.
The State of the Natural Man.   1 Cor. 2 : 14.
Awake, thou that sleepest.   Eph. 5 : 14.
The Nature of Regeneration.   1 Cor. 5 : 17.
The Necessity of Regeneration.   John 3 : 3.
Expostulation with Sinners. (And thou shalt speak my words unto them. . . .)   Ezek. 2 : 7.
Wisdom in Spiritual Things.   Deut. 32 : 29.
Why many of Christ's disciples were offended.   John 6 : 66–68.
On what terms Christ gives life.   John 5 : 40.
Danger of the Wicked.   Ezek. 33 : 7–9.
Creation and Fall of Man.   Gen. 1 : 26.
Now is the accepted time.   2 Cor. 6 : 2.
Killing the heir of all things.   Matt. 21 : 38.
Killing the Prince of Life.   Acts 3 : 14–15.
The Baptism of the Holy Ghost.   Acts 1 : 5.
The three Duties of Zion.   Isa. 52 : 1.
Repentance unto Life.   Acts 11 : 18.
The heart deceitful and wicked.   Jer. 17 : 19.
What Christ is made to us.   1 Cor. 1 : 30.
The Victor sitting on Christ's throne.   Rev. 3 : 21.
Fishers of Men.   Luke 5 : 20.
Not by might nor by power.   Zech 4 : 6–7.
The Penitent Thief.   Luke 23 : 42–43.
The sinner beginning to sink crying, Lord, save.   Matt. 14 : 30.
The true prophet prophesies good. (I hate him, for he doth not prophesy good concerning me. . . .)   1 Kings 22 : 8.
The Riches of the Glory of the Mystery.   Col. 1 : 26–28.
Joseph as a type of Christ.   Gen. 45 : 4.
What is it to preach Christ.   1 Cor. 1 : 23.
Sinners wonder at and despise Christ.   Acts 13 : 40–41.

The cry of Jesus to thirsty souls.   John 7 : 37-38.
The prevailing importunity of Esau.   Gen. 27 : 38.
The Song of the Angels at the time of Christ's birth.   Luke 2 : 14.
Prepare to meet thy God.   Amos 6 : 12.
Anathema, maranatha.   1 Cor. 16 : 22.
The Serpent lifted up.   John 3 : 14-15.
Winning Christ.   Phil. 3 : 8.
Rend your hearts, and not your garments.   Joel 2 : 13.
The Gospel should be received mixed with faith.   Heb. 4 : 2.
Why will ye die, O house of Israel.   Ezek. 18 : 31.

SERMONS BY REV. T. J. FRELINGHUYSEN.

THEMES AND TEXTS.

Christ's Lamentation over Jerusalem.   Matt. 23 : 37.
The righteous scarcely saved.   1 Pet. 4 : 18.
The miserable end of the ungodly.   1 Pet. 4 : 18.
The sins of youth lamented and deprecated.   Ps. 25 : 7.
The Lord's controversy with His people.   Hosea 4 : 1-3.
The judgments of God upon corrupt professors.   Rev. 8 : 13.
The soul seeking and finding Jesus.   John 20 : 11-18.
The soul covenanting with God.   Joshua 24 : 22.

SERMONS BY REV. CHARLES G. FINNEY.

OUTLINES.

SERMON I. SINNERS BOUND TO CHANGE THEIR OWN HEARTS.

Ezekiel 18 : 31.

1. What is *not* the meaning of this requirement.
2. What *is* the meaning of it.

SERMON II. HOW TO CHANGE YOUR HEART.

Ezekiel 18 : 21.

TRADITIONS OF THE ELDERS.

Matt. 15 : 6.

This sermon is intended to expose the errors of the Antinomians, Universalists, and others.

SERMON I. TOTAL DEPRAVITY.

John 5 : 42.

SERM. II. (Same subject continued). Rom. 8 : 7.

Why sinners hate God. John 15 : 25.

God cannot please sinners. Luke 7 : 31–35.

1. Why ?

a. Sinners do not like the *holiness* of God.

b. They do not like the *justice* of God.

c. The *mercy* of God.

d. The *precepts* of His law.

e. The *penalty* of His law.

f. His *Gospel.*

(*a*) They do not like the Gospel *rule of conduct.*

(*β*) The *conditions* of the Gospel.

(*γ*) The *means of grace.*

(*δ*) The *manner the Gospel is preached.*

(*e*) The *lives of ministers.*

(*ζ*) The *conduct of Christians.*

(*η*) *Church discipline.*

2. The sermon is *concluded* with fifteen practical remarks.

THEMES AND TEXTS.

Stewardship. Luke 16 : 2.

Christian Affinity. Amos 3 : 3.

Doctrine of Election. Eph. 1 : 45.

Doctrine of Reprobation. Jer. 6 : 30.

The love of the world. John 2 : 15.

The love of God for a sinning world. John 3 : 16.

Trusting in the mercy of God. Ps. 52 : 8.

The wages of sin. Rom. 6 : 23.

The Saviour lifted up, and the look of faith. John 3 : 14, 15 12 : 32, 33.

The excuses of sinners condemn God. Job 40 : 8.

The sinner's excuses answered. Job 36 : 1–3.

On refuges of lies. Isa. 28 : 17.

The wicked heart set to do evil. Eccles. 8 : 11.

Moral insanity. Eccles. 9 : 3.

Conditions of being saved. Acts 16 : 30.

The sinner's natural power and moral weakness. 2 Pet. 2 : 19.

The atonement as a governmental expedient. 1 Cor. 15 : 3 ; Rom 3 : 25, 26.

Where sin occurs God cannot wisely prevent it. Luke 17 : 10.

The inner and the outer revelation. 2 Cor. 4 : 2.

Quenching the Spirit. 1 Thes. 5 : 19.

The spirit not striving always. Gen. 6 : 3.

Christ our Advocate. 1 John 2 : 1, 2.

God's love commended to us. Rom. 5 : 8.

Prayer and labor for the gathering of the great harvest. Matt. 10 : 36-38.

Converting sinners a Christian duty. Jas. 5 : 19, 20.

Men often highly esteem what God abhors. Luke 16 : 15.

Victory over the world through faith. John 5 : 4.

Death to sin through Christ. Rom. 6 : 11.

The essential el ments of Christian experience. Matt. 5, 6.

LECTURES—THEMES AND TEXTS.

TO PROFESSING CHRISTIANS, DELIVERED IN NEW YORK CITY DURING THE YEARS 1836 AND 1837.

1. Self-deceivers. Jas. 1 : 22.
2. False professors. 2 Kings 17 : 33.
3. Doubtful actions are sinful. Rom. 14 : 23.
4. Reproof a Christian duty. Levit. 19 : 17.
5. True Saints. Exod. 32 : 26.
6. Legal religion. Exod. 32 : 26.
7. Religion of public opinion. John 12 : 43.
8. Conformity to the world. Rom. 12 : 2.
9. True and false repentance. 2 Cor. 7 : 10.
10. Dishonest in one thing, dishonest in all things. Luke 16 : 10.
11. Bound to know your true character. 2 Cor. 13 : 5.
12. True and false conversion. Isa. 50 : 11.
13. True submission. Jas. 4 : 7.
14. Selfishness and true religion. 1 Cor. 13 : 5.
15. Religion of the law and gospel. Rom. 9 : 30-33.
16. Justification by Faith. Gal. 2 : 16.
17. Sanctification by Faith. Rom. 3 : 31.
18. Legal experience. Rom , chap. 7.
19. Christian Perfection. Matt. 5 : 48.
20. Christian Perfection. Matt. 5 : 48.
21. Way of Salvation. Acts 16 : 30, 31.
22. Necessity of divine teaching. John 16 : 7-13.
23. Love the whole of religion. Rom. 13 : 10.
24. Rest of the saints. Heb. 4 : 3.
25. Christ the husband of the Church. Rom. 7 : 4.

SERMONS BY REV. JONATHAN EDWARDS.

Mr. Prince, in his "Christian History," describes Mr. Edwards's manner of preaching : " He was a preacher of a low and moderate voice, a natural delivery, and without any agitation of body or anything else in his manner to excite attention, except his habitual and great solemnity, looking and speaking as in the presence of God, and with a weighty sense of the matter delivered." Mr. Edwards represents his congregation as having been "a rational and understanding people." We need not wonder, therefore, that they understood his "Sermons on Justification," which were delivered in Northampton about the time of the Great Awakening, and were, we are told, the means of great religious concern among his hearers.

THEMES AND TEXTS.

Man's natural blindness in the things of religion. Ps. 94 : 9-11.

Men naturally God's enemies. Rom. 5 : 10.

Justification by Faith alone. Rom. 4 : 5.

The Wisdom of God as displayed in the way of Salvation. Eph. 3 : 10.

God glorified in Man's dependence. 1 Cor. 1 : 29-31.

The excellency of Christ. Rev. 5 : 5-6.

The final Judgment, or the world judged by Jesus Christ. Acts 17 : 31.

The Justice of God in the damnation of sinners. Rom. 3 : 19.

The future punishment of the wicked unavoidable and intolerable. Ezek. 22 : 14.

The eternity of Hell torments. Matt. 25 : 46.

The wicked filling up the measure of their sins. 1 Thess. 2 : 16.

The end of the wicked contemplated by the righteous. Rev. 18 : 20.

Wicked men useful only in their destruction. Ezek. 15 : 2-4.

Sinners in the hands of an angry God. Deut. 32 : 35.

The vain self-flatteries of the sinner. Ps. 36 : 2.

The warnings of Scripture best adapted to the awakening of sinners. Luke 16 : 31.

Indetermination in religion unreasonable. 1 Kings 18 : 21.

The Folly of Procrastination. Prov. 27 : 1.

Unbelievers contemn the excellency of Christ. Acts 4 : 11.

The best manner of seeking salvation.   Gen. 6 : 22.

Pressing into the Kingdom of God.   Luke 16 : 16.

The folly of looking back in fleeing from destruction.   Luke 17 : 32.

Ruth's inflexible resolution.   Ruth 1 : 16.

Pardon for the greatest sinners.   Ps. 25 : 11.

The Peace which Christ gives to His true followers.   John 14 : 27.

The reality of spiritual light.   (For flesh and blood hath not revealed it unto thee....)   Matt. 16 : 7.

True grace distinguished from the experience of devils.   Jas. 2 : 19.

Hypocrites deficient in the duty of prayer.   Job 27 : 10.

The fearfulness which will hereafter surprise hypocrites.   Isa. 33 : 14.

In self examination great care necessary.   Ps. 139 : 23, 24.

A warning to professors who attend divine worship, and yet allow themselves in any known sin.   Ezek. 23 : 37–39.

God the best portion of the Christian.   Ps. 73 : 25.

God's Sovereignty.   (Therefore hath he mercy on whom he will have mercy.)   Rom. 9 : 18.

The Most High a prayer-hearing God.   Ps. 65 : 2.

Joseph's temptation and escape.   Gen. 39 : 12.

The Christian's life a journey toward Heaven.   Heb. 11 : 13, 14.

SERMONS BY REV. EBENEZER ERSKINE.

E. Erskine was born 1680 and died 1754.   He was minister at Stirling.   He was not as popular as his brother Ralph, but as a leader of the Seceders, as a reformer, and an open-air preacher his influence was deservedly great.

THEMES AND TEXTS.

The Holy Spirit as a wind blowing on the Dry Bones.   Ezek. 37 : 9.

The humble soul the favorite of heaven.   (Though the Lord be high, yet hath he respect unto the lowly....)   Ps. 138 : 6.

Christ in the Believer's arms.   Luke 2 : 28.

The Throne of Grace.   (Justice and judgment are the habitation of thy throne : mercy and truth shall go before thy face.)   Ps. 89 : 14.

God in Christ a God of love.   1 John 4 : 16.

Unbelief arraigned and condemned.   John 3 : 18.

The Day-Spring from on high visiting us. Luke 1 : 78.

The Law of Faith issuing from mount Zion. Isa. 2 : 3.

The standard of Heaven lifted up against the powers of Hell. Isa. 59 : 19.

Christ the Resurrection and the Life. John 11 : 25.

Worthless man much regarded in the sight of God. Ps. 144 : 3.

The Wise Virgins going forth to meet the Bridegroom. Matt. 25 : 6.

God's doves flying to His windows. Isa. 60 : 8.

Abraham rejoicing to see Christ's day, though distant. John 8 : 56.

Christ as the breaker opening all passes to glory. (The breaker is come up ..) Mic. 2 : 13.

The Word of Salvation is sent to us. Acts 13 : 26.

Christ in the Clouds coming to Judgment. Matt. 16 : 37.

SERMONS BY REV. RALPH ERSKINE, A.M.

Born 1685, died 1752. Minister in Dunfermline from 1711 to 1752.*

THEMES AND TEXTS.

The Main Question of the Gospel Catechism. (What think ye of Christ?) Matt. 22 : 42.

The Woman of Samaria's sermon to the men of the city. John 4 : 29.

The Great Gathering of the people to Shiloh. Gen. 49 : 10.

The Mediator's Power in Heaven and Earth. Matt. 28 : 18.

Great sinners saved for the sake of God's great name. Ps. 107 : 8.

A strong encouragement to Faith. (The Father loveth the Son, and hath given all things into his hand.) John 3 : 35.

The law of God's house requires that its limits be holy. (This is the law of the house....The whole limit thereof round about shall be holy.) Ezek. 43 : 12.

The Church besieged but delivered by Christ. Eccles. 9 : 14, 15.

Fed by the enthroned Lamb. Rev. 7 : 17.

---

* This reformer, the friend and correspondent of Wesley and Whitefield, is characterized by the latter as " a field-preacher of the Scottish Church, a noble soldier of the Lord Jesus Christ." The Rev. Dr. Stephen H. Tyng, Sr., says : " The works of Ralph Erskine have long been to me a mine of gold." There are two British editions of his works, that of 1777 and that of 1821. A selection of his sermons was published in Philadelphia in 1863, in 2 vols. 8vo.

Faith pleading with God to regard the Covenant. Ps. 74 : 20.

Faith taking God at his word. ("Do as thou hast said.") 2 Sam. 7 : 25.

We are blessed from the day the foundation of the spiritual temple is laid. Hag. 2 : 9.

The giving love of Christ and the receiving faith of Paul. Gal. 2 : 20.

The humiliation and pacification of the Gospel. Ezek. 16 : 63.

The word of salvation sent to sinners. Acts 13 : 26.

Gospel compulsion to fill the house. Luke 14 : 23.

1. The ministerial commission : "*compel them.*"

2. The design of this power : "to compel them *to come in.*"

3. The reason of it : that his *house may be filled.*

4. Make some application of the whole.

The Fountain-head of all Blessings. 2 Cor. 5 : 8.

The tribe vanquished at first is victor at last. (Gad, a troop shall overcome him ; but he shall overcome at last.) Gen. 49 : 19.

Christ the true Moses sent to deliver the true Israel. Acts 7 : 34.

Satan bound and baffled by Christ. Luke 22 : 31, 32.

Redemption of God and to God. 1 Cor. 1 : 30 ; Rev. 5 : 9.

The true Christ no new Christ. Heb. 13 : 8.

Preventing love. 1 John 4 : 19.

Faith in Christ the sure way to relief. Jonah 2 : 4.

The great rain and the great relief. Hos. 13 : 9.

Access to the Holy of Holies by the death of Christ. Matt. 27 : 51.

The nature and excellency of Gospel purity. Prov. 30 : 12.

We ought not to consult with flesh and blood. Gal. 1 : 16.

Witnesses cited for God. (Therefore ye are my witnesses that I am God....) Isa. 43 : 12.

The comer's conflict. Luke 9 : 42.

1. We shall speak a little of coming to Christ.

2. In what respects matters may grow worse to people while they are coming to Christ.

3. The reasons why such may find their distress grow before their rescue come.

4. Make some application of the whole.

The Saints more than conquerors. Rom. 8 : 37.

The day of effectual calling the levelling day. Luke 19 : 5.

Law-death and Gospel-life. Gal. 2 : 19.

The happy hour of Christ's quickening voice. John 5 : 25.

The duty of receiving Christ and walking in him. Col. 2 : 6.

The gradual conquest, or heaven won little by little. Deut. 7 : 22.

The best security for the best life. Col. 3 : 3.

The eagle-winged believer.* (They shall mount up with wings as eagles.) Isa. 40 : 31.

SERMONS BY CHRISTMAS EVANS.

THEMES AND TEXTS.

The time of reformation. Heb. 9 : 10.

The triumph of Calvary. (Who is this that cometh from Edom.... and I will bring down their strength to the earth). Isa. 63 : 1-6.

The smitten rock. 1 Cor. 10 : 4.

The fall and recovery of man.† Rom. 5 : 15.

One God and one Mediator. 1 Tim. 2 : 5.

The living Redeemer. Job 19 : 23-27.

Messiah's Kingdom. Dan. 2 : 44-45.

The sufferings of Christ. 1 Pet. 2 : 24.

The purification of conscience. Heb. 9 : 14.

The Cedar of God. Ezek. 17 : 22-24.

The Prince of Salvation. Heb. 2 : 10, and 5 : 9.

Finished redemption. John 19 : 30.

The Resurrection of Jesus. Matt. 28 : 6.

The Ascension. Acts 3 : 21.

Tribulation conquered. (In the world ye shall have tribulation....) John 16 : 33.

---

* The Scottish celebration of the Lord's Supper in the days of Whitefield and the Erskines was very different from what it is in the Kirk of to-day. Now the ordinance is celebrated once in three months, or in some places once a month. Then the Lord's Supper was administered but once a year in each congregation. The occasion was one of general concourse for Christian people. For three days—Saturday, Sunday, and Monday—there were services for prayer and preaching. As these gatherings were always in the summer, and made up of the faithful of several parishes (the people frequenting a succession of communions) the numbers were so great that tents were pitched near the church for the protection of such as could not find room within. Not only the neighboring flocks but their pastors would be present, and those who did not meet their own pastors at these distant solemnities were admitted to them by "tokens." One part of the duties of the ministers was to "fence the tables," or to make such searching addresses to those who came to the communion as might serve to hinder all that were unqualified from sitting down at any of the successive tables that were provided for the throngs of communicants. It was at these festal seasons that many a revival commenced, and some of the celebrated sermons of Livingstone, Whitefield, and the Erskines were preached with remarkable power and success.

† In this sermon is found his vision of the world as a graveyard.

The Glory of the Gospel. 2 Tim 1 : 11.

The Song of the Angels. Luke 2 : 14.

The Stone of Israel. (Upon one stone shall be seven eyes....) Zech. 3 : 9.

Justification by Faith. Job 9 : 2.

The shield of faith. Eph. 6 : 16.

The Paraclete. John 14 : 16, 17.

The Father and Son glorified. John 16 : 13–15.

Christ knocking at the Door.* Rev. 3 : 20.

SERMONS BY REV. SAMUEL · DAVIES, A.M.

THEMES AND TEXTS.

The nature of Salvation through Jesus Christ. (For God so loved the world....) John 3 : 16.

Sinners entreated to be reconciled to God. 2 Cor. 5 : 20.

The authority and sufficiency of the Christian religion. (If they hear not Moses and the prophets....) Luke 16 : 27–31.

The nature and universality of spiritual death. Eph. 2 : 4, 5.

The nature and process of spiritual life. Eph. 2 : 4, 5.

The poor in spirit and the contrite objects of the Divine favor. Isa. 66 : 2.

The nature and danger of making light of salvation. Matt, 22 : 5.

The compassion of Christ to feeble believers. Matt. 12 : 20.

The divine mercy to mourning penitents. (I have surely heard Ephraim bemoaning himself....) Jer. 31 : 18–20.

The danger of lukewarmness in religion. Rev. 3 : 15,16.

The universal judgment. Acts 17 : 30, 31.

The one thing needful. Luke 10 : 41, 42.

The saints saved with difficulty, and the certain perdition of sinners. 1 Pet 4 : 18.

Ingratitude to God a heinous but general iniquity. 2 Chron. 32 : 25.

Jesus Christ the only foundation. Isa. 28 : 16, 17.

Dedication to God argued from redeeming mercy. (For ye are bought with a price....) 1 Cor. 6 : 19, 20.

---

* This sermon has not been entirely translated into English. The best part of it, however, has been translated and published by the American Tract Society, N. Y., as a tract, under the title, " Welsh Preaching," No. 697.

The enrolment of our names in Heaven the best ground of joy. Luke 10 : 20.

Religion the highest wisdom, and sin the greatest folly. Ps. 111 : 10.

Rejection of Christ a common but unreasonable sin. Mark 12 : 6.

The doom of the incorrigible sinner. Prov. 29 : 1.

The nature of looking to Jesus explained. Isa. 45 : 22.

Arguments to enforce our looking to Jesus. Same text.

Vessels of mercy and vessels of wrath delineated. Rom. 9 : 22–23.

The nature and necessity of true repentance. (And the times of this ignorance God winked at....) Acts 17 : 30.

The wonderful compassion of Christ to the greatest of sinners. Matt. 23 : 37.

The nature and author of regeneration. John 3 : 7.

The way of sin hard and difficult. Acts 9 : 5.

The characters of the whole and the sick contrasted. Matt. 9: 12.

The Gospel invitation. (A certain man made a great supper and bade many....) Luke 14 : 21–24.

The nature of justification by faith. Rom. 1 : 16–17.

The success of the ministry owing to a Divine influence. 1 Cor. 3 : 7.

The rejection of Gospel Light the condemnation of men. John 3 : 19.

Time to awake out of sleep. (It is high time to awake out of sleep.) Rom. 13 : 11.

The happy effects of the pouring out of the spirit. Isa. 32 : 13–19.

Practical atheism in denying the agency of Divine Providence. Zeph. 1 : 12.

The primitive and the present state of man compared. Rom. 5 : 17.

Evidences of the want of love to God. John 5 : 42.

Christmas-day sermon. The song of the angels. Luke 2 : 12, 14.

Christians reminded of their solemn obligations. (Ye are witnesses ....we are witnesses....) Josh. 24 : 22.

The guilt and doom of impenitent hearers. Matt. 13 : 14.

The apostolic valediction considered and applied. 2 Cor. 13 : 11.

SERMONS BY TIMOTHY DWIGHT, D.D.

OUTLINES.

THE HARVEST PAST.

Jer. 8 : 20.*

The state of the people in whose name these words were uttered by the prophet...There are many situations in the life of man to which this lamentation may be applied.

1. Every person who still remains in sin may at the close of a year usefully adopt this lamentation.

2. A season in which religion prevails is also eminently a time of harvest ; and such as lose this season may well adopt with regard to themselves the lamentation of the text.

3. Another situation in which this melancholy reflection is peculiarly applicable is that of a dying sinner.

   a. Human life is a continued scene of delusion, but on a dying bed it often vanishes.

   b. The retrospect of a dying sinner.

   c. His prospects.

A JUST SENSE OF THE CHARACTER AND PRESENCE OF GOD A SOURCE OF REPENTANCE.

Job 42 : 5-6.

THE DANGER OF LOSING CONVICTIONS OF CONSCIENCE.

Matt. 12 : 43-45.

1. The miserable condition of an impenitent sinner before he is awakened to a serious conviction of his guilt ; he is inhabited by an "unclean spirit."

2. Convictions of sin constitute in the eye of God an important change in the state of man. "When the unclean spirit is gone out of a man."

3. We are here taught that beings absolutely sinful find neither rest nor enjoyment but in doing evil. "He walketh through dry places," etc.

4. Persons under conviction are always in danger of falling anew into hardness of heart. "He saith, I will return," etc.

---

* "The delivery of this sermon," says one of Dr. Dwight's biographers, "was in two instances the commencement of a revival of religion among his pupils : in the first of which nearly half of them united with the college church. Similar consequences have been ascribed to its delivery on two other occasions in different

5. The soul from which convictions of sin have been finally banished is more perfectly prepared to become the seat of absolute wickedness than before these convictions began. "He findeth it empty, swept, and garnished."

6. The soul from which convictions of sin are finally banished becomes far more sinful than before its convictions began. "He goeth and taketh," etc.

Remarks.

a. The immeasurable importance of cherishing in the heart convictions of sin.

b. The high interest which persons in this situation have in being directed in their duty by sound wisdom.

c. The miserable situation of unawakened sinners.

THE FOLLY OF TRUSTING OUR OWN HEARTS.

Prov. 28 : 26.

1. What is meant by trusting our own hearts.

2. The folly of this conduct.

THE PRODIGAL SON.

Luke 15 : 11-17. (Sermon First.)

1. Sinners regard God only so far as to gain from Him whatever they can.

2. Sinners waste their blessings and reduce themselves to absolute want.

3. Afflictions are very often means of bringing sinners to a sense of their condition.

4. When sinners first acquire such a sense of their condition, they betake themselves to false measures of relief.

5. The situation of sinners is eminently unhappy.

6. The repentance of the Gospel is the resumption of a right mind.

a. The sinner realizes his own miserable condition.

b. He realizes that in his father's house there is an abundance of good.

c. He begins to realize the hope that this good may be his.

THE PRODIGAL SON.

Luke 15 : 18-24. (Sermon Second.)

1. True repentance is a voluntary exercise of mind.

2. True repentance is a filial temper, disposing us to regard God as our parent.

3. It is followed by the confession of sin.

4. A real penitent feels that his sins are committed against God.

5. Consequently a real penitent is humble.

6. He brings nothing to God but his want, shame, and sorrow.

7. He executes his resolutions of obedience.

8. God is entirely disposed to receive the sincere penitent.

9. The richest provision is made for his enjoyment.

10. There is peculiar joy in Heaven over the repentance of return-ing sinners.

Remark.

What inducements are here presented to sinners to return to God.

THE DANGER OF OPPOSING RELIGION.

Acts 5 : 38-39.

Gamaliel's address to the Sanhedrim.

My purpose is to engage those who hear me to shun all opposition to the revival and prevalence of religion.

Observations : 1. This spirit of hatred is exactly the same as that of the Sanhedrim.

2. The conduct of Gamaliel merits the highest commendation.

1. This hostility and all its malignant effects are *unnecessary and useless.*

a. Because Christians and Christianity will do no harm to good men and such as are seeking their own salvation.

b. Because, if Christianity is a delusion, it will come to nothing of itself.

c. Because, if it is true, all opposition to it will certainly fail.

2. This opposition is in the highest degree *dangerous.*

a. Every person who opposes the commencement or progress of religion in others hardens his own heart.

b. He daily provokes the anger of God against himself.

THOSE WHO BELIEVE NOT THE SCRIPTURES WOULD NOT BE PER-SUADED THOUGH ONE ROSE FROM THE DEAD.

Luke 16 : 31.

THE YOUNG MAN OF NAIN.

Luke 7 : 11-15.

The resurrection of this son of a widow was the first miracle of the kind which our Saviour performed.

Consider this miracle of Christ as symbolical of one of greater in-terest which he performs by His Spirit.

1. Every youth who is thus raised to life is, before this resurrection, spiritually dead.

2. There is still room to hope that among you there may in the end

be found some youths of Nain ; some who, though now dead and to the human eye lost and gone forever, may yet be restored to life.

3. For this resurrection to spiritual life, it is indispensable that such as desire to be interested in it should begin a total change of their conduct.

THE RICH MAN AND LAZARUS.

Luke 16 : 26.

ON REVIVALS OF RELIGION.

Isa. 60 : 8.

The question, Who are these ? plainly indicates that the persons spoken of were either unknown or unexpected. They are said to "fly as a cloud." They were a vast multitude, and were hastening to their place of destination. They are said to fly " as doves to their windows ;" they were considered as returning with dove-like spirit to their final and proper residence. Observe—

1. At some future period a vast multitude will be gathered into the Church of Christ.

2. The multitude will in great measure consist of such persons as are not rationally expected to become Christians.

3. These persons will enter the Church of their own accord and with great earnestness of mind.

4. They will possess a dove-like character.

Remarks.

a. From these observations it is evident that there will hereafter be a general revival of religion in the world.

b. This revival will furnish a solid foundation of joy to the universe.

c. Hence, it follows also, that the same things are partially true of every revival of religion.

d. We are bound faithfully to labor and fervently to pray for the universal revival of religion.

THE COMING OF CHRIST.

Luke 12 : 40.

1. What it is for which we are to be ready.

2. What is included in being ready ?

3. The uncertainty of the event is a motive for immediate preparation.

THE DISAPPOINTMENTS WHICH WILL TAKE PLACE AT THE DAY OF
JUDGMENT.

Luke 13 : 28-30. (Sermon First.)

1. Some of the human race will be shut out from the kingdom of
God who confidently expected admission.

2. Others, whom they expected to be shut out, will be received.

(Sermon Second.)

3. The distress occasioned by this disappointment will be very
great.

Remarks.

a. Carefully determine what the genuine religion, required by the
Gospel, is.

b. Let every one examine the grounds of his hope of salvation.

c. We should entertain very humble apprehensions of our own
character.

d. These considerations compel us to exercise charitable thoughts
toward others.

SERMONS BY REV. WILLIAM DAWSON.

THEMES AND TEXTS.

Sowing in Time and Reaping in Eternity. .Gal. 4 : 7-8. (" Pulpit,"
vol. xxiii. p. 17.)

Pardon to every Penitent Believer. Acts 13 : 38, 39. (Vol. xxiv.
p. 169.)

The Inestimable Value of the Soul. Matt. 16 : 26, 27. (Vol. xxi.
p. 47)

A Warning to Youth. Ps. 144 : 11, 12. (Vol. xxvi. p. 193.)

The Love of God to Man. John 3 : 16. (Vol. xxvii.)

The Servant that was beaten with many stripes. Luke 12 : 47.
(Vol xxxi. p. 499.)

Faith rather than Fear. Mark 5 : 36. (" The Wesleyan Preacher,"
vol. ii. part 3, p. 52.)

Work while it is day. John 9 : 4. (P. 148.)

Invitation to enter the Ark. Gen. 7 : 1.

The axe laid unto the root of the trees. Matt. 3 : 10.

The separation of the wheat from the chaff. Matt. 3 : 12.

The world gained, but the soul lost. Matt. 16 : 26.

The Fear of Man—its Causes, Character, and Folly. Prov. 29 : 25.

The Horrible Pit, the Prayer, and the New Song. Ps. 40 : 1-3.

The Righteous and the Wicked contrasted.   Isa. 3 : 10, 11.

Looking back.   Luke 9 : 62.

Sons of God, the Spirit crying in their hearts, Abba, Father.   Gal. 4 : 4–6.

The Word of God prevailing over the books of magic.   Acts 19 : 20.

The invitation to the Gospel Feasts.   Isa. 4 : 1, 2.

A call to the Sleeper.   Jonah 1 : 6.

Weighed in the Balance and Found Wanting.   Dan. 5 : 27.

The Good Shepherd carrying the lambs in his bosom.   Isa. 40 : 11.

The Prodigal returning home.   Luke 15 : 20.

" Come and see," or, Death on the Pale Horse.   Rev. 6 : 7, 8.

Warning the Wicked.   Ezek. 3 : 17–19.

We would see Jesus.   John 12 : 21.

Who is on the Lord's side ?   Exodus 22 : 36.

God's love to the world.   John 3 : 16.

To-day if ye will hear His voice.   Heb. 3 : 15.

SERMONS BY BENJAMIN COLMAN, D.D.

OUTLINES.

PLEASANT TO SEE SOULS FLYING TO CHRIST.

Isa. 60 : 8.

Preached Oct. 21, 1740, at the close of Whitefield's labors in Boston. *

1. Exposition of the context.

2. Explain the phraseology of the text.

a. Clouds.

a. The clouds driven before the wind.

β. The clouds fly in the open sky, in the sight of all.

γ. They fly irresistibly.

δ. They fly high.

b. Doves.   They are clean and innocent birds, emblems of the Holy Spirit.

a. They fly swiftly.

---

* Dr. Colman ten years before (1730) preached four sermons to persuade young people to give their hearts to God.   He also preached a series of sermons on the " Ten Virgins."   Though he zealously co-operated with Whitefield, he took a middle course between those who fully approved and those who entirely discountenanced the work. He signed a testimonial in favor of Whitefield's labors, and yet he did not hesitate to condemn, both in his letters and published sermons, whatever, after further observation, he found worthy of censure.—Rev. Dr. Sprague's "Annals," vol. i., p. 227.

β. They fly home eagerly at any noise or other cause of fright.

γ. They fly in flocks unto their windows.

δ. They fly for food, company, and rest.

Application.

1. The pleasure God has in this event.
2. The delight all good people take in the spectacle.
3. How pleasant must it be to pious ministers.
4. It calls for wonder and admiration.
5. Address to various classes of believers.
6. To convinced and awakened sinners ; to the new converts and the reclaimed.

SERMONS BY REV. DANIEL A. CLARK.

OUTLINES.

THE CONTROVERSY SETTLED.

2 Cor. 5 : 10.

1. Sinners are in a state of hostility to God, while He is graciously disposed toward them.
2. There is no just cause for these hostile feelings toward God.
3. The terms on which God will receive sinners to favor.
4. Urge some of the motives to reconciliation.

THE LOITERER AT THE VINEYARD.

Matt. 20 : 6.

" Why stand ye here all the day idle ? "

1. Is it because you know not what you have to do ?
2. Is it because it is not an important work to which you are called ?
3. Is it because it is an unreasonable work ?
4. Do you reply that there is time enough yet ?

a. Will it be easier to begin to-morrow ?

b. Will it be painful to be a Christian any longer than is absolutely necessary ?

c. Will God excuse you from beginning the work to-day ?

Remarks.

a. You have reason to fear that God may be about to take back the offer.

b. How horrid will be your regret that you did not accept the offer.

c. The invitation is not one to pain, or danger, or misery.

THE DESPERATE EFFORT.

Matt. 11 : 12.

Let me offer some reasons why you should try to be saved.

a. You cannot expect to be saved without trying.

b. In striving to be saved, you have the assurance of success.

c. You should try, because with a more heavenly temper you can be more useful in life.

d. Because you could be more useful in heaven.

e. Because you could be so happy in heaven.

f. What others have done for your salvation should induce you to try.

g. You should try, because if you do not you must be infinitely degraded in hell.

h. If you are not saved, the most bitter reflections await you.

i. The longer you postpone, the less likely it is that you will ever attempt it.

j. Do you postpone because you have not had your fill of sin?

Remarks.

a. Why does God make it so difficult to get to heaven ?

b. If we reach heaven with difficulty, it will always seem worth more for the cost of it.

THE MERCIES OF GOD NOT RECIPROCATED.

Isa. 1 : 32.

1. God has brought us up as children.

2. We have rebelled against Him.

RECIPE FOR A REVIVAL.

2 Chron. 7 : 14.

1. The Lord has in this world a precious people.

2. They are called by His name.

3. If they shall humble themselves.

4. And pray.

5. And seek God's face.

6. And turn from their evil ways.

7. He will hear from heaven.

8. And forgive their sins.

9. And heal their land.

Remarks.

1. Do you say we depend for a revival too much on human contrivance ? We can only say it is God's own contrivance.

2. Thus the church is a Jacob's ladder communicating between God and the world, presenting to Him its wants, and serving as a medium of His favors.

3. How important and responsible a situation the Christian fills. How important, therefore, that he should perform the duties incumbent on him.

SINNERS WEARY THEMSELVES TO COMMIT INIQUITY.

Jer. 10 : 5.

They are in vexation and conflict of mind because of their opposition to the will of God.

1. The sinner must sustain morality without piety.

2. He must feel secure without a promise.

3. He must hope for heaven while forming a character for perdition.

4. He must resist Christ without a cause.

5. He must try to be happy while guilty.

6. He must have enough of the world to supply the place of God in his heart.

7. He must arrange matters for death, while he is afraid to think of dying.

8. He must read the Bible, while he is afraid to think or pray.

Concluding Thoughts.

1. We should have compassion for a suffering world.

2. We should do all we can to relieve this miserable condition of our fellow-men.

THE KINGDOM OF GOD COME NEAR TO SINNERS.

Luke 10 : 11.

1. When may the kingdom of God (or the Gospel) be said to come nigh to an individual or a people ?

a. When it comes within the hearing of the ear.

b. When it reaches the understanding.

c. When it gains access to the conscience.

2. Why the Gospel is brought nigh to some who are finally lost.

WHY WILL YE DIE ?

Ezek. 33 : 11.

Men have started in a course that must, as they ought to know, end in eternal ruin, for—

1. They break the law of God, knowing what the penalty is.

2. They reject Christ Jesus the only Redeemer.

3. The Holy Ghost, the only regenerator and sanctifier.

4. They are forming a character for perdition when a totally different character is demanded to fit them for heaven.

Remarks.

1. Will it prove you *brave* to dare the Eternal to His face?

2. Will it prove you *wise* to place so small a value on your soul?

3. Will it prove you *good* to place so low an estimate on the blood of Christ and the glory of God?

THEMES AND TEXTS.

The bridgeless Gulf. Luke 16 : 26.

Grieving the Holy Spirit. Eph. 4 : 30.

Terms of Divine Acceptance. Acts 16 : 30.

Salvation made sure. John 6 : 37.

The sinner's desperate pursuit of sin. Jer. 3 : 5.

It is a fearful thing to fall into the hands of the living God. Hebrews 10 : 31.

Where is the blessedness ye spoke of? Gal. 4 : 15.

The righteous saved with difficulty. 1 Pet. 4 : 18.

God be merciful to me a sinner. Luke 18 : 13.

Look and Live, or the Brazen Serpent. John 3 : 14.

Why do revivals cease? Matt. 8 : 34.

The delay of God in punishing sinners. Eccles. 8 : 11.

The duty of immediate repentance. Acts 17 : 30.

The Gospel offer should be accepted without delay. 2 Cor. 6 : 2.

Perdition a dark spot in the moral landscape. Ezek. 18 : 32. ·

SERMONS BY J. A. CLARK, D.D.,

Some time Rector of St. Andrew's Church, Philadelphia. *

THEMES AND TEXTS.

Unconverted men are asleep. Eph. 5 : 14.

Unconverted men must be awakened. Same text.

* These sermons were published in full under the title, "Awake, thou that sleepest," by Robert Carter, N. Y., 1844. (Pp. 244, 12mo.)

Importance of immediate attention to Religion. (Go ·thy way for this time. . .) Acts 24 : 25.

The absurdity, danger, and guilt of procrastination. 2. Cor. 6 : 2, and Acts 24 : 25.

The sinner must be convinced of sin. Jer. 2 : 23.

The sinfulness of the unconverted state. Same text.

Objections to the endless punishment of the wicked answered. Rom. 3 : 9.

How sin is taken away. (Behold the Lamb of God. . . .) John 1 : 29.

If Christ be rejected, there can be no salvation. Heb. 10 : 26.

The freedom of the Gospel salvation. Rev. 22 : 17.

SERMONS BY REV. JAMES CAUGHEY.

OUTLINES.

THE STANDING DOUBT.

1 Thess. 5 : 16-18.

1. Show that it is the privilege of the Christian to rejoice evermore.

2. State the reason why so many professors do not attain to this happy state.

THE OMNIPOTENCE OF FAITH.

Mark 11 : 24.

1. Is there any difference between faith and believing ?

2. Is faith the gift of God ?

3. How can you account for it that there is in some a greater aptness to believe than in others ?

4. Are the objects of faith limited ?

5. How can we reconcile the phraseology of the text and believe that we have in the present what is spoken of in the future tense ?

6. What preparation must a man have in order to believe ?

PURIFICATION BY FAITH.

Acts 15 : 9.

1. Why does God purify the heart by faith ?

2. What is faith ?

3. What is the difference between faith and knowledge ?

4. What degrees of faith are necessary to salvation ?

THE FEAR OF DEATH DESTROYED BY THE SIGHT OF CHRIST.

Luke 2 : 26.

1. God always honors pre-eminently devoted men.

2. Simeon was a man of this description.

3. Yet he had great discouragements in obtaining a sight of Christ.

THE FULNESS THAT DWELLS IN JESUS CHRIST.

Col. 1 : 19.

THE FEAR OF UNCONVERTED MEN IN THE HOUR OF DEATH.

Heb. 2 : 14.

1. The unconverted are afraid to die.

2. Christians are not afraid to die.

QUENCHING THE SPIRIT.

1 Thess. 5 : 19.

1. The Spirit's operations are true.

2. The Spirit's operations may be quenched.

THE STRIVING OF THE SPIRIT.

Gen. 6 : 3.

1. A great fact stated—the striving of the Spirit.

2. A dreadful event predicted.   The Spirit ceasing to strive.

THE STING OF DEATH.

1 Cor. 15 : 56, and Heb. 6 : 1.

Proposition : If a happy death-bed be desirable, and a miserable death-bed is to be deprecated, then go on to perfection.

A CALL TO DECISION.

1 Kings 18 : 21.

1. What are we to understand by halting between two opinions?

2. What are the causes of this halting?

3. You remain undecided because you will not pay the price demanded by decision.

Plain dealing with obstinate sinners.   And shall cast them into a furnace of fire. . . .)   Matt. 13 : 41–43.

A warning to sinners.   Same text.

Alarming cries.   Same text.

An invitation to straitened souls (a farewell sermon). (A broad place where there is no straitness.) Job 36 : 16.

SERMONS BY REV. T. T. CASTLEMAN,

Of Staunton, Va.

(From a volume entitled, " Plain Sermons for Servants." Some of these sermons were given by other clergymen of the Episcopal Church)

OUTLINES.

JONAH CAST INTO THE SEA ; OR, THE SINNER UNDER CONVICTION.

Jonah 1 : 12.

1. When Jonah was awakened, he saw that he had sinned against God.

2. Jonah did not try to excuse himself : he condemned himself.

3. Jonah saw that he had no power to save himself.

4. Jonah was in great darkness and trouble, yet not without hope.

5. Jonah despaired of saving himself, but trusted in God.

THE WAY TO OBTAIN GOD'S FAVOR.

I entreated thy favor with my whole heart.... Ps. 119 : 58.

1. Entreat God's favor.

2. Entreat with the whole heart.

3. Accept the terms of mercy as revealed in God's Word. (This partition is now first suggested. The *original* has none.)

GOD'S WONDROUS LOVE TO SINNERS.

1 John 3 : 1.

1. The love of the Father is too great for man to measure.

2. He offers it to us without money and without price.

3. Yet the Father's love to us was a costly love.

4. His love to us is full of strength and tenderness.

5. The love of the Father to us is abundant.

6. His love extends to the worst sinners.

THEMES AND TEXTS.

Sin a disease cured by Jesus Christ. (And as Moses lifted up the serpent in the wilderness....) John 3 : 14, 15.

Beginning a religious life. "Grow in grace." 2 Pet. 3 : 18.

How the Christian grows in grace. Mark 4 : 28.

The Christian like a tree by the water side. (For he shall be like a tree....that spreadeth out her roots by the river ...) Jer. 17 : 8.

The careless Christian warned. Matt. 25 : 8.

All of us must give account to God. Rom. 14 : 12.

Outward religion not enough to fit us for heaven. Matt. 7 : 21.
The refreshing grace of the Gospel. Prov. 25 : 25.
The faithful Christian shall wear a crown. Rev. 2 : 10.

SERMONS BY REV. DAVID BRAINERD.

(Preached while missionary among the Indians of New Jersey and Pennsylvania.)

THEMES AND TEXTS.

" Truly in vain is salvation hoped for from the hills," etc. Jer. 3 : 23.

Behold these three years I come seeking fruit, etc. Luke 13 : 7.

Blessed is the people that know the joyful sound, etc. Ps. 89 : 15.

Jesus stood and cried, saying, If any man thirst, etc. John 7 : 37.

Will ye also go away ? John 6 : 67.

As I live, saith the Lord God, I have no pleasure in the death, etc. Ezek. 33 : 11.

Yet it pleased the Lord to bruise him, etc. Isa. 53 : 10.

I shall be satisfied when I awake with thy likeness Ps. 17 : 15.

And whosoever will, let him take of the water of life freely. Rev. 2 : 17.

Herein is love, not that we loved God, etc. 1 John 4 : 10.

He is despised and rejected of men, etc. Isa. 53 : 3-10.

Then said he unto him, a certain man made a great supper, etc. Luke 14 : 16-23.

Behold a sower went forth to sow, etc. Matt. 13 : 3-23.

Come unto me, all ye that labor, etc. Matt. 11 : 28.

For the Son of man is come to seek and to save that which was lost. Luke 19 : 10.

Parable of the Prodigal Son. Luke 15 : 11-32.

Apostle Peter's sermon at Pentecost. Acts 2 : 1-40.

Of a truth, I perceive that God is no respecter of persons. Acts 10 : 34.

And he came to Nazareth, etc. Luke 4 : 16-21.

Ye seek me not because ye saw the miracles, etc. John 6 : 26-34.

I am the bread of life, etc. John 6 : 35-40.

Ho ! every one that thirsteth, etc. Isa. 55 : 1.

No man can come unto me except, etc. John 6 : 44-50.

But I would not have you ignorant, etc.   1 Thess. 4 : 13-17.

Parable of the Lost Sheep.   Luke 15 : 3-7.

Behold, I stand at the door and knock, etc.   Rev. 3 : 20.

I am the living bread which came down from heaven, etc.   John 6 : 51-55.

And others, tempting him, sought a sign, etc.   Luke 11 : 16-23.

Ye have sold yourselves for naught, etc.   Isa. 52 : 3-6.

Therefore let the house of Israel know assuredly, etc.   Acts 2 : 36-39.

Let not your heart be troubled, etc.   John 14 : 1-6.

I am the door of the sheep, etc.   John 10 : 7-11.

The conversion of the jailer.   Acts 16 : 16-33.

Exposition on the restoration of Eutychus.   Acts 20 : 1-12.

Jesus answered and said unto her, If thou knewest, etc. John 4 : 13, 14.

The resurrection of the dead.   Luke 20 : 27-36.

The marriage of the king's son.   Matt. 22 : 1-13.

It is easier for heaven and earth, etc.   Luke 16 : 17.

The resurrection of Lazarus.   John, 11th chap.

The account of Zaccheus.   Luke 19 : 1-9.

The miracle at Bethesda.   John 5 : 1-9.

The Transfiguration.   Luke 9 : 28-36.

Parable of the rich man and Lazurus.   Luke 16 : 19-26.

The prayer of the rich man for his brethren.   Luke 16 : 27-31.

The account of the blind man.   John, 9th chap.

The Parable of the Ten Virgins.   Matt., 25th chap.

The Master teaching to pray.   Luke 11 : 1-13.

Striving to enter in at the strait gate, etc.   Luke 13 : 24-28.

The wicked sentenced.   Matt. 25 : 31-46.

The rich young man.   Matt. 19 : 16-22.

The parable of the barren fig-tree.   Luke 13 : 6-9.

The necessity of regeneration.   John 3 : 1-5.

The withered hand healed.   Matt. 12 : 10-13.

Seek ye the Lord while He may be found, etc.   Isa. 55 : 6.

Let the wicked forsake his way, etc.   Isa. 55 : 7.

Blind Bartimeus healed.   Mark 10 : 46-52.

Philip preaching in Samaria.   Acts 8 : 5-8.

And Jesus said unto them, I am the bread of life, etc.   John 6 : 35-37.

Ye have not chosen me, but I have chosen you, etc.   John 15 : 16.

The one thing needful.   Luke 10 : 38-42.

The great salvation.   Heb. 2 : 1-3.

"O Israel, thou hast destroyed thyself." Hosea 13 : 9.

Repent ye therefore, and be converted, etc. Acts 3 : 19.

The day of judgment. Matt. 25 : 31–40.

"Not every one that saith unto me, Lord, Lord," etc. Matt. 7 : 21–23.

"Who gave himself for us," etc. Titus 2 : 14.

"Ye will not come to me that ye might have life." John 5 : 40.

High feelings not to be sought for their own sake." Acts 20 : 18–19.

"He that believeth on me, believeth not on me," etc. John 12 : 44–48.

If any man be in Christ, he is a new creature, etc. 2 Cor. 5 : 17.

Take my yoke upon you, etc. Matt. 11 : 29.

And I will pour upon the house of David, etc. Zech. 12 : 10.

Behold the Lamb of God, etc. John 1 : 29.

————

SERMONS BY REV. JOHN BERRIDGE, M.A.

Berridge's sermons were for the most part practical and experimental. Although a humorist by nature, his sermons are marked by uniform gravity. After considerable research we have discovered what we hardly hoped to find—a number of the revival texts of this gifted but eccentric preacher. Almost all of those which have come down to us were intended for young converts. A special work of grace began in his parish during the summer of 1759, when he invited Wesley to assist him in field-preaching. The Journal of Wesley (No. 11, from May 28th to Nov. 25th, 1759) gives a short account of this awakening in the region of which Everton was the centre. Within a single year about two thousand souls were awakened in connection with his ministry and that of Mr. Hicks. At this time Berridge preached ten or twelve sermons a week, more or less in the open air, although he then suffered from great bodily weakness. But when he was feeblest the Spirit so strengthened him that his voice sounded out to a very great distance. "I have," said an ear-witness, "heard Whitefield speak as loud, but not with such a continued, strong, unbroken tenor." In 1776 Mr. Berridge labored for three months in London. He had the largest congregations that were ever known, considering the average attendance ; and greatly were his sermons and prayers owned of the Lord in that city. One saying of his is worth remembering : " Much reading and thinking may make a popular preacher, but much secret prayer must make a powerful preacher." His little book, "The Christian World Unmasked," gives one some notion of the humor, good sense, and closeness of application which marked his sermons. A volume, his "Life and Letters," was republished in London in 1864 (12mo, pp. 632).

THEMES AND TEXTS.

With the Lord there is plenteous redemption. Ps. 130 : 7, 8.

Every man to till his own heart as a piece of land. (He that tilleth his land shall have plenty of bread. . . .) Prov. 28 : 19.

Christ giveth His bread to the poor. Prov. 22 : 9.

In the Lord Jehovah is everlasting strength. Isa. 26 : 3, 4.

Seeking and finding mercy, Isa. 55 : 6, 7.

Breaking up fallow ground. Jer. 4 : 3, 4.

Christ the Great Physician. Jer. 33 : 6.

Our Redeemer successfully pleading our cause. Jer. 50 : 33, 34.

Salvation is of the Lord. Ezek. 36 : 25–27.

God delights in mercy. Micah 7 : 18.

An example of importunity. Matt. 15 : 28.

The Kingdom is righteousness, peace, and joy. Luke 12 : 31, 32.

Keeping the commandments. John 14 : 15–17.

The Lord's commission to Paul. Acts 26 : 17, 18.

The blessed effects of tribulation. Rom. 5 : 3–5.

The carnally minded and the spiritually minded. Rom. 8 : 6, 7.

The Father giving to us all things freely. Rom. 8 : 32.

Ministers pens, grace the ink, the heart the parchment. (Ye are our epistle written in our hearts, known and read of all men.) 2 Cor. 3 : 2.

Christ dwelling in us as the hope of glory. Col. 1 : 27, 28.

Thanks to God for the conversion of sinners. 2 Thess. 2 : 13, 14.

The faithful saying. 1 Tim. 1 : 15.

Fight the good fight of faith. 1 Tim. 6 : 12.

Be strong in the grace of Christ. 2 Tim. 2 : 1.

Able to save to the uttermost. Heb. 7 : 25.

The Law written in the heart. Heb. 8 : 10.

The double-mindedness of believers and unbelievers. Jas. 4 : 8.

Christ precious to believers. 1 Pet. 2 : 7.

Having the form of godliness, but denying its power. 2 Tim. 3 : 5.

Justification not by works, but by faith. Gal. 3 : 10, 11.

The gospel invitation to the hungry and thirsty. Isa. 55 : 1.

Farewell Sermon : God our refuge and trust. Ps. 62 : 8.

SERMONS BY DANIEL BAKER, D.D.

THEMES AND TEXTS.

The truth and excellence of the Christian Religion. (For their rock is not as our Rock....) Deut. 32 : 31.

The greatness of God. Ps. 104 : 1.

Christ the Mediator. Philip. 2 : 6-11.

The uses of the law. Gal. 3 : 19.

The sinner weighed and found wanting. Dan. 5 : 27.

The character and reward of the earthly minded. Prov. 3 : 35.

The Deluge. Gen. 7 : 1.

War in Heaven. Rev. 12 : 7, 8.

On seeking the Lord. Isa. 55 : 6.

The duty of coming to Christ. John 6 : 44.

Vain excuses. Luke 14 : 18.

Idleness reproved. Matt. 20 : 6.

The necessity of preparation for death. John 9 : 4.

Precious Faith. 2 Pet. 1 : 1.

The fulfilment of prophecy. 2 Pet. 1 : 21.

The nature, sinfulness, and consequences of unbelief. Mark 16 : 16.

Justification. Rom. 5 : 1, 2.

Naaman. 2 Kings 5 : 12.

The example of Eli. 1 Sam. 3 : 13.

Prove your own work. Gal. 6 : 4.

The sufferings of Christ and their design. Mark 15 : 13.

The tomb of Jesus. Matt. 28 : 6.

Christian morality. Philip. 4 : 8.

A sermon to young men. 1 Chron. 28 : 9.

The sovereignty of God. Rev. 19 : 6.

The blessedness of being a Christian. 1 John 3 : 2.

The danger of procrastination. (And he said, To-morrow.) Exod. 8 : 10.

SERMONS BY REV. ALBERT BARNES.

Mr. Barnes was in many points a model revivalist for a cultivated community, and his lectures on revivals in the "National Preacher" are of value and interest to such preachers as have prejudices against these works of grace to remove, either in themselves or others. We subjoin a list of his sermons from a volume entitled " The Way of Salvation," prepared in 1835 at the suggestion of British publishers, Messrs. Knight & Son, London.

THEMES AND TEXTS.

Man not benefited by the rejection of Christianity.   John 6 : 68.

The earth a place of probation.   Acts 17 : 26, 27.

It is wise to submit to the Divine Government.   Matt. 25 : 26, 27.

The state in which the Gospel finds man.   Matt. 18 : 11.

What must I do to be saved?   Acts 16 : 30.

Conviction of sin.   Ps. 51 : 4.

The struggles of a convicted sinner.   Mark 10 : 22, 23 ; Matt. 8 : 21, 22 ; Luke 9 : 61, 62.

The remedy for a wounded spirit.   Prov. 18 : 14.

Permanent peace for the convicted soul.   Jer. 6:14 ; Luke 7 : 48–50.

The atonement giving peace to the convicted.   1 John 1 : 7.

The atonement in its relation to pardon.   Col. 1 : 20.

The necessity of regeneration.   John 3 : 3.

The nature of regeneration.   2 Cor. 5 : 17.

The Spirit's agency in regeneration.   Titus 3 : 5.

The nature of repentance.   Acts 20 : 21.

Repentance in its relation to pardon.   Acts 3 : 19.

The evidence of true repentance..   2 Cor. 7 : 9–11.

Faith a condition of salvation.   Mark 16 : 16.

The importance of faith.   Heb. 11 : 6.

Faith as a principle of action.   2 Cor. 5 : 7.

How shall man be just with God ?   Job 25 : 4.

Man cannot disprove the charge of guilt.   Rom. 3 : 20.

Man cannot show that his conduct is right.   Rom. 3 : 20.

Men cannot merit salvation.   Job 35 : 5–8.

What is meant by the merits of Christ ?   John 1 : 16.

How are we justified by the merits of Christ ?   Rom. 3 : 24.

The relation of faith to justification.   Rom. 1 : 16, 17.

The prime importance of justification.   Rom. 1 : 17.

SERMONS BY REV. JEDEDIAH BURCHARD.[*]

THEMES AND TEXTS.

Prayer for the restoration of saving joy. Ps. 51 : 12, 13.

The conduct of Bartimeus recommended to sinners.   Mark 10 : 46–52.

Coming to Christ as illustrated by Peter walking on the water. Matt. 14 : 22–31.

The necessity of regeneration.   John 5 : 3.

Sermon addressed to young converts on watchfulness, etc. (no text).

SERMONS BY REV. EMERSON ANDREWS.

THEMES AND TEXTS.

CHRIST WEEPING OVER JERUSALEM.

Luke 19 : 41, 42.

1. Why did Christ weep?
2. What belonged to their peace?
3. The Jews had their day of grace.

Filled with the Spirit.   Eph. 5 : 18.

The new birth.   John 3 : 7.

The Christian lawsuit.   Matt. 5 : 25.

1. God has an action against sinners.
2. Notice the only terms of reconciliation.
3. Why you should settle your case quickly.
4. Beware of deferring reconciliation until the judgment day.
5. Behold the blessings of gracious reconciliation.

THE IMPORTUNATE CRY.

Habakkuk 1 : 2.

1. How long ministers may cry and not be heard.
2. How long churches and Christians may cry and not be heard.

---

[*] This zealous but eccentric evangelist, who was popular in New York and New England about the years 1831-35, was very unwilling that any one should report his sermons. On one occasion, having detected a reporter taking notes of his sermon, he invited him to come forward to the anxious-seat to be prayed for, assuring him that taking notes was a bad business for his soul.

3. How long convicted sinners may cry and not be heard.

The Great Salvation.   Heb. 2 : 3.

Spiritual Farming.   Hosea 10 : 12.

The soul's gain or loss.   Mark 8 : 36, 37.

Christ knocking at the door.   Rev. 3 : 20.

The sinner's hard way.   Prov. 13 : 15.

The power of the Spirit.   Zech. 4 : 6.

The spiritual looking-glass.   Jas. 1 : 23.

Preparation for meeting God.   Amos 4 : 12.

Revivals.   Hab. 3 : 2.

Effectual prayer.   Jas. 5 : 16.

Possessing the land for God.   Josh. 13 : 1.

Sin hunting sinners.   Num. 32 : 23.

Not caring for souls.   Ps. 142 : 4.

The Barren Fig-tree.   Luke 13 : 7.

Love to God.   Matt. 22 : 37.

God's inquisition for blood.   Ps. 9 : 12.

Reasons why we should accept salvation.   Acts 13 : 26.

The tokens of perdition.   Phil. 1 : 28.

The great election day.   Josh. 24 : 15.

The worth of the soul.   Ps. 49 : 8.

Bringing in the tithes.   Mal. 3 : 10.

The sinner's excuses.   Luke 14 : 18.

The General Judgment.   2 Cor. 5 : 10.

God's witnesses.   Isa. 43 : 10.

The Resurrection.   Acts 26 : 8.

Gospel power.   Rom. 1 : 16.

The Prodigal Son.   Luke 15 : 18.

A good hope.   1 John 3 : 3.

Christ's Kingdom.   John 18 : 36.

Christian conversion.   Acts 3 : 19.

Glorying in the Cross.   Gal. 6 : 14.

Christian union.   Eph. 4 : 3.

The Christian race.   Heb. 12 : 1.

The sinner's shipwreck.   1 Tim. 1 : 19.

Intemperance.   Prov. 23 : 21.

A minister's responsibility.   Acts 20 : 26.

The great change.   2 Cor. 5 : 17

Awakening.   Rom. 13 : 11.

Constraining love.   2 Cor. 5 : 14.

Gracious election.   Rom. 8 : 33.

The spiritual voyage.   Acts 27 : 31.

The unspeakable gift.   2 Cor. 9 : 15.
Benevolence.   Gal. 6 : 10.
Christ precious.   1 Pet. 2 : 7.
The evangelist.   2 Tim. 4 : 5.
Christ our Beloved.   Song of Sol. 2 : 16.
Direction to inquirers.   Acts 2 : 37.
The great change.   Mark 5 : 19.
Converting souls.   Jas. 5 : 20.
Christian reforms.   Isa. 66 : 8.
Harvest-time.   John 4 : 35.
A time to dance.   Eccles. 3 : 4.
Christian union.   Ps. 133 : 1.
Gospel reformation.   Acts 3 : 19.
Revival Triumphs.   2 Cor. 2 : 14.
Cheerful Christians.   John 16 : 33.
Sufficiency in God.   2 Cor. 3 : 5.
Bible conversion.   Ps. 51 : 13.
Why not saved?   Jer. 8 : 20.
Glorify God in the fires.   Isa. 24 : 15.
Their way is their folly.   Ps. 19 : 13.
The Christian's farewell.   2 Cor. 13 : 11.

REVIVAL SERMONS FROM VARIOUS SOURCES.

FROM "SKETCHES OF SERMONS PUBLISHED BY THEIR RESPECTIVE AUTHORS."

(American edition, Philadelphia, 1844.)

SINNERS RETURNING TO GOD.

Jer. 50 : 4, 5.

1. In those days the children of Israel shall come, they and the children of Judah together.

2. Going and weeping.

3. To seek the Lord their God.

4. They ask the way to Zion, with their faces thitherward.

5. Come and let us join ourselves to the Lord In a perpetual covenant.   GAMMA.

THE HOLY GHOST OBTAINED IN ANSWER TO PRAYER.

Luke 11 : 13.

1. These words *exhibit our privilege* as the followers of Christ.

a. Who is meant by the Holy Ghost.

b. His presence is enjoyed by all Christians.

c. For what purpose he is received by them.

2. Prescribe our duty. This is to ask as God requires.

a. Ask sincerely.

b. Ask evangelically, *i.e.* in entire dependence on the mediation of Christ.

c. Ask importunately.

d. Ask believingly.

3. *Encourage our hope.* If, then, ye, etc.

a. Mankind naturally evil.

b. Yet they know how to give good gifts to their children.

(*a*) *Good* gifts.

(β) They *give* them.

(γ) *Know how*, etc. Sufficient wisdom to adapt them to the character and wants of the child.

c. But God is certainly your Father if you ask the Holy Spirit as He requires. 2 Cor. 6 : 17, 18.

d. And God being your Father, you cannot fail of obtaining the gift of the Holy Spirit ; He is all-sufficient, He is engaged to give the Spirit. He is a good, a wise, and a gracious Father.

Application.

a. Recollect you privilege, with self-examination.

b. Recollect your duty, with perseverance in it.

c. Recollect your encouragement, with steadfast hope.

ALPHA.

THE IMPORTANT QUESTION.

Dost thou believe on the Son God ? John 9 : 35.

1. The nature of the question.

2. Offer some helps to assist you in answering it.

3. State some reasons why an answer should be given.

BETA.

PAUL'S DISCOURSE BEFORE FELIX.

Acts 24 : 25.

1. The manner of the Apostle's preaching.   He reasoned, etc.

2. The effect of his preaching.   Felix trembled.

3. The conduct of his hearer.   " And answered, Go thy way," etc.

ETA.

SINNERS BROUGHT NIGH BY THE BLOOD OF CHRIST.

Eph. 2 : 13.

1. We were sometimes far off.
2. Now are we made nigh. These words convey to the mind ideas of—
   a. Relationship.
   b. Friendship.
   c. Union.
   d. Fellowship.
3. In Christ Jesus, by the blood of Christ.

GAMMA.

ADDRESS TO THE FALLEN.

Rev. 2 : 5.

1. The fall.
2. The means by which they may rise again.

I N D E C I S I O N.

1 Kings 18 : 21.

1. The evidence of indecision in religion.
   a. The undecided keep the ordinances of God only in part.
   b. Rest in external acts of public worship or other duty.
   c. Engage more heartily in secular pursuits than in eternal concerns.
   d. Without spiritual comfort.
2. The evil of it.
3. Means suggested for the abandonment of this habit.

ALPHA.

MANASSEH'S REPENTANCE.

2 Chron. 33 : 12, 13.

1. His character as a sinner.
2. His conduct as a penitent.
3. His salvation as a believer.

ETA.

THE REVIVAL OF THE WORK OF GOD AT HOME INTIMATELY CONNECTED WITH ITS EXTENSION ABROAD.

Ps. 67 : 1, 2.

OMEGA.

THE REDEEMER'S COMPLAINT.

John 5 : 40.

1. We have our natural state evidently implied : the opposite of "life," a state of *death.*
2. We are pointed to the source of life : "Ye will not come unto *me.*"
3. We are instructed how to obtain the life we need : "Come."

4. We learn what is the immediate cause of man's eternal destruction. Ye *will* not.   ZETA.

PETER FOLLOWING AFAR OFF.

Luke 22 : 54.

1. Survey the marks of declension represented in the text.
a. He felt some attachment to his Master.
b. Peter's love was in a decaying condition.
c. His heart was undecided and irresolute.
2. Advert to its causes.
a. Presumption.
b. Shame.
c. Fear and worldly prudence.
d. Unbelief.
3. Reflect on its consequences.
a. A dreadful fall.
b. Gross dishonor to the cause of Christ.
c. Bitter remorse.

Application.

a. A word of *reproof* to those who do not follow Christ at all.
b. A word of *incitement* to those who follow him afar off.
c. A word of *caution* to those who follow him closely.

DELTA.

FROM THE "NATIONAL PREACHER."

A Dreadful Meeting. Isa. 47 : 3. By the Rev. Dr. H. Humphrey. (Vol. iv. No. 6.)

Persuasives to Immediate Repentance. Acts 24 : 25. By the Rev. Dr. B. Tyler. (Vol. v. No. 6.)

The sinner, and not the believer, deranged. Acts 26 : 24, 25. By the Rev. E. W. Hooker. (Vol. v. No. 11.)

Means of a revival of religion. Amos 7 : 2. By the Rev. Dr. Tucker. (Vol. vii. No. 9.)

Alarm to the Careless. Isa. 32 : 11. By the Rev. Dr. Tucker. (Vol. vii. No. 9).

A Solemn Question answered. Jer. 8 : 6. By the Rev. Dr. Nevins. (Vol. vii. No. 12.)

Ground of the Difficulty of Conversions. Jer. 2 : 25. By the Rev. Mr. Dickinson. (Vol. ix. No. 3.)

The Moral Insanity of Irreligious Men. Eccles. 9 : 3. By the Rev. Mr. Ide. (Vol. xv. No. 12.)

The great Separation which Religion makes in Families. Matt. 10 : 35. By the Rev. A. Barnes. (Vol. xvii. No. 2.)

Fathers invited into the Ark. Gen. 7 : 1. By the Rev. Milton Badger. (Vol. xvii. No. 4.)

Why should the work cease? Nehemiah 6 : 3. By the Rev. W. B. Lewis. (Vol. xvii. No. 4.)

The Tokens of Perdition. Phil. 1 : 28. By the Rev. G. B. Ide. (Vol. xvii. No. 6.)

The Salvation of the Gospel great, and not to be Neglected. Heb. 2 : 3. By J. M. Whiton. (Vol. xviii. No. 5.)

The Guilt of Continued Impenitence. Matt. 11 : 21. By the Rev. Dr. Mark Tucker. (Vol. xviii. No. 7.)

The Blessed Consequence of Repentance. Acts 3 : 19. (Vol. xviii. No. 12.)

The Superior Glory of the Ministration of the Spirit. 2 Cor. 3 : 8. By the Rev. Dr. Magie. (Vol. xix. No. 1.)

A Revival of Religion in God's Work. Ps. 119 : 126. By the Rev. Dr. Tucker. (Vol. xix. No. 7.)

The Christian's Need of a Revival of Religion. Ps. 51 : 12, 13. By the Rev. G. A. Lintner. (Vol. xx. No. 5.)

The withdrawal of the Spirit deprecated. Isa. 51 : 11. By the Rev. A. D. Smith. (Vol. xxi. No. 2.)

How long we may pray, and God not hear. Habakkuk 1 : 2. By the Rev. D. A. Clark. (Vol. xxi. No. 3.)

The Fatal Tendencies of Unbelief. Heb. 3 : 18. (Ibidem.)

The Four Lepers. 2 Kings 7 : 3. (Vol. xxi. No. 4.)

Waiting for a Revival. Hab. 5 : 3. By the Rev. Dr. Humphrey. (Vol. xxi. No. 6.)

The funeral of the Soul. Matt. 25 : 46. By the Rev. H. B. Hooker. (Vol. xxi. No. 12.)

Submission to God. By the Rev. Dr. G. W. Bethune. (Vol. xxii. No. 1.)

The Place and Importance of the Individual. 1 Cor. 12 : 20, 21. By the Rev. Albert Barnes. (Vol. xxiv. No. 14.)

The Demands of Sinners Unreasonable. Matt. 27 : 42. By the Rev. S. Harris. (Vol. xxvii. No. 3.)

To whom shall we go? or the Church Member in doubt. John 6 : 66–68. By the Rev. Dr. Adams. (Vol. xxvii. No. 4.)

Climbing up some other Way. John 10 : 1. By the Rev. Emerson Davis. (Vol. xxvii. No. 12.)

The Sin of Consulting with Familiar Spirits. Lev. 20 : 27. By the Rev. Dr. Pond. (Vol. xxviii. No. 5.)

The Two Sides. Exodus 32 : 26. By the Rev. Dr. Magie. (Vol. xxviii. No. 8.)

No Communications from the Dead to the Living.   2 Cor. 15 : 1–4.
By the Rev. T. L. Shipman.   (Vol. xxx. No. 11.)

Escape for thy Life.   Gen. 19 : 17.   By the Rev. Dr. Jeremiah Day.
(Vol. xxxi. No. 5.)

FROM "THE HOMILETIC MONTHLY."

GOD'S IRRECONCILABLE ENEMY.

The carnal mind is enmity against God ; for it is not subject to the law of God, neither indeed can be. Rom. 8 : 7.

1. A description of this enemy of God.

It is the fleshly mind, the mind that serves the flesh and lives on the flesh.   It is the lower and base nature which breeds the lusts of the flesh.   It is the nature that binds living fast to the present world, and refuses men any delights or hopes higher than a dinner or a dram.   It is the "law in the members" warring against the "law of the mind" cr spirit.   It is the ground in human nature, out of which spring all the vices, shames, crimes, and sins of mankind.   This mind is not *at* enmity ; it is enmity itself.   It is not estranged ; it is not, and cannot be, subject to the law of God.   That there is such a hostile force in the soul of man, all history, every daily newspaper, all experience proves ; for the disorderly and malignant spirit is continually breaking forth in vice, crime, and sin.   It is a totally depraved spirit.

2. Have we the carnal mind ?

Right reason will answer the question.   If we behave or feel as loyal subjects of God ought not to behave and feel, we must have the carnal mind.   We may also have the "mind" which Paul describes as approving and serving the law of God, but the carnal mind may be master.

Tests.

a. Do we do what our consciences condemn ?

b. Do we try to reform, and fail ?

c. God is our Father : have we a true child's love for Him ?

d. God is dear to true men : do we love Him, love to think of Him, to go to Him in prayer, to be alone with Him ?   Is the thought of Him often in our minds, a refreshment and joy ?

3. The carnal mind cannot be treated with, compromised with, or made an ally of.

It must be cast out.   Christ casts out devils still.   Every sinner is a sufferer, torn and sore rent by devils of carnality ; Christ still heals all that are brought unto Him.   He heals the patient by casting out the evil spirit.   There is no other healing except by this deliverance from the carnal mind.

THE WANT OF SPIRITUAL APPETITE.

Blessed are they which do hunger and thirst after righteousness, for they shall be filled. Matt. 5: 6.

1. Desire is a condition and a prophecy of religious attainments.

Wanting things enough to seek them earnestly goes before getting them. The successful men of this world are the men who hunger after wealth, honor, fame, or wisdom. It is a law of even the lower life that an appetite goes before eating, and that the desire for a dinner urges men to seek it. We cannot get either the lower or the higher in life without wanting it. God puts spiritual attainments under this condition. We become righteous after and through desiring to become righteous.

2. This law of desire explains our spiritual poverty.

We do not want to be righteous in the fullest sense—in the high sense of likeness to God. We are often even afraid to be righteous, lest we may not prosper in life, or may have to surrender some cherished sin. If we want righteousness, as we want human love, riches, honor, power, fame, or wisdom, we should become "rich in faith."

3. This want of appetite for righteousness is the curse of mankind.

The sweet blessing of Christ is for us in such small measure! A little crumb suffices us. We have no true hunger. Grace has to be forced upon us, and is then refused by many. To be "filled"—who dares desire this as starving men want food, or thirsty men seek water? Wanting spiritual desire, we lack spiritual manhood; lacking such manhood, we fall from our best estate and wander outside of the spiritual Eden, because we do not wish to return to its blessed life.

AN AWFUL MISTAKE.

Thou sayest I am rich and increased with goods, and have need of nothing; and knowest not that thou art wretched, and miserable, and poor, and blind, and naked. Rev. 3 : 17.

1. Which of these estimates is correct?

It is a difference of judgment between God, on the one hand, and a Church whose faults have just been summed up in the charge that they are "lukewarm," "neither cold nor hot." It describes any of us who are content with *appearances* of religious or moral character, and have no heat of purpose or zeal. God must be right for three reasons.

a. He knows all about us.

b. Morals and religion, pure conduct and spiritual vitality, are too important to be lukewarmly preferred, or sought or lived.

c. Great numbers of witnesses testify that, having been stimulated to careful self-examination, they have discovered that God's description of them in their lukewarm life was awfully true.

2. The mistake of the lukewarm carries an awful burden of consequences.

a. It keeps him poor, wretched, blind. It shuts him out from all sweet sights of goodness and holiness, and leaves him empty of the best treasures.

b. It sets up for our children and our neighbors a false standard of religion. Lukewarm people are teaching just what God denounces as deadliest error.

c. The lukewarm state a great peril : " I will spew thee out of my mouth."

CHRIST'S FIRST CARE WAS FOR PENITENTS.

Zaccheus, make haste and come down ; for to-day I must abide at thy house. Luke 19 : 5.

A man who has led a well-known wicked life has difficulties to face in coming to Christ. None but a determined man will succeed. The man who is anxious to see Jesus will throw away his so-called dignity. He will run and climb a tree like Zaccheus. It was not curiosity that led him to do this. He had been deeply impressed with what he had heard of Christ, and he wished to know more. Christ looked lovingly on Zaccheus, went to dine with him, and gave him salvation.

1. We should never be so absorbed in great things as to neglect little things at our side. When you are building a college don't forget Lazarus.

2. It is a comfort to know that our Lord is never too busy to meet a soul that really desires Him.

3. Jericho was a city of priests, yet Jesus preferred to dine with a penitent publican.

THE SINNER'S FRIEND.

Thou gavest me no kiss. Luke 7 : 45.

1. Defects of the life that is free from heinous and public sin, but is destitute of love to Christ ; honors Christ in outward forms, but refuses Him affection, and the service which love inspires.

2. *Loving Christ the proof of repentance.* The conduct of the woman which was a sinner showed her repentance.

3. *Love to Christ is the spring of obedience.* Notice the tender assiduity, the all-surrendering *giving* of the woman.

Exhortation : You are denying Christ the kiss of affection and the alabaster box of personal sacrifice for His cause.

THE TRIBUNAL OF GOD.

I the Lord search the heart, I try the reins, even to give every man according to his ways, and according to the fruit of his doings. Jer. 17 : 10.

1. It is a searching tribunal.

It gets all the facts, measures all the motives, studies all the circumstances, of our ways and doings. "The truth, the whole truth, and nothing but the truth," comes out only to the eye of God.

2. We are tried and judged before this tribunal, and cannot escape it.

Every man's ways and doings are put to this trial. Our fellow-men neither know all, nor judge of and by all. They see the shell with which we cover our lives : God sees all that we hide from human eyes. We ourselves acquit ourselves by turning away our eyes from the bad places, by weighing temptation on one side, and our personal choice on the other, in false balances. We deceive our neighbors, we deceive our own hearts, but we cannot escape from all-revealing trial by the just and wise judgment of God.

3. The tribunal of God is final ; execution follows without appeal.

He gives to every man according to the facts—his ways and the fruit of his doings. We are under law ; we are tried by Infinite Justice ; there is no appeal, no stay of sentence, no reprieve, no new trial, no revision of judgment, no interference by an executive, no being pardoned out in answer to the petitions of our friends.

> How careful, then, ought we to live,
> With what religious fear,
> Who such a strict account must give,
> For our behavior here !

FROM "THE HOMILETICAL QUARTERLY,"

January, 1880, pp. 133, 134.

Why abodest thou among the sheepfolds ? Judges 5 : 16. (Words of Deborah to the tribe of Reuben.)

We have no right to sacrifice—

1. Duty to comfort.
2. Duty to peace.
3. Duty to gain.

REVIVAL SERMONS

*Preached in New York and Brooklyn during the year 1858.**

The Holy Flock.   Ezekiel 36 : 37, 38.   By the Rev. Dr. James W. Alexander.

* The sermons here suggested are printed in "The New York Pulpit in the Revival of 1858," published by Sheldon, Blakeman & Co., 1858.

Religious Conversation. Malachi 3 : 16. By the Rev. Rufus W. Clark.

Past Feeling. Eph. 4 : 19. By the Rev. Theo. L. Cuyler.

Why will ye die ? Ezek. 18 : 31. By the Rev. Dr. B. C. Cutler.

The Wise Decision. Heb. 11 : 24–26. By the Rev. Dr. Edward Lathrop.

Christ at the Door. Rev. 3 : 20. By the Rev. Dr. G. W. Bethune.

Unanswered Prayer. James 4 : 3. By the Rev. Dr. George Potts.

Man's Pride against God's Grace. 1 Cor. 1 : 30. By the Rev. J. P. Thompson.

Tears at the Judgment. Matt. 22 : 13 : There shall be weeping.'' By the Rev. Dr. J. M. Krebs.

True Repentance. Heb. 6 : 1. By the Rev. Dr. Wm. Hague.

Seeking the Lord so as to find Him. Jer. 29 : 12, 13. By the Rev. Dr. Joel Parker.

No Exempts and no Quarter in that War. Eccles. 8 : 8. By the Rev. Dr. W. R. Williams.

Coming to Christ. John 4 : 37. By the Rev. Dr. M. S. Hutton.

What shall I do to be saved ? Acts 16 : 30, 31. By the Rev. Dr. W. I. Budington.

Men to be reconciled to God through Christ. 2 Cor. 5 : 20 (last clause). By the Rev. Dr. R. S. Storrs.

The Ancient Worthies our Example. Heb. 6 : 12. By the Rev. Dr. T. E. Vermilye.

Incentives to seek companionship with Israel. Num. 10 : 29. By the Rev. Dr. J. Kennedy.

The Cross Contemplated. Matt. 37 : 36. By the Rev. Dr. E. T. Hiscox.

The Strait Gate. Luke 13 : 23, 24. By the Rev. Dr. J. McClintock.

Man's Perdition not of God. Ezek. 18 : 23. By the Rev. Dr. E. F. Hatfield.

The Duty of Repentance. Acts 17 : 30. By the Rev. Dr. Asa D. Smith.

Religious Insensibility. Eph. 4 : 19. By the Rev. Dr. S. D. Burchard.

Religion a Service. Matt. 7 : 21. By the Rev. Dr. R. D. Hitchcock.

The Life Battle. 1 Tim. 6 : 12. By the Rev. Dr. Jesse T. Peck.

Not far from the Kingdom of God. Mark 12 : 28–34. By the Rev. Dr. Wm. Adams.

THE GOSPEL INVITATION.

Sermons Related to the Boston Revival of 1877 (Boston, 1877).

The Christian Believer's Burden. Rom. 9 : 1-3. By the Rev. Dr. E. K. Alden.

The Old Faith and the New. Jer. 6 : 16. By the Rev. Dr. C. G. Lorimer.

Learn of Me. Matt. 11 : 29. By the Rev. Dr. G. Z. Gray.

The Separation of the Soul from God. Isa. 59 : 1-2. By the Rev. Dr. W. F. Mallalieu.

The Decay of Will. Luke 15 : 18. By the Rev. S. E. Herrick.

Coming to One's Self. Luke 15 : 17, 18. By the Rev. Dr. A. P. Peabody.

The Cry for a Cleansed Heart. Ps. 51 : 10-13. By the Rev. A. E. Dunning.

God's Controversy with His People. Micah 6 : 3. By the Rev. Dr. A. H. Vinton.

God a Consuming Fire. Heb. 12 : 20. By the Rev. A. J. Gordon.

God Dismissed. Job 21 : 14. By the Rev. S. L. Caldwell.

Jesus of Nazareth Passeth By. Luke 18 : 37. By the Rev. A. McKenzie.

Nothing to do with Christ. Matt. 27 : 19. By the Rev. W. W. Newton.

The Door Opened, and Christ within. Rev. 3 : 20. By the Rev. H. M. Grout.

Faith the Source of Faithfulness. Acts 26 : 18. By the Rev. Joseph Cook.]

Our Two Harvests. Gal. 6 : 7, 8. By the Rev. Dr. Rufus Ellis.

The Gospel Invitation. Rev. 22 : 17. By the Rev. Dr. W. F. Warren.]

The Permanence of Moral Character. No text. By the Rev. Joseph Cook.

The Prominence of the Atonement. 1 Cor. 2 : 2. By the Rev. Dr. E. A. Park.

MISCELLANEOUS.

OUTLINES.

IF THOU DOEST NOT WELL, SIN LIETH AT THE DOOR.

Gen. 4 : 7.

As for the meaning of these and other connected words, the learned differ in opinion. They interpret them in one of two senses, either of which agrees with the analogy of the faith and is rich in practical sug- ·gestions. We intend, therefore, to examine and apply both these chief interpretations.

1. According to many high authorities, the passage may be ren- dered, " If thou doest well, shalt thou not be accepted ? and if thou doest not well, sin (*i.e.* the punishment of sin), or s·n personified, lies at the door like a ravenous beast of prey ready to seize thee. (It is remarkable that Dr. Julius Müller's " Christian Doctrine of Sin" and Principal Tulloch's lectures on the same subject ignore this difficult passage.) Admitting, however, that Cain could know what sin in our modern sense signified, what does this Scripture from this first point of view teach us?

a. Mere reason would prefer Cain's offering as more cleanly, more beautiful, and more humane.

b. Kindness to brutes is not always associated with mercy to man. He who made the first unbloody sacrifice was the first man of blood.

c. Unbelief and disobedience go together. God accepted neither Cain nor his offering.

d. We generally sin against God before we sin against our brother.

e. The example of the good often makes the bad envious, and fills them with persecuting hate.

f. Sin, not repented of. leads to still greater sin.

g. Guilt pursues the guilty and drives them to despair.

2. Or, the passage may be rendered : " If thou doest well, shalt thou not be accepted? And if thou doest not well, a sin-offering coucheth at the door, and to thee shall he [the lamb] be subject, and thou shalt have rule over him." The word here rendered "sin" is rendered "sin-offering" in Exod. 29 : 14 ; Levit. 4 : 1-35, 6 : 17, 25, and elsewhere. The word translated "lieth" is often used for the couching of tame animals which lie on the breast with the limbs gathered under them like sheep. See Gen. 29 : 2 ; Isa. 11 : 7, 17 : 2 ; Ezek. 34 : 14 ; Zeph. 2 : 14. The word which translates the Hebrew word "sin-offering" in the Septuagint is employed in 2 Cor. 5 : 21, where Jesus is said to be made "sin" for us, *i.e.*, a sin-offering. If

this is the true interpretation, it is one of the many instances in which the New Testament opens the Old.*

Practical deductions :

a. Every kind of professed worship of God, however pleasing and attractive, that is offered without faith, and its inseparable attendant, obedience, is sinful. 1 Sam. 15 : 22 ; Prov. 15 : 8 ; Matt. 15 : 9.

b. The Father of all mercies shows us our sin, and at the same time shows us the only remedy for sin.

c. The Lamb of God became obedient even to the death of the cross. Not more in subjection was a lamb to Cain. Let the same self-denying, lowly, and obedient mind be in us. Philip. 2 : 5–8.

d. Have faith in the atoning blood of the Lamb.

e. The same Divine Victim is ever near, at our very doors, still offering His life's blood to atone for our sins.

f. The neglect of this one sacrifice may be followed by other sins, for which there is no forgiveness. Heb. 10 : 26, 27.

WATCHMAN, WHAT OF THE NIGHT ?

Isa. 21 : 11–12.

The prophet in vision hears Edom asking him a question in the character of a watchman on a tower of Jerusalem, looking eastward for the light of the morning. . . . Of the sense of this obscure passage of prophecy no Hebrew scholar will speak with undoubting certainty ; and yet, happily, one of two views has been approved by the most learned interpreters, either of which has weighty and close applications.

1. The question and answer are by some supposed to have been uttered in irony and derision. If this be the correct opinion, the text will convey to us these lessons.

a. Beware lest your mornings of grace be followed, not by days of probation, but immediately by nights of despair. This agrees with the history of Edom, which, between brief periods of freedom, was oppressed in succession by Assyria, by Chaldea, by Persia, by Greece, and by Rome.

b. Once abandoned to judicial hardness of heart, all your inquiries about salvation, however frequent and anxious, will be in vain.

---

* The "Speaker's Commentary" *in loco*, p. 54, says : "The chief objection to this interpretation is that there is no instance of this use of the word before the giving of the Law." This objection holds equally good of the first interpretation ; for the word is not again employed until the giving of the Law. The primitive man was quite as able to understand the import of a literal sin-offering as of generic and personified sin. See Bishop Kip's " Unnoticed Things of Scripture."

c. How dreadful our doom, if in our rebellion against the Almighty we incur His derision.

2. The other alternative explanation is that the question is serious and the answer encouraging.

a. In doubt, despondency, and fear, we do well to inquire at the oracle of God.

b. We know not how short our time for inquiry is : our morning of youth may be followed, not by the day of middle life, but by the unexpected night of death.

c. We are left to our free choice whether we will inquire or not. " If ye will inquire."

d. The Lord deigns to hear and answer our questions.

e. His offers of mercy to His worst enemies, *e.g.*, Edom.

f. Seek salvation in good earnest.

g. Repent or " turn back " before night.

h. Not only repent, but " come " to Zion.

THE SMALLEST CHURCH MAY STILL BE A BEACON.

Isa. 30 : 17.

This originally said of Jerusalem, when almost deserted of its inhabitants.

The uses of the beacon fire :

a. A fire kindled on the top of a mountain in time of invasion in order to point out to the fighting men in the darkness of night a place of rendezvous.

c. A series or line of fires on mountain-tops or prominent hills to convey speedily important intelligence. Thus after the Captivity, the remnant of the Jewish nation would communicate to the exiles in Babylon the time of the rising of the paschal moon by beacon lights, beginning on Mt. Olivet, and gleaming eastward from mountain to mountain and hill to hill, " until they were mirrored in the Euphrates." Similar appear to have been the signals by which the man who led away the scapegoat, flashed back the intelligence to the high-priest in Jerusalem that the goat had been conducted to the border of the wilderness. In Arabia on festive occasions beacon-fires are kept burning in the night along the roads leading to and from the residence of the giver of the feast.

Lessons : 1. As a church reduced in numbers, you may be despised ; and yet you are not useless. The top of a towering crag may be of little present interest to the mountain climber—a little space of barren rock showing only a few large stones stained and rent by fire. The coals and ashes were long ago blown or washed away. But let an invasion of the land begin, etc. You and such as you are, through grace, of the greatest service, as great perils bear witness. Particularize the mission of such a church—

a. To warn.

b. To send good tidings.

c. To direct along shadowed and obscure paths.

2. "But we are not only few, but feeble. We have very few who can do anything," etc. Remember that a little cripple can light a beacon-fire on an Alpine ledge.

3. "But we are timid and full of doubts and misgivings." Consider that you occupy a high and almost inaccessible position. The Almighty is your defence.

4. Is it not time to light the beacon-fires? Is not the enemy coming in like a flood?

5. Or have you not good news of salvation to flash to other beacon stations? Every Sunday is Easter, a holy festival in commemoration of the resurrection of Christ. See how the Greek Church observes Easter at Athens by a general lighting of torches and by the salutation, "Christ is risen!" *

THE SUBDUING OF OUR INIQUITIES. (TO YOUNG CONVERTS.)

Micah 7 : 19.

To "subdue" imports in Hebrew to "tread under foot." For what purpose? The first part of the text may be understood in one of two allowable senses. (Handle according to the alternative method.)

1. That God will trample our iniquities under foot as enemies. The Hebrew word is used in Gen. 1 : 28, where Jehovah commands our first parents to subdue the earth—*i.e.*, to bring into subjection the animal kingdom. According to this view, He will subdue our passions, appetites, our imagination, our pride, and selfishness. He promises also to incline and dispose our will to submit to and obey Him. Without the regenerating and sanctifying work of the Holy Spirit the pardon of our sins through the sacrifice of Christ would avail little to make us happy. A very pious educator once said, "Have we a subdued spirit? It is precious to be and to feel subdued under God." Or, the text may mean :

2. That God will tread our iniquities under foot—*i.e.*, He will disregard them or refuse to resent them. The word is employed in Zech. 9 : 15 to express the trampling upon sling-stones in contempt.

---

* The above sketch was composed without any knowledge that the Rev. J. Reynolds Hole, Canon of Lincoln, had about the same time (Aug., 1880) published a sermon on the same text. The latter contains some fresh illustrations of the subject.

Comp. Job 41 : 28. The second view harmonizes with the following words : "And he will cast all their sins into the depths of the sea." Agreeably to this import—

a. God will forgive our sins in the most thorough sense : *all* our sins. He will pass them by and put them out of His sight ; He will throw them as far away from Him as possible ; He will forget them ; He will never recall His assurance of pardon. Comp. Isa. 38 : 17, 44 : 22 ; Jer. 50 : 20 ; Ps. 103 : 12 ; Micah 7 : 18. The Almighty will treat His redeemed as if they had never sinned.

Some Encouragements.

1. We have an all-sufficient Saviour. He rescues from the power of sin and Satan ; from the burden of leprosy and captivity of sin ; from the punishment of sin. Making a total oblivion of our iniquities, he justifies, adopts, and glorifies us.

2. Who is a God like him ? (v. 18). What system of idolatry, what false system of Christianity, can compare with the glad tidings of a full and free salvation ? Sin is totally destroyed. The old-time races of animals are not so completely swept away ; they have left their bones or the impressions of them in the rocks. But our sins shall not reappear even in the memory of God.

HUNGERING AND THIRSTING AFTER RIGHTEOUSNESS.
Matt. 5 : 6.

1. "The righteousness" here ardently desired. In the original Greek we find the article which is translated *the.* The righteousness of faith is here intended. It means—

a. A personal righteousness, or the removal of the defilement and power of sin and the fulfilment of God's revealed will in our hearts, consciences, and conduct.

b. But in order to this, there must be imputed to us the righteousness of Christ, whereby we through faith are formally justified, and through the grace of the Holy Spirit we grow in personal righteousness, both negative and positive.

2. The hungering and thirsting here expressed.

a. It is either preceded or attended by a sense of privation. The order in which this beatitude is placed is instructive. It comes after the beatitude to those who are " poor in spirit," to such as " mourn," and to as many as are " meek." These lowly conditions of privation and suffering are certainly good preparations for the righteousness of the Gospel.

b. It involves the idea of anxious and painful desires as yet not satisfied.

3. The blessedness of all such.

a. "They shall be filled;" gradually if not quickly shall they gain full evidence that they are justified, that they are growing in grace, and that they shall at last drink to their satisfaction of the fountain of the water of life. Rev. 21 : 6.

b. That Divine Spirit who created these hungerings and thirstings has made abundant provision to satisfy them.

c. These hungry and thirsty ones are not without some present refreshments. They have antepasts and prelibations. Already, long ago, Jesus pronounced them "blessed."

THE HID TREASURE.

Matt. 13 : 44.

Introductory : The preciousness of free grace.

1. The secret and individual operations of free grace. The treasure was twice hid.

a. The true believer secretly finds and guards the treasure of grace.

b. Experiences a secret joy, which ends in a purpose at any cost to secure the grace of salvation.

c. He makes choice of the treasure, does not merely wish for it.

d. He finds it; he has not *earned* it. It was earned by another, who buried the coin.

e. He discovers it providentially. The gracious providence of God in our conversion.

f. He does not conceal because of shame or fear, but in order to secure.

g. In no long time he must acknowledge and confess his great riches. The cherishing of secret hope is but a stage in true experience.

h. There is a progress in joy. The joy of discovery does not equal the joy of possession.

i. Suppose this man had been content to discover the treasure.

j. How ignorant are the children of this world of the buried treasures of grace, over which they have walked a hundred times.

THE EFFECT OF UNBELIEF.

Matt. 13 : 58.

1. It may *limit*, although it cannot *prevent* in any place.

2. Although it may limit in one place, it cannot limit in all.

3. The power of the Lord Jesus cannot be lessened, although His goodness and forbearance may prove fruitless.

THE DARKENED SOUL HEARING OF AND CRYING TO JESUS OF NAZARETH.

Luke 18 : 36–38.

1. Clear apprehensions not necessary to prevailing prayer.

2. Great gloom of *mind* consistent with faith.

LET YOUR LIGHT SO SHINE, ETC.

Matt. 5 : 16.

1. The light of Gospel truth and grace ought not to be concealed.

2. We should cause this light so to shine as to lead men to glorify God, not praise us or admire our good works.

3. By what means may we cause our light so to shine?

a. By showing that the doctrines we believe, the precepts we practise, and the examples we follow, are from the Word of God.

b. By proving that our experiences are from the grace of God.

c. By subjecting our hearts and conforming our *conduct* to the Christian code of morals.

THE BACKSLIDER RETURNING.

Ps. 119 : 59.

1. We should think of our ways.

2. We should turn *back* our feet (see the original Hebrew).

THE POWER OF PRAYER.

Matt. 15 : 28.

Prayer moveth all the wheels of heaven and earth ; overcometh God and Satan.

1. Prayer is a post dispatched up to the Court of Heaven. Job 33 : 5 ; Ps. 18 : 6.

2. Prayer demands an answer as a right on the ground of His covenant and promise. Ps. 22 : 2 ; Isa. 63 : 17, 18 ; Lam. 2 : 20.

3. It brings God into great straits and sufferings. Jer. 31 : 20.

4. It wakes up God. Ps. 7 : 6 ; 18 : 6, 7 ; 44 : 23 ; Isa. 64 : 1.

5. It layeth chains on God's hands and binds Him. Isa. 64 : 7 ; Ezek. 22 : 30.

6. It useth a heavenly violence with God, Isa. 62 : 6, 7 ; striving, Rom. 15 : 30 ; wrestling, Exodus 32 : 10 ; Deut. 9 : 14. Let me alone, etc. Importunate widow in the parable. Luke 18 : 2–5.

7. It commandeth God. Isa. 45 : 11 ; Ps. 32 : 15 ; 65 : 2 ; 145 : 18, 19 ; Mark 7 : 7, 8 ; John 14 : 13, 14.

8. It putteth the crown on Christ's head, and heighteneth the footstool of His throne; "thy Kingdom come ;" " Even so come, Lord Jesus."

Use 1. If prayer thus prevail over God and Christ, then it can prevail against Satan and his angels.

Use 2. You lament the want of means, etc. If you can pray, you can set the wheels of Omnipotence at work. Prayer divided the Red Sea. What a rescue was wrought by the prayers of Esther and her maids. Prayer opened the prison doors for Peter, Paul, and Silas.

SAMUEL RUTHERFORD (b. 1600 ; d. 1661).

FEAR NOT ; FOR I KNOW THAT YE SEEK JESUS, ETC.

Matt. 28 : 5.

1. What these holy women are doing.

a. Not merely desiring, wishing, resolving, but seeking.

b. They seek the crucified and risen Redeemer.

2. The angelic encouragement, "Fear not," "I know." These pious women had some cause to fear. The earthquake, the angel, etc. How the seekers are encouraged.

a. By removing all obstacles ; the soldiers lying on the ground as if dead ; the great stone rolled away ; the angel proving a messenger of good tidings.

b. By removing all remaining unbelief.

(*a*) Giving them a view of the vacant place in the sepulchre.

(*β*) Assurance that they should meet the risen Jesus in Galilee.

(*γ*) Twofold evidence of miracle and prophecy. The strength they derived from divine power and foreknowledge. "I know," etc.

Application.

a. All such as sincerely seek Jesus are already found by Him.

b. We will then seek Him in His appointed way.

c. To those who thus seek Him every obstacle is removed.

d. The faith of such will be confirmed by new evidence.

e. Our all-knowing Lord anticipates our wants and dangers. "I know," etc.

f. Almighty energy is engaged in behalf of all true seekers.

g. Let us rejoice as these holy women did in the fact of Christ's resurrection.

METHODS ORDINARY AND EXTRAORDINARY.

Luke 5 : 18-20.

This miracle, so uncommon in its methods and surroundings, regarded as an acted parable. The principle here suggested is that perishing souls should, if necessary, be brought to Jesus, the Saviour, by irregular and out-of-the-way methods.

1. This principle is reasonable and practical.

a. It is acted on in secular affairs. If one kind of business does not prosper, men try some other, perhaps before unheard of. In war, *e.g.* soldiers let down in baskets before the mouth of the cave. In the siege of Tambi, an African town,* the Portuguese were repulsed by hives of bees thrown over the walls.

b. In religious transactions, *e.g.* the victory over Sisera ; Paul let down over the wall in a basket ; Peter smitten on the side by an angel.

c. The atonement of Christ was a remedial expedient without a parallel—an interposition.

2. But while this is admitted, we are not hence to infer that the ordinary means and methods of grace are to be neglected or despised. These are of the first importance ; the regular is ever more valuable than the occasional and exceptional.

3. Lessons.

a Do not make too much of religious ceremonies, observances, and usages.

b. As Jesus does not always walk our ways, we must seek Him whenever and wherever we can find Him.

c. To seek salvation is *ever opportune.* In this case the Great Teacher's sermon was interrupted. He brings a funeral procession to a stand-still in order to raise the dead. While Peter was speaking at Cæsarea the Holy Spirit fell on the hearers, and they began to magnify God. Acts 10 : 44–46.

d. Ordinary means will not be employed by all.

e. The regular and common services of the Lord's house sometimes become a hindrance rather than a help to the inquirer. In this instance the audience blocked up the doorways, etc.

f. A certain unity, however, is desirable in such proceedings. Here four men chose to co-operate.

g. Redeem time wasted. Perhaps these men had neglected a better opportunity.

h. No time to be lost now. They do not wait for the congregation to break up.

i. Christian laborers, rest not at any stage in your progress. Not in the way to the house, not at the door, not on the roof.

j. The ingenuity of true benevolence and compassion !

k. The rescue of others depends on the faith of the workers. "He seeing their faith." Not a word said. Here work was the prayer of faith.

l. Greater blessings found than were sought. *Sins forgiven.*

* See a Dutch book on Old Age and Country Life, by Jacob Caats.

m. Possibly one or more of these hearers had himself been healed. He felt that he was in *gratitude* bound, etc.

n. What if they had said to the paralytic, "You have violated some *natural law*, and now you must take the necessary consequences? Neither God nor man can do anything to cure you." *

THE IMPORTANCE OF INDIVIDUAL EXERTION IN SEEKING THE CONVERSION OF SINNERS.

John 4 : 5-9.

Many awakened sinners complain that no one had spoken to them privately about their religious interests. They ought rather to complain of their own insensibility in not having been moved by any of the hundreds of sermons which were publicly addressed to them ; in giving no heed to the invitations and warnings to be found throughout their own Bibles ; in not hearkening to the testimony God gives of Himself in Creation and Providence. But still, the example of our Saviour and His first disciples, no less than the conduct of all winners of souls in times of awakening, encourage personal interviews ; facts also without number prove that the Master blesses this kind of service. . . . It is also worthy of attention that it was our Lord's freedom from prejudice in respect of a secular matter which prompted the woman of Samaria to commence religious talk, and that it was she and not He, that introduced the subject. Our success in Christian interviews depends much on the spirit we manifest in the common affairs of life. See "Christian Effort," by Sarah Baker : Methodist Book Concern, N.Y., 1852 ; "His Own Brother," a sermon on John 1 : 41, by Mr. Moody ; also "The Conversion of Sinners a Christian Duty," Jas. 5 : 19, 20, a sermon by Mr. Finney.

THE WOMAN OF SAMARIA.

John 4: 28, 29.

Upon the text and its connection we shall make the following plain observations :

1. That Jesus Christ is possessed of the greatest excellences. We shall confine ourselves to those illustrated in His conversation with the woman of Samaria.

a. Profound humility. Though He was rich in the glories of His divine nature, He humbled Himself and became a man, and so as not to be above holding conversation with a poor woman at a well. Let proud mortals contemplate this and be ashamed.

b. Consummate wisdom. He knew where to find this woman ; He

---

* Some few young preachers may possibly need to be told that these lessons are too numerous for a single sermon.

knew all her circumstances, and what kind of words to address to her.

c. Ardent benevolence. He exerted Himself for the instruction and conversion of this poor woman.

2. That those who are able to discover His excellences feel an attachment to Him.

The affection of the soul which has by faith contemplated and discovered the excellences of Christ, is—

a. Reasonable or rational.

b. Fervent

c. Influential.

3. That those who really love Him are anxious to recommend Him to others—

a. By earnest entreaty.

b. By bringing them under the sound of the Gospel.

c. By prayer to God for them.

d. By a holy life.

Improvement.

a. We see that there is no worthiness in the instrument employed in the conversion of a sinner. The Samaritan woman was useful in directing others to Christ.

b. This subject affords a test whereby we may try our characters.

c. Are there here any desirous to see Jesus?

REV. THOMAS SPENCER.

THEN WERE THE DISCIPLES GLAD WHEN THEY SAW THE LORD.

John 20 : 20.

1. We are disciples of the same Saviour.

a. A renunciation of all other moral teachers.

b. We must spiritually forsake the world.

c. We must dedicate ourselves to the service of Christ.

2. It is the privilege of disciples to see the Lord.

a. How do we now see Christ? By a believing realization.

b. Where do we see Christ?

c. What are the evidences of having seen Christ.

3. A sight of Christ is always gladdening to the souls of His people.

a. See it in the accepted penitent.

b. See it in the spiritual worshipper.

c. See it in the afflicted Christian.

d. See it in the dying saint.

e. See it the beatified glory.

Application.

a. Have you ever had a believing view of Jesus Christ?

b. A sight of Christ leads to still greater desires after Him.

c. Men do not know the excellences of Christ.

d. A sight of Christ at the last day will be terrible to his enemies.

ANONYMOUS.

A RESURRECTION TO RIGHTEOUSNESS THE GREATEST NEED.

1 Cor. 15 : 34.

This exhortation is made in the midst of the Gospel revelation as to the great doctrine of the resurrection, in making known to us for the first time in the history of the world many wonderful facts concerning the general resurrection. The Holy Spirit, ever mindful of our salvation from sin, breaks off for a moment the doctrinal discourse to call on us to awake to righteousness.

a. The question of our personal righteousness here more important than that of our resurrection on the last day.

b. The knowledge of God connected with holy living.

c. To be ignorant of God's righteousness is shameful.

d. Personal righteousness one of the ends of a true awakening.

e. It is the first proof of the coming of the new kingdom into our hearts. Rom. 14 : 17.

THE LAW WAS OUR SCHOOLMASTER (CHILD-LEADER) TO BRING US UNTO CHRIST.

Gal. 3 : 24.

The word here rendered "schoolmaster" is in the Greek *paidagōgos*, "child-leader," a slave or servant who had charge of boys on their way to and from school. He was also a guardian of the school boys in the time of waiting and recreation, and responsible for their safety and good behavior. Here the law is the child-leader conducting pupils to school, and shutting them up until Christ, who is the *didascalos* or teacher, shall come and instruct them. See v. 23.

1. The law and conscience convict and condemn, and so shut us up to wait for Jesus, who teaches us how to be justified by faith in Him Verse 23.

2. The doctrine of natural laws, on the contrary, with their unavoidable penalties, knowing no priest, no prophet, no sacrifice, no interposition to save the transgressor, leads us to the school of Satan and shuts us up there. This is "the school of Tyrannus" (Acts 19 : 9), the scene of the severest discipline and most hopeless toil and suffering ; whither no apostle daily comes to preach the love of Christ in atoning for our sins.

3. The conscience, without faith, leads to despair; with faith it leads to Jesus, the soul's only light and hope and joy.

THE FULNESS OF THE HOLY SPIRIT OVERFLOWING IN PRAISE AND THANKSGIVING.

Eph. 5: 18-20.

The state here mentioned is not unlike that of those who were "endued with power from on high" (Luke 24 : 49), and "baptized with the Holy Ghost" (Matt. 3 : 11 ; Acts 1 : 5). The miraculous gifts, as speaking foreign languages, etc., were withheld as soon as they ceased to be needed as signs and evidences, but prophesying was retained because it built up the church. The meaning of this word in the primitive church appears to have included sacred song. Prophesying on the day of Pentecost seems to have chiefly consisted of praising God or "speaking the wonderful works of God (compare Acts 10 : 46 ; Luke 1 : 46). By comparing Acts 10 : 46, and 19, 6, we find "praising God" put in the place of prophesying. Again, "a psalm," in 1 Cor. 14 : 26, is placed where we find "prophesying" in 1 Cor. 12 : 28 ; 13 : 27 ; 14 : 7. And this elucidates 1 Cor. 11 : 5, where a woman is mentioned as prophesying. As the singing of hymns and psalms was ever permitted to women, they could share their part of the public service of God. This also explains how the four daughters of Philip could be said to prophesy (Acts 21 : 9). "Being filled with the Holy Spirit" is perhaps a figure called synecdoche, by which a part of what is intended is expressed. *Running over with* would, we think, express the idea more exactly, although not more popularly. It was probably alluded to by our Lord on the last day of the feast of Tabernacles, where he compares the "belly" of a believer to the belly of the golden vessel in which the priest carried the sacred water from the spring of Siloam into the fore-court of the temple (John 7 : 38, 39).

This state is not a necessary attendant either of regeneration or of sanctification. The apostles were for the most part regenerate before the day of Pentecost.

It is not the only cause of great joy and rejoicing. The disciples returned from the scene of the Ascension to Jerusalem "with great joy."

Nor is full assurance of faith always one of the fruits of this plenitude of the Spirit.

It is different from the permanent presence of the Spirit, though it is not incompatible with the latter.

It is often attributed to those primitive disciples who are moved by it to speak or act with promptness, power, and good effect.

In the text, as in some other Scriptures, it finds an overflowing voice in praise and thanksgiving to God.

Lesson 1—*a.* The plenitude of the Holy Spirit manifests itself not in a life of contemplation, but in worship and Christian work.

b. It inspires forgetfulness of ourselves and our adoring and greatful remembrance of God. The tongues of fire flamed heavenward.

A SERMON FOR YOUNG CONVERTS.

DOING ALL IN THE NAME OF THE LORD JESUS.

Colos. 3 : 17.

What is meant by the phrase "in the name of?" It has various significations, which are to be determined by the connection. The text is comprehensive, taking in all Christian duties : "whatever ye do in word or deed." Here the sense may embrace Christ Himself in all His offices and powers.

1. Prayer and thanksgiving are offered in the name of Jesus when we exercise faith in Jesus as our Intercessor at the right hand of the Father and in the Holy Spirit as sent by Him from the Father (John 16 : 24, 26 ; Eph. 5 : 20). This involves "praying in the Holy Ghost" (Jude 20), and the intercession of the Spirit (Rom. 8 : 26, 27). This is a light additional to that which the Lord's Prayer gives. In the use of this prayer we do not ask anything in Christ's name.

2. In our works of beneficence we act in the name of Christ when we give to others as if we were giving to Him (Matt. 25 : 40), because the receivers belong to Christ (Mark 11 : 41) in obedience to Christ (Matt. 10 : 8 ; 2 John 6), with the hope of sharing His reward (Heb. 11 : 24 ; 12 : 2, etc). The Golden Rule we are to apply as enlightened Christians. "Whatsoever ye would " (*i.e.* the disciples).

3. In acts of self-denial we recognize the name of Jesus when we are willing, if necessary, to become poor in imitation of the Lord of Glory (2 Cor. 8 : 9) ; to sacrifice ourselves for the good of our brethren according to the new command.

4. While toiling, praying, and suffering for the salvation of men, we are to look to the power of Christ for guidance, support, and success. The word "name," sometimes in the Old Testament as well as the New Testament, signifies force or efficacious power (2 Chron. 14 : 11 ; Ps. 52 : 9 ; 54 : 1 ; Isa. 64 : 2 ; Acts 3 : 12, 16 ; 4 : 7 ; Matt. 7 : 22). Hence the Holy Spirit is sent from God the Father through Jesus to take the place of the latter, and to exert the same gracious power. It is this import that the word "name" is employed twice in Philip. 2 : 9–11. [To convey the idea of authority, another Greek word is always used—*exousia.*]

5. Whatever we do "in the name of Christ" "must be done in the exercise of faith in that power" (Acts 3 : 16 ; 14 : 9 ; John 20 : 31), "that believing ye might bear life in His name."

6. If we would obey the injunction in the text we must likewise acknowledge that it is in this power that everything is to be said, done, and suffered. We are to profess our faith in the divine energy exerted for us and in us (Col. 2 : 2 ; 2 Tim. 2 : 25 ; Philemon 6 ; Rev. 2 : 12).

Our time does not permit us to do more than glance at some principal branches of this duty, which should attend every other.

Application.

a. Our conversion brings us into a new sphere and element. We live, walk, pray in the Holy Spirit, who prompts us to refer everything to Christ.

b. Fully to discharge this duty we need the continual presence of the Spirit, forming in us right habits of heart and mind. We ought perpetually to consult the oracles of God, to meditate much, and to be vigilant.

c. To do all things in the name of Christ is to renounce all power of our own, and to be prevented from thinking too highly of our experience and service.

d If you do all things in the name of Jesus, you will not fail to do all things for His glory.

THE SAVIOUR SEEKING ADMISSION TO THE HEART.

Behold I stand at the door and knock. Rev. 3 : 20.

These words were addressed to each member of one of the primitive churches.

1. The relation of Jesus to some church-members.

a. To some He is as a stranger.

b. To others He is as a neighbor.

c. To some He is as a boarder.

d. To others He is as a visitor or guest.

e. He ought to be to every heart as an elder brother, who is also the greatest of benefactors.

f. With every member of a church He ought to be on such terms of love and intimacy that He need not knock when He walks in.

2. If Jesus returned to the church of Laodicea, He returned to them as individuals. "If any man," etc. The same is true to-day.

a. At each church-member's door He stands, knocks, speaks.

b. To each one is the promise of gracious intimacy made.

c. If any man refuse to answer to the call of the Saviour, he must suffer the consequences.

d. Do not inquire, "Are my brethren opening the door?" the question is, "Am I?'

HEAR WHAT THE SPIRIT SAITH UNTO THE CHURCHES.

Rev. 3 : 22.

This admonition repeated more than once.

1. How does the Divine Spirit now speak to churches?

a. By the Scriptures read or preached.

b. By the works of creation and Providence.

c. By His most important operations in regeneration and sanctification.

d. By the symbolical teachings of Baptism and the Lord's Supper.

2. How did the Spirit speak to the seven churches of Asia.

a. By the written word, not the oral, which had become more or less corrupt.

b. The matter of these letters was chiefly warning and encouragement.

c. The churches of to-day have similar faults and dangers to consider.

d. The primitive churches of Asia had not ears to hear; will the churches of to-day hearken?

THEMES FOR REFORMS.

THE NECESSITY OF REFORMS.

The emblem of the ephah. Zech. 5 : 5-11.

According to the previous vision (that of the Flying Roll) the judgment of God would destroy those who were guilty of perjury and theft. A transgression is taken as a sample from both tables of the law. In the text idolatry and sorcery are seen departing from the land. The word "wickedness," literally the wickedness or the wicked woman, is supposed to allude to Athaliah, the daughter of Jezebel, 2 Chron. 24 : 7, or to Jezebel herself, Rev. 2 : 20, as the national type; idolatry and sorcery, 2 Kings 9 : 22, 34.

The prophecy was first fulfilled in the attempted suppression of these vices, their increase in consequence of coercion, and their ultimate departure, further increase and establishment in Babylon. Its second and often-repeated fulfilment has been shown in exertions for the removal of the vices which proceed from covetousness and underhand dealings, sensuality, and witchcraft, with all their criminal brood.

Lesson : *a.* To limit and so to license crime is only to establish it in all the land. The ephah was the largest dry measure. The exhibition of the restricting bushel causes no alarm.

b. Hearken to no compromises aiming at a partial suppression of vice or an avoidance of its publicity, profanity, and sauciness. Some expositors suppose that the weight of lead was cast merely on the mouth of the woman, but it was cast on the mouth of the ephah, and so at once silencing the advocate of vice and putting a stop to the traffic in wickedness.

c. The legal and forcible suppression of vice in a community will at fi st occasion its seeming increase. The temporary imprisonment of one woman in the ephah is followed by the uprising of two other women to be the helpers of the first, while wings are given to both.

d. When a community or the churches therein will employ all the spiritual and evangelical means at their command, vice will voluntarily rise and depart to a more congenial place. It will fly away on broad and powerful pinions. The Holy Spirit, that like a refreshing wind blesses the churches, will at the same time waft it away ; '' The wind was in their wings.'' He will distinguish and separate.

e. Let the churches flee all connivance and complicity with vice, and drive it away to the mystical Babylon for refuge and protection.

f. Any church or any community that guards and fosters vice is destined to share the doom of Babylon.

SELF-WROUGHT REFORMS AND THEIR CONSEQUENCES.

Luke 11 · 24-26.

1. They lead to self-righteousness.
2. And self-righteousness leads back to worse iniquities,

THE BRAND PLUCKED OUT OF THE FIRE.

Zech. 2 : 3.

1. Saved from destruction.
2. Reserved for better use.
3. Yet bears the scars of fire.
4. More liable to take fire again than wood not charred.
5. But still we hope that He who who has plucked it out will not throw it back.
6. It is implied that there is a fire, and that some fuel remains in it.
7. We should try and help pluck out other brands before it is too late.

SHIFTING RESPONSIBILITY. ''WHAT IS THAT TO US? SEE THOU TO THAT.''

Matt. 27 : 4. (Rev. S. Baring-Gould.)

THE RIGHT USE OF THE LOT.

Prov. 18 : 18.

The profanation of the lot is very scriptually discussed in the works of the Rev. Dr. John M. Mason.

READINGS ON THE NATURE AND REWARDS OF OVERCOMING.

The doctrine of victory is taught most fully by the apostle John.

1. Victors over whom or what? Victors over Satan, the world, Babylon, and the Beast. I John 2 : 13, 14 ; Rev. 17 : 14.

2. We overcome through Christ. John 16 : 32 ; Rev. 5 : 5 ; 6 : 2 ; 17 : 14.

3. Through faith in His blood. I John 5 : 4, 5 ; Rev. 12 : 11.

4. The personal character of the victors. Born of God. I John 5 : 4. Called chosen and faithful. Rev. 17 : 14. Compare Rev. 2 : 10, 6 : 29.

5. Promises to the victors. Rev. 2 : 7 ; 10-11, 17, 26-28 ; 3 : 4, 5, 11, 12, 20, 21 ; 15 : 2-4 ; 21 : 7.

TEMPERANCE THEMES FOR REVIVAL SERVICES.

THE EXTENT OF THE PLAGUE OF INTEMPERANCE ILLUSTRATED.

Rev. 8 : 10, 11.

The interpretation of this part of the Revelation is still unsettled. The best expositors think that by the great star falling from heaven, Gregory the Great, or Pelagius, or Arius is symbolized, while the embittering of the waters of the fountains and rivers represents the poisoning of the grace and truth of the Gospel to such a degree as to cause the moral death of a third part of those who partake of them. We now employ these words solely as an illustration. The late Dean Alford, in his comment on them, uses the following language : " It is hardly possible to read this third plague and not to think of the deadly effect of those strong spirituous drinks, which are in fact water turned into poison. The very name *absinthe* is not unknown in their nomenclature ; and there is no effect which could be so aptly described by the falling of fire into water, as this, which results in *ardent* spirit—or that which the simple islanders of the South Sea call *firewater.* That this plague may go on to destroy even this fearful proportion of the ungodly in the latter days is far from impossible, considering its prevalence even now. . . . But I mention this rather as an illustration than as an interpretation."

Temporal evils of intemperance. Prov. 23 : 29-35.

The eternal destiny of the drunkard. I Cor. 6 : 10.

The effects of intemperance on the heart and conscience. Isa. 5 : 12.

On the evils and remedy for intemperance. Sermons by the Rev. Lyman Beecher on Hab. 2 : 9, 11, and 15, 16.

Am I my brother's keeper ? Gen. 4 : 9.

THEMES AND OUTLINES CONCERNING SPIRITUALISM.

For a series of sermons preparatory to a revival in communities where Spiritualism prevails.

I. THE TRUE GOD CONCEALS AS WELL AS REVEALS.

Prov. 25 : 2.

II. THE REVEALED THINGS OF GOD HAVE OBEDIENCE TO HIM FOR THEIR END.

Deut. 29 : 29.

III. A SPECULATIVE OR HISTORICAL BELIEF IN IMMORTALITY DOES NOT IMPROVE THE HEART AND LIFE.

Acts 23 : 8.

[The Sadducees denied the existence of both angels and spirits, and yet were not so deadly enemies of Christ as the Pharisees were.]

IV. THE WITCH OF ENDOR.

1 Sam. 28 : 6, 7.

V. THE WONDERS WROUGHT THROUGH SPIRITUALISTS ARE NOT EQUAL TO THOSE WROUGHT BY THE LORD JESUS CHRIST.

2 Tim. 3 : 8.

[Jannes and Jambres, aided by Satan, wrought marvellous works ; but they were outdone by Moses, who was assisted by the Almighty. Spiritualists must raise the dead before the followers of Christ can leave Him and go over to their company.]

VI. SIMON, THE SORCERER DECEIVING HIMSELF AND THE APOSTLES.

Acts 8 : 22, 23.

1. Simon honestly conceded that the power of the Holy Spirit was greater than any that he could invoke.

2. Yet he totally misunderstood the religion of Christ.

3. Not beyond repentance and forgiveness.

4. He was not too wicked to pray (v. 22).

5. The reason why we hear nothing further about him is, perhaps, his unwillingness to pray for himself, and his exclusive reliance on the prayers of the apostles (v. 24). For traditions, see Bible Dictionaries.

VII. SPIRITUALISTS SIN IN CONSULTING THE CREATURE MORE THAN THE CREATOR.

Rom. 1 : 25.

VIII. BY HONORING NOT THE SON, THEY HONOR NOT THE FATHER.

John 5 : 23.

IX. THE SCRIPTURES THE ONLY STANDARD OF DOCTRINE, EXPERIENCE, AND DUTY.

Isa. 8 : 19, 20.

X. THE DEMORALIZING INFLUENCE OF SPIRITUALISM.

John 8 : 48, 49.

"Thou art a Samaritan, and hast a demon." The Jews seem to have associated a demoniac inspiration with Samaria. If we turn to Acts 8, we observe how generally, "from the least to the greatest," the Samaritans gave heed to Simon the sorcerer. The colonists from various parts of Babylonia, who repeopled the cities of Samaria, did not supplant the peasantry scattered all over the land, who had derived from Egypt through Jeroboam, and from Tyre through Jezebel, the witchcraft which was believed and practised there in the time of Christ and the Apostles. See articles on "Magic," "Demon," and "Divination" in Smith's Bib. Dic. ; also Abp. Trench on the Miracles, "Demoniacs in Gadara," chap. 5.

As for the moral character of the Samaritans, all authorities agree that it was no better than that of the Gentiles.

XI. SPIRITUALISM HAS NOTHING THAT EQUALS CHRISTIAN LOVE.

1 Cor. 13 : 1.

1. Christian love in its sources. 1 Tim. 1 : 5.

2. Its works as seen —

a. In hospitals, asylums, reformatories, missions, Bible and tract societies.

b. In family and social life.

3. Admitting that Spiritualism can perform all the wonders of which it boasts, it is nothing without Christian love.

4. Has it any equivalent for this ? No.

XII. IF THE WORD OF GOD FAILS TO PERSUADE MEN TO REPENT, THE VISITS OF DEPARTED SPIRITS WILL EQUALLY FAIL.

Luke 16 : 31.

XIII. CHRIST HEALS THE BROKEN HEART ; THIS SPIRITUALISM CANNOT DO.

Luke 4 : 18.

XIV. CHRISTIANS IN THEIR PERPLEXITIES HAVE THE GUIDANCE OF THE ALL-KNOWING ONE.

Prov. 3 : 6.

XV. CHRISTIANS ENJOY THE SERVICES OF ANGELS, WHO ARE SUPERIOR TO US.*

Heb. 1 : 14.

XVI. THE DIVINE SPIRIT IS PROMISED TO US AS A GUIDE INTO ALL THE TRUTH.

The truth *i e.* respecting the gospel (see original Greek).   John 16 : 13.

OUTLINES ON VARIOUS SUBJECTS.

AND THE SPIRIT OF GOD MOVED ON THE FACE OF THE WATERS.

Gen. 1 : 2.

1. The Holy Spirit begins His work amidst disorder and darkness.

2. There is no movement toward a new creation before the Spirit of the Lord begins to move.

AND GOD SAID, LET THERE BE LIGHT, ETC.

Gen. 1 : 3, 4.

1. The Holy Spirit moves before God speaks.

2. God speaks before the dawn of the first day.

3. The first day dawns before the limits of night are fixed.

WHILE HE LINGERED, THE MEN LAID HOLD UPON HIS HAND.

Gen. 19 : 16.   (Sermon on the departure of Lot, by Rev. M. Grafton.)

1. The believer, while dwelling in the world of iniquity, is exposed to danger.

2. Examples of rescue to such as have lingered: Moses, David, Isaiah, Jeremiah, Peter, Paul.

3. In death angels remove us beyond the city.

AND THE CUP WAS FOUND IN BENJAMIN'S SACK.

Gen. 44 : 12.

This text is used by way of illustration to teach how Satan artfully introduces groundless doubts and fears into the minds of men.

1. How Satan sometimes troubles and alarms true believers.

2. How he often seeks to drive convicted sinners to despair.

3. Christ Jesus affords the only hope in this conflict with the prince of darkness.

---

* One of the best preventives of and antidotes to Spiritualism is the preaching of the Scripture doctrine concerning angels.

LET THINE EYES BE ON THE FIELD THAT THEY DO REAP.

Ruth 2 : 9. (The advantages of relating facts concerning former revivals.)

1. See the love of God.
2. The grace of Christ.
3. The work of the Spirit.
4. The fruit of faith.
5. Answers to prayers and exertions.
6. Gather the scattered stalks of wheat.
7. Share the food of the reapers.

A PRESENT SALVATION.

Num. 13 : 30. (From Sermons by Rev. Joseph Sutcliffe.)

1. The children of Israel could not enter the Land of Promise until they were proved in respect of self-will and obedience.
2. They were to expect immediate victory.
a. The atonement is already made.
b. Regeneration is instantaneous.
c. The Holy Spirit present.
d. Christ intercedes.
e. Progress in sanctification not to be denied. To enter Canaan, one thing ; to possess it all, another.
3. Unbelievers are disheartened by appearances.
4. These unbelieving and timid Israelites did not reach the Land of Promise.
5. Let the example God here makes of unbelieving fathers be a warning to their children. Jehovah has to punish fathers in order to save their children.

CHILDREN OUGHT NOT TO BE NEGLECTED ON ACCOUNT OF THE BACKSLIDINGS OF THEIR PARENTS.

Num. 14 : 28-31.

The predictions of murmurers do not often come to pass, even in part.

1. Disobedience in, unfaithfulness and discord in a church should not keep us from seeking the salvation of the young.
2. Important as an awakening in the church is, yet it is not absolutely necessary to the conversion of the young.
3. Such is the declension of piety in some churches, that our chief encouragement is that the children of their members may be converted.

MEN OF PUBLIC SPIRIT OFTEN MORE CAREFUL OF THEIR HONOR THAN FOR THE CAUSE OF CHRIST.

2 Sam. 6 : 20-23.

[The reproachful words of Michal were probably not according to truth. David still wore his dress of fine linen and an ephod. His uncovering himself was only the divesting himself of the royal robe and crown. Michal was wrong and David was right, as the event proved.]

Let the example of David reprove those public men who fear that if they be zealous for the religion of Christ, they will expose themselves to derision and contempt.

THE SEVEN SNEEZES.

The child sneezed seven times.   2 Kings 4 : 34.

1. The first clear evidence that the child was restored to life.

a. The evidence very simple. The first tear of penitence. We ought not to expect too much from inquirers. The first signs of new life ought to encourage us.

b. This evidence of life was in itself unpleasant. To the child it was no pleasure to sneeze. To those who heard the sneeze, it was not very musical. Repentance is not an agreeable exercise, either to its subjects or to their friends who witness. The evidences of life were very monotonous. "The child sneezed seven times." Much of the talk of inquirers is very wearisome.

2. It was a sure evidence. It was evidence of life. Give us proof that a soul has passed from death to life, and we rejoice. We must have indisputable marks of grace.

Conclusion : The more watched the better. This service requires graces rather than gifts. Be ready to take care of the newly quickened one.   REV. CHARLES H. SPURGEON.

AN ANCIENT REVIVAL.

And when Asa heard these words....And the Lord gave them rest round about.
2 Chron. 15 : 8-15.

1. The heart of a revival is the renewal of the covenant with God (v. 12).

2. The public proclamation of a revival faith before the world (v. 14).

3. It was attended with a great coming in of converts from without (v. 9).

4. Thorough reformation of public and private morals (v. 8).

5. Often such awakenings are followed by periods of temporal prosperity (v. 15).   REV. DR. AUSTIN PHELPS.

CURSE YE MEROZ, ETC.

Judges 5 : 23.

[Meroz was probably a city somewhere within the territory of Zebulun and Naphtali that neglected to send its contingent or quota of warriors against Sisera. Some suppose that the inhabitants of Meroz incurred a curse because, being near the field of battle, they did not join in pursuit of the flying enemy.]

1. All are not equally bound to active service in a work of grace. Two tribes here exclusively engaged in the battle. Of other tribes, Reuben, Gilead, Dan, and Asher receive reproachful mention, while the other tribes escape all censure.

2. The duties of private life form no sufficient apology for neglecting the public service of God. Reuben took good care of his flocks.

3. Beware of delay. The Reubenites had "great searchings of heart;" they inquired, reflected, and deliberated until it was too late.

4. Guard against mere neglect. The crime of Meroz was one of omission.

SERMON FOR BEGINNING OF A REVIVAL.

Ps. 132 : 9.

1. The nature of the priesthood of all true Christians.

2. The righteousness of the Lord Jesus is imputed to them.

3. Let them be clothed with this.

4. Let them shout for joy.

SERMON FOR THE FEAST OF INGATHERING.

Ps. 132 : 16.

1. The relation of imputed righteousness to salvation.

2. This righteousness and this salvation are alike from the Lord.

3. The saving presence of the Lord is the joy of His disciples.

THE SOUL FLYING AS A BIRD.

Ps. 11 : 1.

Alternative senses :

1. Some high authorities would render the words, " Flee *from* your mountain." In this view it is regarded as the advice of the enemies of David to induce him to forsake his trust in the Lord and wander from trust to trust.

2. Others consider the words as signifying, " Flee as a bird to your place of greater security." In this sense it becomes the counsel of David's friends.

According to the first interpretation, we have a warning to all such as do not put their trust in the Lord. They are doomed, as Luther and Calvin teach us, to go from one refuge to another as a bird flying from one mountain covert to another, but finding no rest anywhere. Agreeably to the second apprehension of the sense, we are exhorted to make the Lord Jesus our only refuge, and to ask ourselves whether we are in earnest search of His salvation and protection.

AWAKE, O NORTH WIND, AND COME, THOU SOUTH.

Canticles 4 : 16.

1. The Holy Spirit as producing a divine light.
2. A divine warmth.
3. The joint agency of both at work in the soul.

WHEN JESUS DOES NOT APPEAR FOR THE HELP OF THE CHURCH, LET HER NOT BE IMPATIENT AND HASTY.

Canticles 8 : 4.

These words repeated three times— 2 : 7, 3 : 5.

1. Christ has an appointed time for coming to bless the Church.
2. He only knows what preparations are to be made by the Spirit and by Providence.

Application.

a. Let the Church show forbearance toward the weak, the back-slidden, and the lukewarm.

b. Let her beware of unseasonable importunity to Christ.

c. Let her beware of impatiently forestalling the Lord.

d. Shows unbelief.   Isa. 28 : 16.

THE LORD'S TENDER CARE OF YOUNG CONVERTS.

He shall gather the lambs with His arms, and carry them in His bosom.   Isa. 40 : 11 (compare verses 12, 15).

The Good Shepherd lifts the lambs to a place of security in His arms, and carries them near His heart.   They are more precious to Him than all the rest of His works.

a. They are near His heart while seas, lakes, and rivers He keeps at arm's length, measuring their waters in the hollow of His hand.

b. They are next to His heart while the dome of heaven He keeps at his finger's ends, meting it out with the span.

c. While all the earth beneath us He comprehends in a measure.

d. While the hills and mountains He weighs in scales.

e. While He takes up the islands as a very little thing.

f. While all nations are in comparison as the drop of a bucket or the small dust of the balance.   REV. SAMUEL ALMAN.

SHALL THE LAWFUL CAPTIVE BE DELIVERED?
Isa. 49 : 25.

1. Satan holds unregenerate souls in captivity.

2. Christ Jesus came to deliver them.

OUR BONDAGE AND REDEMPTION.
Isa. 52: 3.

1. We have sold ourselves ; Jesus offers to redeem us.

2. We have sold ourselves for nought ; He offers to redeem us with His precious blood.

3. We use our freedom to enslave us ; He employs His sovereign power to emancipate us.

HE THAT WINNETH SOULS IS WISE.
Prov. 11 : 30.

1. That man is wise who makes the winning of souls one of the chief objects of his ministry.

a. The edification of the living Church is indeed not to be neglected.

b. But there can be no building up before the foundation has been laid.

c. And in laying foundations, we should follow the wise Master-builder. 1 Cor. 3 : 10; Rom. 15 : 20.

2. To win souls demands a wise use of means.

3. Wisdom from above is required. Jas. 3 : 17, 18.

4 Souls are to be won, not driven.

GOD DESIROUS OF SAVING MEN.
Woe unto thee, O Jerusalem, etc. Jer. 13 : 27.

1. The woes which impenitent sinners have reason to expect.

2. How unwilling God is to inflict them.

Address : *a.* Those who imagine they have no need of cleansing.

b. Those willing to be cleansed.

c. Those who desire to be cleansed. REV. CHARLES SIMEON.

ENCOURAGEMENT TO CAPTIVES.
Micah 2 : 13.

The Messiah fulfilled this prophecy *the first time,* when he led the Jews out of Babylon. He had emancipated them in Egypt, Exodus 33 : 14 ; Isa. 63 : 9; *in the second and last period,* in which he appears as the incarnate Redeemer of all men.

AS THE BREAKER, JESUS GOES BEFORE ALL BELIEVERS.

1. Conquering sin and Satan, the world and death.

2. Opening the gates of hope, liberty, service, victory, and heaven.

AND BARAK CALLED ZEBULUN AND NAPHTALI TO KADESH.

Judges 4 : 10.

1. All the Lord's battles are fought by chosen men.
2. A general rally of a church against the common enemy is not to be expected.
3. Those who are already in the field, though few, should not wait for reinforcements, but advance.

AND SALT, WITHOUT PRESCRIBING HOW MUCH.

Ezra 7 : 22.

1. We may not limit the action and sphere of regenerating and sanctifying grace.
2. There cannot be too many Christian people in the world.
3. We ought not, therefore, to restrict the use of the means of grace.

THE BLOOD OF THE LAWFUL SACRIFICE CANNOT BE IMPROVED BY ADDING TO IT OUR OWN BLOOD.

1 Kings 18 : 28.

1. Our sufferings cannot atone for our sins.
2. Repentance toward God cannot supersede the necessity of faith in Christ.

THE HIDING-PLACE DESTROYED.

Isa. 28 : 17.

1. The refuge of lies condemned by the plumb-line.
2. The righteousness of God sweeps it away.
3. The common justice of men overflows it.

THE DISEASE AND THE BALM.

Jer. 8 : 21, 22.

1. The disease deplored : "For the heart of the daughter of my people," etc.
2. The assurance that there is a remedy : " Is there no balm," etc.
3. Why is it that health is not restored ? " Why then is not, " etc.

ENCOURAGEMENT FOR YOUNG PILGRIMS.

Jer. 31 : 9.

1. The way is smooth.
2. The way is straight.
3. Rivers of water flow by the side of it.

A REASONABLE CHOICE.

We will go with you ; for we have heard that God is with you.   Zech. 8 : 23.

UNION IN PRAYER.

And the children of Israel cried unto the Lord ; for he had nine hundred chariots of iron. Judges 4 : 3.

1. By united supplication we may be enabled to subdue the most powerful opposition.

2. May be enabled to convert the wickedest men.

3. May be enabled to do these things by means of few and feeble instrumentalities.

A REVIVAL ACCORDING TO SCRIPTURE.

Ps. 119 : 25.

1. Cleaving to the dust.

2. Quickening prayed for.

3 Agreeably to the word of God.

THE CO-OPERATION OF FATHERS AND CHILDREN IN REVIVALS.

Mal. 4 : 5, 6 (compare Luke 1 : 17).

1. The effect of Gospel repentance is not only to reconcile us to God, but to compose the differences which exists between parents and children.

2. To secure their co-operation in the service of the Lord.

3. Such union prepares the way for the coming of the King into many hearts.

4. Disharmony between the Church and the Sunday-school, or the old and the young, is a curse to any congregation or community.

WHEN THEY SAW THE STAR THEY REJOICED WITH EXCEEDING GREAT JOY.

Matt. 2 : 10.

1. The light of reason leads us along many dangerous ways.

2. The light of faith conducts us to our Saviour and King.

3. Those who are thus led to Jesus share the joy of the Wise Men.

SHAME FOR SIN A PREPARATION FOR DISCOVERING THE TRUE CHURCH.

And if they be ashamed of all that they have done, shew them the form of the house. Ezek. 43: 11.

THE SPIRIT'S LIFE-GIVING OPERATIONS.

John 6 : 63.

1. Necessity. *a.* Men are legally dead. *b.* Spiritually dead.

2. Subjects. *a.* The will. *b.* The attention. *c.* The intellect. *d.* Conscience.

3. Mode. *a.* Mysterious. *b.* Instantaneous. *c.* Sovereign. *d.* Powerful. REV. GEORGE BROOKS.

THE BLIND AND DUMB MAN HEALED.

Matt. 12 : 22.

This man illustrates the moral condition of many.

1. They neither discern their spiritual interests, nor speak of them.

2. But still they can hear the joyful sound of salvation.

3. The Spirit of God can cause all such not only to hear, but see and speak.

4. It is only through Christ that the Holy Spirit heals the soul.

5. Every such instance of conversion is a fresh proof that the Kingdom of God is come to us (see verse 28).

TRIAL AND TRIUMPH OF FAITH IN THE EXPERIENCE OF THE WOMAN OF CANAAN.

Matt. 15 ; 21-22 (compare Mark 7 : 24-26).

THE BLINDNESS OF THE BACKSLIDER PARTIALLY CURED.

Mark 8 : 22-25.

The blind man healed at Jericho must have once been able to see, otherwise he would not have instantly recognized either man or tree ; it is not said that he was born blind.

1. View this man at that stage of his cure when he sees men as trees walking about.

a. A partial restoration of moral vision causes prejudices, misjudgments of character and conduct, and such misdoings as short-comings as result from one-sided views of facts and obligations.

b. Inadequate notions of our fellow-man.

(*a*) We regard man as if he were a being without intelligence or feeling—a living and walking tree !

(*β*) We live as if our fellow-man were to perish like a tree.

(*γ*) We regard them as timber produced for our exclusive use.

c. We forget man's destiny.

d. Our business is not to walk about (Gr. *peripatountas*) in a circle, but to walk forward with the great purpose of life in view.

2. The duty of the backslider that is partially cured.

a. Let him permit the Great Physician to put His hands on his eyes once more.

b. Let him first prove his cure to his own family rather than to the general public.

SCIENCE DOES HOMAGE TO CHRIST.

Matt. 2 : 1-12.

1. True science leads first to Scripture, then directly to Christ. [The wise men go first to Jerusalem, then to Bethlehem.]

2. At best it has inadequate views of Christ. He is not merely "King of the Jews."

3. It pays a rich though late tribute to the Messiah. [The shepherds went immediately. The Magi did not perhaps arrive until more than a year later.] Compare Matt. 2 : 16.

4. Yet is science under the divine guidance and protection. [They were warned of God in a dream.]

5. Finally it disappears, to be heard of no more. [Knowledge shall vanish away. 1 Cor. 13 : 8.]

THE WAY HOME.

Sermon to converts. Matt. 2 : 12.

1. We are by nature lost.
2. Our finding of Christ.
3. The charge not to return to Herod.
4. We are to go to our own country.
5. And that by another way. THOMAS ADAMS.

OUT OF EGYPT HAVE I CALLED MY SON.

Sermon to young converts. Matt. 2 : 15.

1. As the child Jesus found in Egypt a refuge from His enemies, so the young convert finds security in the afflictions of the Gospel.

2. Be not alarmed, then, if great temptations and disappointments soon overtake you.

3. Satan, like Herod, would destroy his enemy while yet young.

a. Be vigilant, therefore.

b. And trust in the guidance and protection of the Almighty.

EVANGELISTS FISHERS OF MEN.

Matt. 4 : 19.

The kingdom of God does not always advance gradually, like leaven in a mass of dough. Conversions do not always take place occasionally, one here and another there at long intervals of time, as when Peter caught with a hook only one fish having a piece of silver in its mouth. But sinners were also expected to come into the kingdom in large numbers at once, as when fish come into a net. And yet Christ Jesus alone can make men-fishing a real and lasting success.

1. He alone can make us fishers of men. "Follow me, and I will make you," etc.

a. He alone can make us Christians.

b. He alone can give us the requisite simplicity and wisdom.

c. He alone can bestow upon us and upon our audiences the Holy Ghost.

2. The Lord alone can direct us when and where to cast in the net. (Compare Luke, chapter 5 and John, chapter 22.)

3. He alone can save us from the consequences of too large and too mixed a membership.

A PUBLIC PROFESSION OF RELIGION.

Matt. 10 : 32, 33.

1. It is due to the world.
2. Due to the Church.
3. Due to yourself.
4. Due to Christ.   REV. DR. GEORGE W. BETHUNE.

THE WEDDING GARMENT INDISPENSABLE.

Matt. 22 : 22.

1. Clad in this, the most miserable and criminal were admitted to the feast.

2. To enter without it was to neglect to show a proper respect to the son.

OUR DUTY TO A DEAD-ALIVE CHURCH.

Matt. 24 : 12.

1. Iniquity abounds.
2. Hence complacency grows cold.
3. Our love should now take the form of compassion.

MEETING OF OPPOSITE CHARACTERS AT THE JUDGMENT.

Matt. 25 : 32.

Noah and the unbelievers to whom he preached ; Moses and Pharaoh ; David and Saul ; Elijah and Jezebel ; Paul and his persecutors ; we shall meet our kindred friends and enemies.

FOLLOWING CHRIST AFAR OFF.

Matt. 26 : 58.

1. Indicate those who follow Jesus afar off :
a. Those who have some love, but grace in them is weak.
b. Such as are ashamed to confess Christ.
c. Those who walk inconsistently.
d. Such as do not heartily promote the kingdom of Christ.
2. The causes of following Jesus afar off.
a. Weakness of faith. *b.* Fear of man. *c.* Attachment to the world. *d.* Self-confidence.

3. The evils of this course.

a. It is not honorable. *b.* It is not reasonable. *c.* It is not comfortable. *d.* It is not safe. REV. DUNCAN MATHESON.

THE DAY OF GOD'S POWER.

Thy people shall be willing in the day of thy power. Ps. 110 : 3.

1. The persons spoken of : " Thy people ;" God's elect, those given to Christ by the Father.

2. The promise of the Father to Emmanuel regarding these persons : they shall be willing.

a. They are willing to be saved by Christ's imputed righteousness.

b. They are willing to be subject to His kingly power.

c. They are willing to bear the cross in following Him.

3. The time of the promise—the day of Emmanuel's power.

a. It is the time of His exaltation to the mediatorial throne (verse 1).

b. It is the day of the free preaching of the gospel.

c. It is the day in which Christ crucified is the centre and sum of the doctrine taught.

d. It is the day of the outpouring of the Holy Spirit (verse 2).

Conclusion : An invitation to sinners respecting Isa. 55 : 1–3 and Rev. 22 : 17. REV. WILLIAM C. BURNS, Scottish Evangelist.*

THE TEMPTATIONS OF CHRIST AFTER HIS BAPTISM.

Sermon addressed to young converts. Matt. 4 : 1.

The temptations of our Saviour may for our present purpose be summed up in these three suggestions of the Wicked One.

1. Take the most hidden way to the prizes of life.

2. Take the shortest path to what you most desire.

3. Take the newest road to wealth or power, pleasure or honor.

HOW MUCH THEN IS A MAN BETTER THAN A SHEEP?

Matt. 12 : 12.

1. The life of a man is of more value than the life of a brute.

a. Yet there are those who would help pull a sheep out of a ditch who will do nothing for the reform of the drunkard, for the sick or the poor.

b. There are those who do more for pet horses and dogs than for their sick or disabled servants.

2. The soul of a man is worth more than the life of a sheep.

---

* The sermon of which the above is an outline was preached in the parish church at Kilsyth, July 23d, 1839. The awakening that attended it is related in this preacher's memoir, by Rev. Dr. Islay Burns, pp. 83–130. Full notes of parts of this sermon are given in the appendix of the memoir, pp. 561–568.

a. There are those who would rescue a sheep from death while they are doing nothing to save their own souls.

b. Some show great compassion for all the lower animals and for the afflicted bodies of human beings, and yet they are helping to destroy the souls of their fellow-men.

TAKE MY YOKE UPON YOU.

Matt 11 : 29.

1. Human beings cannot be saved by destroying their will.
2. The service of Christ is a voluntary service.

WHY STAND YE HERE ALL THE DAY IDLE?

Matt. 20 : 1.

1. Why? The vineyard is so spacious.
2. Why? The reward is so liberal.
3. Why? The Master is so kind.
4. Why? The time of working is so short.

J. J. VAN OOSTERZEE.

FOR INGATHERING—THE EFFECTS OF CHRIST'S ENTRY INTO THE TEMPLE.

Matt. 21 : 12-16.

1. The restoration of the temple to sacred uses.
2. The healing of the blind and the lame.
3. The conversion of children ; their hosannas.
4. The displeasure of the chief priests and scribes.

WHAT THE GOSPEL DOES FOR US.

Luke 8 : 35.

Many of our Lord's miracles may fairly be employed as acted parables.   In conversion, we received—

1. Soundness of mind—" in his right mind."
2. The vesture of Christ's righteousness—"clothed."
3. True peace—"sitting at the feet of Jesus."

THE FIELDS OF EVANGELISTIC WORK.

Luke 14 : 21-24.

Three invitations :

1. To those who " were bidden" (vs. 16, 20).
2. To those who lived and begged in the open streets and lanes of the city (v. 21).
3. To those who were found in the highways and hedges of the suburbs—drunkards, thieves, robbers, tramps, etc. (v. 23).

Conclusion :   *a.* They were to go out *quickly.*

b. They were to keep in mind the extent of the feast.

c. The third class they must compel to come.

THE LOST COIN.

Luke 15 : 8-10.

A striking image of the soul :

1. Its original brilliancy.

2. Its present deterioration.

3. Its worth when it is found.   J. J. VAN OOSTERZEE.

THE PHARISEE IN THE PARABLE.

Luke 18 : 11, 12.

1. The self-righteous spirit is harsh in its judgments of others.

2. It is inconsistent in its utterances. (He is no sinner, and yet he fasts as if he were a very great sinner.)

3. It is ever prone to magnify a service of rites and forms.

REV. DR. HENRY CALDERWOOD.

CHRIST MORE MIGHTY THAN THE POWER OF SIN AND SATAN.

Lu ke 11 : 21-23.

1. An encouragement to sinners to fly to Jesus for help and refuge.

2. A motive to weak believers to continue the Christian warfare.

MEMORANDA OF THE PRODIGAL SON.

Luke 15 : 11-24.

1. Wilful. 2. Wandering. 3. Wasteful. 4. Wanting. 5. Wretched. 6. Walking home again. 7. Welcome.

REV. DR. JOSEPH SANDERSON.

Another. 1. Rebellious. 2. Roaming. 3. Revelling. 4. Ruined. 5. Reflecting. 6. Remembering. 7. Resolving. 8. Returning. 9. Received. 10. Rejoicing.

THE LAMB OF GOD.

John 1 : 29.

1. The sin of the world.

2. The Lamb of God, who takes it away.

3. Behold Him.

THE DAY OF OUR PROBATION.

The night cometh, when no man can work. John 9 : 4.

1. We ought to give our first attention to the most important work.

2. We should commence work by believing in Christ's work.

3. The night may come unexpectedly ; it must come soon.

4. When the night is upon us, it is too late to commence work.

THE END OF THE SPIRIT'S MISSION IS TO GLORIFY CHRIST.

He shall glorify me.   John 16 : 14.

1. Explain this prediction.
2. Show what this prediction explains.
3. Show the relation of this subject to our experience and duty.

BEHOLD THE MAN.

John 19 : 5.

With very different feelings we may regard him :

1. With wonder.   2. With pity.   3. Admiration.   4. Penitence.
5. Faith.

SAVE YOURSELVES FROM THE WORLD.

Acts 2 : 40.

1. A testimony.
a. Expressed : " this untoward generation."
b. Implied : that his hearers were in danger of being lost.   " Save yourselves."
2. An exhortation : " Save yourselves."
a. Not merely from perdition.
b. Not merely from an accusing conscience.
c. But from this present world.
3. How save yourselves ? (v. 38).

WHO ARE THEY THAT RESIST THE HOLY GHOST ?

Acts 7 : 51.

1. The stiff-necked.
2. The uncircumcised in heart.
3. In ears.

REPENTANCE A GIFT OF GOD.

Then hath God also to the Gentiles granted repentance unto life.   Acts 11 : 18.

1. As to time.
2. As to grace.
3. As to instrumentalities.

THE AWAKENING AT ANTIOCH.

Acts 11 : 20–21.

1. The primitive evangelists preached the Lord Jesus.
2. The hand of the Lord was with them.
3. And a great number believed.
4. And turned unto the Lord.

THE TWELFTH COMMANDMENT.

God....now commandeth all men everywhere to repent.   Acts 17 : 30.

Archbishop Ussher used to call the " New Commandment" the

eleventh ; and accordingly we may, not without good reasons, reckon as next in order the command to repent. Repentance is not a mere privilege to which the Gospel invites us ; it is an imperative duty, an act of obedience demanded by divine authority and enforced by eternal penalties. Were we able to dig deep enough, we would find that Sinai and Calvary have a common foundation. Both rest on the law of God. Many words of Scripture imply this. Luther confessed that he was never able to draw a line of demarkation between the Law and the Gospel.

SAILING WAS NOW DANGEROUS.

Acts 27 : 9.

1. There are perilous seasons in the voyage of life.
2. To take warning is reasonable and wise.

ALL ESCAPED SAFE TO LAND.

Acts 27 : 43.

1. Some called to active, and others to passive Christian life.
2. Active not required to wait for passive Christians.
3. The passive should not complain that the active leave them behind.

DIVINE WRATH A REVELATION FROM HEAVEN.

Rom. 1 : 8.

1. It is not a mere deduction of reason.
2. Not a mere voice of conscience.
3. Not a mere sentiment of the heart. It is a revelation of God.
a. To our faith.
b. To our reason.
c. To our conscience.
d. To our heart.
e. To our senses.

THE EFFECTIVE CHARACTER OF PRIMITIVE CHRISTIAN ADDRESSES.

But he that prophesieth speaketh unto men to edification, and exhortation, and comfort. 1 Cor. 14 : 3.

The reputation of being insane not to be sought (v. 23).

1. Their object was edification.
a. By exhortation.
b. By consolation or encouragement.
c. Instruction (v. 31).
d By variety of exercises. (vs. 6, 26-32).
e. By communications intended for the intellect as well as the heart (vs. 15-17, 19, 20).

f. By the observance of propriety and order.

2. Their effect was the conversion of inquirers. (See Neander's " Planting and Training" on 1 Cor. 14 : 22-24.) Describe the successive stages (vs. 24, 25).

LET US NOT BE WEARY IN WELL DOING.

Gal. 6 : 9.

St. Paul includes himself.

1. It is here supposed that Christian laborers can be weary in well doing.   Why?

2. Dissuasives from yielding to weariness.

3. The consequences of fainting in the time of harvest.

ABEL BEING DEAD, YET SPEAKS.

Heb. 11 : 4.

1. He speaks by His faith.

a. His faith obeyed Jehovah in the choice and offering of the sacrifice.

b. It was with him an individual matter.   The Lamb of God dies for every believer individually.   Imagine yourself the only believer on earth.   You would need an atonement all the same.

c. Imagine how Abel felt on being received by Christ into glory.

2. To whom does Abel speak?

a. To those who would invent a religion of their own.

b. To those who say it matters not what you believe or do, so your heart is only right.

c. To such as trust in obedience or affliction.

THE DANGERS OF YOUNG CHRISTIANS.

1 Pet. 5 : 8.

1. Point out some of the most common of these dangers.

a. A feeling of security.

b. A slothful spirit in regard of religious duties.

c. Worldly-mindedness.

d. Bad examples.

e. A love of popular approbation.

2. How may we escape these dangers?

a. Be always on the lookout.

b. Resist the beginnings of temptation.

c. Look to the Lord for help.   REV. A. C. BALDWIN.

GOD IS LOVE.   GOD IS LIGHT.

1 John 4 : 8.   1 John 1 : 5.

1. God is love.

a. God has love in His heart or will.

b. He manifests love in His word and works.

2. God is light.

a. He is the author of the Scriptures.

b. He sends to us the Divine Spirit to teach us the meaning of Scripture.

c. Hence we should inquire what light God throws on His love.

a. According to the light of Scripture, God's love respects divine justice, holiness, and faithfulness.

b. It defines the sources and limits of Christian love or charity.

THE GRACE OF SALVATION.

Titus 2 : 11.

1. The grace of God.

2. That bringeth salvation.

3. Hath appeared to all men.

"THESE THINGS SAITH HE THAT IS HOLY, HE THAT IS TRUE."

Rev. 3 : 7.

1. Christ and His witnesses are holy ; hence they are worthy of belief.

2. The enemies of Christ are unholy, and therefore not to be credited.

THE FINAL INVITATION.

Rev. 22 : 17.

1. The Divine Spirit says, " Come."

a. In the inspired Word.

b. In creation.

c. In Providence.

d. In preachers and all believers, and especially in young converts.

e. The Spirit whispers the invitation in the hearts of convicted and anxious hearers.

2. The Bride or the Church triumphant says, "Come."

a. The glorified saints in all past ages.

b. Our departed kindred and friends.

3. To whom is the invitation given ?

a. To every thirsty soul.

b. To every willing heart.

c. To every one that will " take."

4. The inducement to come.

a. The water of life.

b. Freely (*a*) as being without price.

(*β.*) As being abundant.

(*γ.*) Every hearer is requested to invite others.

THE SECOND COMING OF CHRIST.

R-v. 22 : 20.

1. The Lord's final coming may be soon.
2. To multitudes it must be sudden and unexpected.

PROMISCUOUS THEMES AND TEXTS.

The Ark of Salvation the only security for families. Gen. 7 : 7.

The Divine Spirit reveals to the heart its newness of life. Gen. 8 : 11.

Angel hands rescuing the lingerers. Gen. 19 : 16.

The break of day was not what Jacob wrestled for. Gen. 32 : 26.

Are we under the wings of the God of Israel? Ruth 2 : 12.

Encouraged by superior numbers. 2 Kings 6 : 16.

Self justification condemns God. Job 40 : 8.

The Good Shepherd leading His sheep along a bend in their path. Ps. 23 : 3.

The folly of that human wisdom which is at war with God. Prov. 21 : 30.

Regeneration rather than affliction demanded. Isa. 1 : 5.

The conversion of the heathen a motive for seeking the conversion of nominal Christians. Isa. 52 : 10.

The danger of delay and the necessity of making haste. Ps. 119 : 60.

An apology for zeal. Ps. 119 : 139.

The backslider should not delay his return. Ps. 119 : 60.

[The Hebrew word for delay is applied to a trifling and unreasonable tarrying in great emergencies. Gen. 19 : 16 ; 63 : 10 ; Exodus 12 : 39.—*A. J. Alexander.*]

Pride deceives us in regard of God's purpose and power. Obadiah 3, 4.

Rowing against the Divine Command. Jonah 1 : 13.

Active service among the young removes the doubts and fears of the Church. Canticles 1: 8.

Neglecting the lambs, " He shall carry the lambs in His bosom." Isa. 40 : 11.

Killing the Lambs. "He that sacrificeth a lamb," etc. Isa. 66 : 3.

Feeding the Lambs. " Feed my lambs." John 21 : 15.

Preconceptions and prejudices in religion. 2 Kings 5 : 11, 12.

The alternatives offered, or the choice of Moses. Hebrews 11 : 25.

The sinner in fleeing one evil meets another. Amos 5 : 19.

Sin a burden—past, present, and future. " Bow down their back," etc. Rom. 11 : 10.

Lest that I myself should be a castaway. (To converts.) 1 Cor. 9 : 27.

The inseparable connection of Christ and the Spirit in the work of salvation. John 16 : 7-15.

The wearisome wanderings of such as are ignorant of the way of salvation. (He knoweth not how to go to the city. Eccl. 10 : 15.)

The woman of Samaria before conversion is controversial. John 4 : 20.

Seek ye me, and ye shall live (see repetitions in verses 6, 8, 14). Amos 5 : 4.

The new commandment. John 13 : 34. [The newness here consists in our making the self-sacrificing love of Jesus the example of our love to one another " As I have loved you."]

I was not disobedient to the heavenly vision. Acts 26 : 19.

Who then is willing to consecrate his service this day unto the Lord ? 1 Chron. 29 : 5.

The two sons. [Lessons from this parable for close of revival.] Matt. 21 : 28-32.

The midnight importunity in behalf of a hungry friend. Luke 11 : 5-8.

[Be thou ashamed, O Zidon ; for the sea hath spoken ; Isa. 23 : 4. Commercial cities have reason to be ashamed of the moral and spiritual condition of sailors.]

Caleb's exhortation : " Let us go up at once," etc. Num. 13 : 30.

Saul as a rejected inquirer. 1 Sam. 28 : 6.

The struggles of the will overcome through prayer. Luke 22 : 41-43.

Apology for the fact that there are unconverted persons in the Church drawn from the Parable of the Tares. Matt. 13 : 28.

Lost opportunities. " And as thy servant was busy here and there, he was gone." 1 Kings 20 : 40.

Broken cisterns preferred to the fountain. Jer. 2 : 13.

The neglect of the duty of believing. John 12 : 37.

The madness of mankind. [Sermon by the Rev. George Finley.] Eccles. 9 : 3.

The importance of seeking the Lord early : " When the sun waxed hot, it melted." Exod. 16 : 21.

We are forever to be learners in the school of Christ. " Mary hath

chosen that good part, which shall never be taken away from her."
Luke 10 : 42.

Your joy no man taketh from you.   [Sermon to converts.]   John
16 : 22.

Nicodemus, or secret discipleship.   John 3 : 1, 2.

The servants sent to dry wells.   Jer. 14 : 3.

Wise unto salvation.   2 Tim. 3 : 15.

How can I endure to see the destruction of my kindred?   Esther
8 : 6.

Touching the hem of the Messiah's garment.   Matt. 14 : 34–36.

They were waiting for Him. · Luke 8 : 40.

While ye have light, believe in the light, etc.   John 12 : 36.

And Abram fell on his face : and God talked with him.   Gen. 17 : 3.
[Reverence and humiliation before God prepare us to learn His will.]

The Church well equipped, yet retreating on the day of battle.   Ps.
78 : 9. (The battle alluded to may possibly have been the affray
mentioned in 1 Chron. 7 : 21, but most probably it was the victory of
the Philistines on the day when the ark was captured near Shiloh, in
the land of Ephraim.)   Sam. 4 : 1–18.

The revival in the summer at Samaria.   John 4 : 6.   (The great revival at Nineveh in the days of Jonah, the revival at Everton in
England in 1759, at East Hampton, L. I., in 1764, and in Ireland
in 1859, occurred in the summer.)

A warning against pride.   1 Tim. 3 : 6.   "Nothing," says Tholuck,
"creeps so easily into the heart of a man after conversion, as
pride."

Bartimeus.   Luke 18 : 41, 42.

The Master requires our intelligent and deliberate choice.   Luke
9 : 58.

For ye were as sheep going astray, etc.   [Sermon to converts.]   1
Pet. 2 : 25.

A false profession makes the service of Christ slavery.   Joshua
9 : 21.

The cry of despair heard.   Gen. 21 : 16.

Be of good cheer ; thy sins be forgiven thee.   Matt. 9 : 2.

Our own resources are inadequate.   "This man began to build,
and was not able to finish."   Luke 14 : 28–32.

What is it to be an enemy of Christ?   John 15 : 23.

The ten days' prayer-meeting in the upper room.   Acts 1 : 14.

The friends of Christ here and hereafter.   Matt. 12 : 47–50.

What scene it is our privilege to approach.   Heb. 12 : 22–24.

The fatherhood of God in His compassion for doubters.   Ps. 103 : 13.

The Lord as viewed by the convicted and the converted. Ps. 18 : 11, 12.

God the Author both of the Winter and the Spring of the soul. Ps. 147 : 15–18.

Invading Canaan without God's command, presence, and promise. Numbers 14 : 40–45.

Be not afraid ; only believe. [Sermon to parents.] Mark 5 : 36.

Christ the sinner's only Refuge. " The hail shall sweep away the refuge of lies.... Isa. 28 : 17.

Our Religion tried at the altar of Sacrifice. 1 Kings 18 : 17–46.

Why are ye the last to bring the king back to his house? 2 Sam. 19 : 11.

Waiting for God's salvation. Gen. 49 : 18.

One effect of the outpouring of the Spirit is righteousness. Isa. 32 : 16, 17.

Come before Winter. [Sermon on the difficulty of death-bed repentance.] 2 Tim. 4 : 21.

The answer which ministers are to return to God. 2 Sam. 24 . 13.

Bring him hither to me. Mark 9 : 14.

Is the young man Absalom safe ? 2 Sam. 18 : 29.

Importance of maturing wishes into purposes. Neither did he set his heart to this also..... Exod. 7 : 23.

Those whom reform cannot chain the Religion of Jesus can tame. Mark 5 : 4.

Lord, open the eyes of these men, that they may see. 2 Kings 6 : 20.

The new Kingdom within the heart goes on seeking till it finds Christ. Matt. 13 : 45, 46.

The Lord Jesus manifested to destroy the works of the devil. 1 John 3 : 8.

Those who will not rejoice at the feast of the Lord's ingathering are not to enjoy the showers of His grace. Zech. 14 : 16–19.

Go the one way or other, either on the right hand or the left. Ezek. 21 : 16.

O that Ishmael might live before thee ! Gen. 17 : 18.

And there was great joy in that city. Acts 8 : 8.

Waiting for Christ. Luke 8 : 40.

Come down ere my child die. John 4 : 49.

My spirit shall not always strive with man. Gen. 6 : 3.

The Spirit of the Lord causing the excellency of the natural man to wither. Isa. 40 : 7.

The Holy Spirit inspiring the feeble with the power of the eagle. Isa. 40 : 29–31.

The lepers of Samaria. 2 Kings 7 : 9.

And as he was yet a coming, the devil threw him down and tare him. Luke 9 : 42.

Yet doth he devise means that his banished be not expelled. 2 Sam. 14 : 14. [Sermon to and in behalf of backsliders.]

Then all those virgins arose and trimmed their lamps. Matt. 25 : 7.

He that regardeth the clouds shall not reap. Eccles. 11 : 4.

They received not the love of the truth, that they might be saved. 2 Thess. 2 : 10.

Conviction, if not followed by conversion, is dangerous. Luke 11 : 24-26.

Is the Lord among us or not ? Exod. 10 : 17.

Behold our desolations, and the city which is called by thy name. Dan. 9 : 18.

Repentance and faith are not to be separated. Acts 20 : 21.

Uses and abuses   a sense of unworthiness. " I am not worthy that thou shouldst come under my roof." Matt. 8 : 8.

That they which come in may see the light. Luke 11 : 33.

Neutrality in our religion impossible. Matt. 12 : 30.

Compel them to come in. Luke 14 : 23.

Your professed subjection unto the Gospel of Christ. [Sermon to converts.] 2 Cor. 9 : 13.

The covetous deride Christ. Luke 16 : 14.

Invited to believe the Good News. Mark 1 : 15.

The Father honors those who serve the Son. John 12 : 26.

Christ by His Spirit has come to bring us home. John 14 : 3.

And now Lord what wait I for ? My hope is in thee. Ps. 39 : 7.

Simplicity of purpose leads to unity of action. 1 Chron. 12 : 33.

They departed quickly from the sepulchre with fear and great joy. Matt. 28 : 8.

Doubting prayer heard. Mark 9 : 22.

The timid and concealed seeker. Luke 8 : 43-48.

The sinner and manslayer compared. Num. 35 : 9-15.

Stumbling on dark mountains. Jer. 13 : 16.

The resurrection of Lazarus. John 11 : 43, 44.

To revive the spirit of the contrite ones. Isa. 57 : 15.

By faith the harlot Rahab perished not, etc. Heb. 11 : 31.

By faith the walls of Jericho fell down, etc. Heb. 11 : 30.

The Wise and the Foolish Virgins. Matt. 25 : 1-12.

The character of God as a pardoner. Micah 7 : 18.

The prayers of very imperfect men heard in the name of Christ. Jas. 5 : 17, 18.

Toil and suffering in behalf of the conversion of sinners [that I may know the fellowship of his sufferings. Phil. 3 : 10].

Let us alone, that we may serve the Egyptians. Exod. 14 : 12.

The Refuge of the new convert in a time of persecution. (Trust ye not in a friend. . . . I will wait for the God of my salvation ; my God will hear me.) Micah 7 : 5-7.

Is the Spirit of the Lord straitened? Micah 2 : 7.

Every one over against his house. Neh. 3 : 28.

After him repaired Meshullam, over against his chamber. Neh. 3 : 30.

Let not the gates of Jerusalem be opened till the sun be hot. Neh. 7 : 3.

The rocks rent. Matt. 27 : 51.

What should I wait for the Lord any longer? 2 Kings 6 : 33.

They shall not find him ; he hath withdrawn himself from them. Hos. 5 : 6.

And he went on his way rejoicing. Acts 8 · 39.

Prejudice as hindering our salvation. John 1 : 46.

Master, I have brought unto thee my son. Mark 9 : 17.

Address to young converts on cleaving to the Lord. Acts 11 : 23.

Despising God's goodness and forbearance. Rom. 2 : 4.

The sower and the reaper rejoicing together. John 4 : 36.

The sin of neglecting the rescue of others. (If thou forbear to deliver them that are drawn unto death. . . .) Prov. 24 : 11, 12.

Lost sheep to be looked after first. Luke 15 : 3-7.

The penitent thief. Luke 23 : 39-43. (This narrative leads us (1) into the heart of the sinner ; (2) into the heart of the Saviour.— ADOLPH SAPHIR.)

The captive hasting to be set free. Isa. 51 : 14.

Gather out the stones. Isa. 40 : 3, 4.

And when the ship was caught, and could not bear up with the wind, we let her drive. Acts 27 · 15.

[The wisdom of the Church cannot control the Spirit. Rev Dr. A. J. Burlingham.]

They will reverence my son. Mark 12 : 6.

Say unto my soul, I am thy salvation. Ps. 35 : 3.

Christ becomes our light by curing our blindness. John 9 : 5-7.

The Hebrew maid in the house of Naaman. [Sermon to servants.] 2 Kings 5 : 3.

A revival experience. (Wilt thou not revive us again : that thy people may rejoice in thee?) Ps. lxxxv. 6.

The son of the widow of Nain. [Sermon to parents.]   Luke 7 : 11–13.

Do your first duty, then will the second be revealed.   Acts 9 : 6.

Formal professors pray that the anxious may be sent away.   Matt. 15 : 23.

The conversion of a child is a mercy to the parent.   Matt. 17 : 15.

An invitation addressed to quiet and afflicted believers to rise and welcome Christ and witness His power.   John 11 : 28, 29.

The guilt and penalty of sin as seen in the light of the Cross.   Luke 23 : 48.

When is it the eleventh hour with us ?   Matt. 20 : 6.

Salvation for great sinners [sermon to backsliders].   Ezek. 36 : 26, 27.

Call the poor, the lame, and the blind.   Luke 14 : 13.

Faith before wisdom, and wisdom before knowledge.   Ps. 119 : 66.

Prayer for Divine knowledge the best preparation for studying and teaching science.   Ps. 119 : 27.

If the enemy is near us, the Lord also is near us.   Ps. 119 : 150, 151.

The wandering professor like a lost sheep.   Ps. 119 : 76.

True life from the true source.   Ps. 119 : 50.

Awake ! awake ! put on strength, O arm of the Lord.   Isa. 51 : 9.

It is high time to awake out of sleep.   Rom. 13 : 11.

I go that I may awake him out of sleep.   John 11 : 11.

Awaking out of the snare of the Dev l [marginal reading].   2 Tim. 2 : 26.

Awake thou that sleepest, and rise from the dead, etc.   Eph. 5 : 14.

But he awaketh, and his soul is empty.   Isa. 29 : 8.

Awakening without the Gospel drives to despair.   Acts 16 : 27.

Christ did not answer every prayer.   Mark 5 : 18, 19.

Insignificance no excuse for neglected duty.   Jer. 1 : 6.   (Compare what the same prophet says in Ps. 119 : 141.)

What will you do with Christ?   Matt. 27 : 22.

Christ as regarded by His friends and by the multitude.   Mark 3 : 20, 21.

Spiritual resurrections attend God's visits.   Luke 7 : 16.

The city destroyed because she knew not the time of her visitation.   Luke 19 : 44.

They who receive Christ become sons of God.   John 1 : 12.

While the disciples are rowing amidst darkness and tempest, Jesus appears.   John 6 : 17, 19.

The evidence of Christian Experience.   John 9 : 25.

The relation of proof and grace to saving faith.   John 12 : 37.

Glad tidings of the terms of reconciliation.   Acts 10 : 36.

The Word of God's grace [a farewell sermon]. Acts 20 : 32.

Felix as the father of bribe-takers. Acts 24 : 26.

The lies of the market and the exchange. Prov. 21 : 6.

The profanation of the lot in games of chance. Prov. 16 : 33.

Thou shalt not sow thy field with mingled seed. Levit. 19 : 19.

[A sermon on the adulteration of food and medicine. Other texts on the same subject : Isa. 5 : 20 ; 2 Kings 4 : 38–41 ; Rev. 8 : 10, 11.]

The Gospel shows us the way to quietness and assurance. Isa. 32 : 17.

Prayer for God's gracious return to His people. Isa. 63 : 17, 19.

The young convert's prayer for the Father's guidance. Jer. 3 : 4.

The golden sons of Zion are as earthen pitchers on the day of doom. Lam. 4 : 2.

The Lord's face no longer hid. Ezek. 39 : 29.

Woe to them that are at ease in Zion. Amos 6 : 1.

But if ye be led by the Spirit, ye are not under the law. Gal. 5 : 13.

Paul a great sinner ; Christ a great Saviour. 1 Tim. 1 : 15.

To every man his work. Mark 13 : 34.

Avoid exaggeration. Come see a man which told me all things, etc. John 4 : 29.

Say not ye there are four months, and then cometh the harvest. John 4 : 35.

The revival in the summer at Nineveh. Jonah 4 : 5–11.

Be not too attentive to signs and seasons. Eccles. 11 : 4.

No room for Jesus in the inn. Luke 2 : 7.

My soul cleaveth unto the just. Ps. 119 : 25.

The woman searching for the lost piece of silver representing the Holy Spirit seeking the lost soul. Luke 15 : 8–10.

The cords of moral obligation which bind us to the Messiah not to be cast away. Ps. 2 : 3.

Dead in God's way ; alive again in His way. Ps. 119 : 37.

Prayer before and prayer after revival. Ps. 80 : 18.

A revival causes rejoicing in God. Ps. 85 : 6.

The last Adam was made a quickening spirit. 1 Cor. 15 : 45.

Unwillingness to hear of rest and refreshing. Isa. 28 : 12.

To lighten our eyes and give us a little reviving. Ezra 9 : 8.

The Church healed and revived. Hos. 6 : 1, 2.

Repent in order that times of refreshing may come. Acts 3 : 19.

When they were awake, they saw his glory. Luke 9 : 32.

Awake and sing, ye that dwell in the dust. Isa. 26 : 19.

Becoming diseased about questions, and a strife of words. 1 Tim. 6 : 4.

The providential protection of youthful piety. Matt. 2 : 13.

When they persecute you in this city, flee ye unto another. Matt. 10 : 23.

How Satan, by scattering, destroys a church ; the devil as a roaring lion. 1 Pet. 5 : 8. (A traveller is of opinion that the roaring of the lion by scattering a flock of animals causes some in terror and darkness to run heedlessly to him, instead of from him.)

The Lord Jesus tempted immediately after his baptism. [To young converts.] Matt. 4 : 1.

Inaction is reaction, sometimes. Since the fathers fell asleep, etc. 2 Pet. 3 : 4.

THE IMPORTANCE OF CONFESSING JESUS BEFORE THE WORLD.
Luke 8 : 45-48

1. Why did our Lord sometimes enjoin concealment?

2. Did he ever request any to confess Him before they were healed ?

3. When is a public confession clearly demanded?

ASA'S TIMELY PRAYER.
2 Chron. 14 : 10-12.

1. Asa made a proper disposition of his army.

2. He cried unto the Lord his God.

The Gospel sometimes occasions a tumult. Acts 19 : 23.

The Gospel may be represented as revolutionary. Acts 17 : 6.

For the beginning. Isa. 51 : 9.

For the ingathering. Isa. 53 : 1.

The advantages of union in revival work illustrated by contrast. Gen. 11 : 6.

The promise is to those who search with the whole heart. Jer. 29 : 13.

Sermon to strangers. (And it shall come to pass that in what tribe the stranger sojourneth....) Ezek. 47 : 23.

The effects of a primitive work of grace. Acts 2 : 42-47.

Amusements unseasonable in time of danger. Ezek. 21 : 9-10.

Trust not for peace with God in doing and suffering. Isa. 30 : 15.

Bring him hither to me. Mark 17 : 17.

Make haste and come down. Luke 19 : 5.

The atonement an occasion of rejoicing. Rom. 5 : 11.

The liberty of the children of God. Rom. 8 : 21.

Christ answering the demands of the law. Rom. 10 : 4.

Abounding in hope through the power of the Holy Ghost. Rom. 15 : 13. [A farewell sermon. Another, 2 Cor. 13 : 11.]

A review of a primitive work of grace. 1. Thess. 1 : 5-7.

Christianized service is the most profitable. Philemon 11.

Immediate action a remedy for forgetfulness and self-deception. Jas. 1 : 22–24.

The scoffers of our time witness for the truth of prophecy. 2 Pet. 3 : 3.

The parable of the Good Shepherd as illustrating the stupidity of some sinners in their wanderings. [Bengel.] Luke 15 : 1–7.

The parable of the lost piece of money as showing the ignorance of some sinners concerning their lost condition. [Bengel.] Luke 15 : 8–10.

The parable of the Prodigal Son as exhibiting the wilfulness of some sinners. [Bengel.] Luke 15 : 11–32.

Truth, peace, and equity as evangelizing forces. Mal. 2 : 6.

The revival lessons of spring. (Floods upon the dry ground.... willows by the water-courses.) Isa. 44 : 3,4.

It is time to seek the Lord. Hos. 10 : 12.

The Lord be with us, as he was with our fathers. 1 Kings 8 : 57,58.

The men of Gibeon asking help of the hosts of the Lord. Josh. 10 : 6.

To cease to pray for others is to sin against the Lord. 1 Sam 12 : 23.

The zeal of Jehu wanting in obedience to God 2 Kings 10 : 31.

Parents are to give Christian training to their converted children. ' Take up thy son." 2 Kings 4 : 36, 37. [This subject may also be proper for a sermon to the church concerning its duty to new converts.]

If the people will not hearken to God, He will not hearken them. Zech. 7 : 13. [Compare Hosea 5 : 6; Micah 3 : 4; Jer. 11 : 14; 14 : 12.]

Except your righteousness shall exceed the righteousness of the scribes and Pharisees, ye shall in no case enter into the kingdom of heaven. Matt. 5 : 20. [Spener was converted while preaching on this text.]

I gave her space to repent. Rev. 2 . 21.

Satan's great wrath and little time. Rev. 12 : 12.

Wonder-working croakers. (And I saw three unclean spirits like frogs, working miracles.) Rev. 16 : 13–15.

The grace of our Lord Jesus Christ be with you all. Rev. 22 : 21.

ERRATA.

Page 11, Kelsyth *read* Kilsyth.

" 29, line 18 from foot of page, these *read* those.

" 86, " 12 " " " teaching *read* teasing.

" 90, " 6 " " " of *read* or.

" 124, " 20 " " " *omit* s in travellers.

" 127, " 19 " " " Luke 15 : 7 *read* Luke 1 : 15.

" 147, " 23 " " " moved *read* led.

" 166, " 34 " " " John 1 : 38, 56, *read* John 1 : 35, 36.

" 178, " 22 " " " *add* text 1 Tim. 6 : 12,

" 208, " 11 " " " *add* text Matt. 13 : 46.

" 213, " 20 " " " Heb. 3 : 2 *read* Hab. 3 : 2.

" 223, " 33 " " " Madley *read* Madeley.

" 255, " 11 " " " published *read* preached.

" 259, " 14 " " " to title of sermon *add* text Rom. 10 : 3. -

" 297, " 22 " " " respecting *read* by repeating.

INDEX OF TEXTS.

INDEX OF SUBJECTS.

C.

D.

Parents, Deut. 5 : 29, 188 ; John 4 : 49, 213 ; 2 Kings 2 : 14, 217 ; 1 Sam. 3 : 13, 251, 258 ; Mark 5 : 36, 307 ; Matt. 8 : 8, 308 ; Mark 9 : 17, 309 ; Luke 7 : 11-13, 310 ; to help their children in the ways of Christ, 2 Kings 4 : 36, 37, 313.

Party spirit to be guarded against, 134.

Pastor, the true, will not disdain the aid of the evangelist, 143.

Pastors to co-operate with evangelists, 137-143 ; the ox and the ass, Isa. 32 : 20, 140, 141.

Pastors who have done good evangelistic work in their churches, 141.

Pastors are not to neglect their own duties while assisted by evangelists, 139.

Pharisee, 299.

Philosophy not to be preached, 27.

Philpot quoted, 32.

Physical manifestations and seizures, 99.

Political troubles, 109.

Power of God may prevail over many bad means and measures, 135.

Power, waiting for, 126-130 ; not a permanent force, 126 ; new investitures, 126 ; scripture views of, 127.

Prayer the right arm of revivalism, 9 ; secret, rewards of, xxi. ; of doubt heard, 308 ; of imperfect men, 308 ; of despair heard, 306 ; importunate, Hab. 1 : 2, 253 ; Job 27 : 10, 228.

Prayer as a preparation for a revival, 3 ; as a sign, 16.

Prayer cure, 62-71 ; in the present and in the past, 62 ; the advocates of the faith cure, 51 ; why revived in our day, 63 ; opposed to materialism, 63 ; the efficacy and application of the Divine Sacrifice, 63, 64 ; how far we resemble the primitive churches in our relation to the world, 64 ; did the gift of healing pass away with the Apostles ? 64 ; argument from probability, 65 ; testimony of honest witnesses, 65 ; the use of oil, 66, 70, 71 ; the prayer of faith, 66, 67 ; the laying on of hands, 67 ; calling for the elders, 67, 69 ; a churchly not a clerical rite, 69 ; must recognize exceptional cases, 69 ; Dr. Gordon's caution, 70 ; abuse of the rite, 67, 71 ; the prayer cure not unfriendly to medical science, 71 ; St. Luke set no limits to the healing power of God, 71.

Prayer exchanged for praise, 7 ; power of, 218, 272.

Prayer-meetings as preparations, 17 ; to be reformed, 4.

Praying devils are scarce, 102.

Preaching, amount of, 40 ; can there be too much ? 40 ; the question answered, 40-42 ; frequent when necessary, 45 ; in revivals aims at immediate results, 45 ; of pastors improved by evangelists, 141 ; one-sided view of, xix. ; effects of collecting materials without converting them into a building, xx. ; true ends of, xix.

Premature joy and rejoicing, 25, 26.

Preparation for an awakening, 123 ; by preaching, 21 ; should not be noisy, 12 ; outlines for, by *Wesley*, Amos 3 : 6, 153 ; Mark 9 : 38, 154 ; Psalm 73 : 20, 155 ; Matt. 16 : 24, 155 ; Matt. 16 : 26, 155 Psalm 147 : 20, 155 ; Matt. 3 : 2, 156 ; Matt. 6 : 33, 156 ; Jer. 6 : 16, 157 ; Zech. 4 : 7, 158 ; Eph. 5 : 18, 166 ; *Welsh*, Rev. 2 : 2-5, 168 ; *Woodhouse*, various texts, 170 ; *Spencer*, Psalm 51 : 8-10, 172 ; *Tyng*, Amos 4 : 12, 171 ; *Spurgeon*, Heb. 3 : 2, 174 ; Matt. 9 : 37, 38, 175 ; *Swan*, same text, 176 ; Mark 26 : 20, 177 ; Acts 1 : 8, 177 ; Gen. 45 : 20, 178 ; *Payson*, Psalm 90 : 8, 179 ; *Parker*, Neh. 2 : 17, 18 and other texts, 181 ; *Nettleton*, Rom. 13 : 11, 183 ; *Moody*, John 11 : 39, 188 ; *Knapp* (*J.*), Acts 26 : 24, 204 ; *Little* (*W. J. K.*), 192-3 ; *Knapp* (*H. W.*), 1 Kings 18 : 44, 206 ; Hos. 10 : 12, 207 ; Matt. 9 : 37, 208 ; John 4 : 42, 209 ; Acts 2 : 27, 209 ; *Kirk*, 210 ; *Krummacher*, Canticles 2 : 12, 211 ; *Hole* (*S. R.*), Isa. 30 : 17, 212 ; *Humphrey*, Isa. 40 : 3 and other texts, 213 ; Matt. 16 : 26, 222 ; Luke 16 : 2, 225 ; Psalm 139 : 23, 24, 228 ; Micah 2 : 13, 229 ; 1 Cor. 3 : 7, 233 ; Josh. 24 : 22, 233 ; 2 Chron. 7 : 14, 241 ; Canticles 8 : 4, 290 ; Judges 4 : 10, 292 ; Ezek. 43 : 11, 293 ; Matt. 22 : 12-16, 298 ; Luke 14 : 21-24, 298 ; Luke 8 : 40, 306 ; 2 Sam. 19 : 11, 307 ; Gen. 49 : 18, 307 ; Eccles. 11 : 4, 308 ; Exod. 11 : 17, 308 ; Dan. 9 : 18, 308 ; Isa. 63 : 17-19, 311 ; Psalm 80 : 18, 311.

Pride, spiritual, 105.

Primitive addresses, 301.

Private talks, in what spirit they should be commenced, 27, 28.

Privileges to be preached, 25.

Professor, the meaning of the word, 34.

Professors, formal, 310.

Professors of theology and evangelism, 140.

Proselyting and the Salvation Army, 44, 45.

Proselytism, 107.

Proselytism gone to seed, *e.g.*, Salvation Army, 44, 45.

Prostrations and seizures, 99.

Providences, afflictive, may cause conviction and fear without conversion, 134, 135.

Providences seemingly adverse yet favorable, 14 ; examples, 14–16.

Providence and revivals, 7.

Psalm one hundred and nineteen written by Jeremiah, 133.

Public profession, 296, 312.

Punishment, future, to be preached, 26.

Q.

QUOTATION better than argument in revivals, 50 ; example of a sceptic silenced by quotations, 50.

R.

RATIONALISM, Prov. 21 : 30, 304.

Rationalistic preaching noticed, 148.

Readings and expositions, 47–51 ; for what class most suitable, 47 ; examples of, 47, 48 ; readings on particular doctrines and duties, 48 ; incidental applications, 48, 49 ; use of such exercises in advancing the work, 49 ; a caution concerning them, 50, 51 ; one-sidedness to be avoided, 51.

Readings, books on, 51.

Reason, Gospel restores us to, 298.

Reconciliation of two kinds, xi.

Refined culture and awakenings, xii.

Reform, *Tyng*, Zech. 3 : 2, 171 ; *Spurgeon*, Ezek. 16 : 54, 174 ; Ps. 94 : 16, 188 ; *Moody*, Dan. 1 : 8 and 11 : 32, 188 ; Luke 5 : 32, 192 ; Prov. 23 : 21, 254 ; Isa. 28 : 17, 292 ; Isa. 66 : 8, 255 ; Zech. 2 : 3, 282 ; Zech. 5 : 5–11, 281 ; Matt. 27 : 4, 282 ; Mark 5 : 4, 307 ; Mark 17 : 17 ; Luke 11 : 24–26, 282.

Reformation, tracts in aid of, 91.

Relatives, conversion of, Esther 8 : 6, 306 ; Gen. 17 : 18, 307 ; John 4 : 49, *Ib.*

Repentance to prepare for the Gospel, 21 ; 168, 212, 213, 234 ; a preparation for revival, Acts 3 : 19, 311 ; 2 Pet. 3 : 4, 312 as a gift, 300.

Reports of revivals much blessed, 13, 93.

Resist beginnings, 100.

Resurrection of Christ, 308.

Resurrection to righteousness, 277.

Retirement, devotional uses of, xx.; testimony of Cecil and Tholuck, xxi.; discrimination needed here, xxi.; necessity of, 133 ; example of the prophets of old, 133.

Retirement and publicity, Carlyle on Loyola, xiii.; who should be urged to devote themselves to Christian work, xxiii.

Revival prolonged, *Spurgeon*, Matt. 14 : 16, 175 ; *Payson*, Luke 4 : 42, 181 ; *Parker*, 2 Kings 4 : 6, 182 ; Neh. 6 : 3, *Id.*; Isa. 51 : 11, 259 ; Micah. 2 : 7, 309 ; various effects of, Matt. 21 : 12–16 ; Isa. 60 : 8, 237, 251–254, 258, 259, 273, 274 ; false, resemble the true, 134 ; rejected, lead to the moral ruin of communities, Luke 19 : 44, 310 ; and ingatherings, 42 ; books on, 143, 144.

Revivals, in former days, 1 Kings 8 : 57, 58, 313, 288 ; at Antioch, 300 ; long continued, 111, 112.

Righteousness, Christian, 313.

Righteousness of Christ imputed, Matt. 22 : 22, 296.

S.

SACRIFICE, Jesus the only, 292 ; remedial, 266.

Sacrifice as a test, 307.

Sailors, revival among, Isa. 23 : 4, 305 moral and spiritual condition of, *Id.*

Salvation Army, 44.

Saplings set up as pillars, 108.

Satan exalting the Spirit at the expense of the Son, 22 ; his method of scattering a church, 312.

Science leading to Christ, 294, 295.

Scoffers, 313.

Seasonable preaching, 3–6.

Second Advent, Rev. 22 : 20, 304.

Secret societies, 223.

S337001

CPSIA information can be obtained
at www.ICGtesting.com
Printed in the USA
FSOW03n0738031216
27912FS